LOVE GAMES

Also by Mark Robert Waldman

The Art of Staying Together

Dreamscaping

JEREMY P. TARCHER / PUTNAM *a member of*
Penguin Putnam Inc.   *New York*

LOVE GAMES

How to Deepen Communication,
Resolve Conflict, and Discover
Who Your Partner *Really* Is

MARK ROBERT WALDMAN

WITH CONTRIBUTIONS FROM:
Harville Hendrix · Nathaniel Branden · Jean Houston
Jack Kornfield · Susan Page · Aaron T. Beck
Sharon Salzberg · Thich Nhat Hanh · The Dalai Lama
Herbert Benson · Margo Anand · *and others*

Jeremy P. Tarcher/Putnam
a member of
Penguin Putnam Inc.
375 Hudson Street
New York, NY 10014
www.penguinputnam.com

Library of Congress Cataloging-in-Publication Data

Love Games : how to deepen communication, resolve conflict, and
discover who your partner really is / [edited by] Mark Robert
Waldman.
p.   cm.
ISBN 1-58542-005-0
1. Intimacy (Psychology) Problems, exercises, etc.   I. Waldman,
Mark Robert.
BF575.I5   L68   2000   99-32737 CIP
302—dc21

Printed in the United States of America
1   3   5   7   9   10   8   6   4   2

This book is printed on acid-free paper. ∞

Book design by Lee Fukui

To Adam, Lauren, and all young lovers of the future:
May you never lose your sense of imagination and
playfulness as you wrestle with the game of love

Contents

Games at a Glance

CHAPTER FIVE
Sensual Games: Awakening Your Pleasure Zones

CHAPTER SIX
Fire-Fighting Games: Transforming Anger into Love

CHAPTER SEVEN

Problem-Solving Games:
Refining Your Relationship Skills

Watson, where's my cape and hat? The game's afoot!

THE HONORABLE SHERLOCK HOLMES

Would You Like to Play a Game?

Love Games began as an experiment with a stranger, at a difficult time in my life. My marriage had collapsed, I was separated and living alone, and I was about to go out on a date. I hadn't felt such vulnerability in years.

A thousand voices were arguing in my head: Was I still attractive, would I be rejected, what should I say and do? I had all the questions of a teenager with a middle-aged body and mind.

I decided to apply a principle that I had used in meditation and perfected on the analytic couch: I would simply try to stay in the present moment and, at the appropriate time, speak directly of my vulnerabilities and fears. I was going to be as open as I possibly could. Now this can be a risky thing to do, particularly on a first date, but I needed to know if my potential lover could handle self-disclosure. In the dating game, I found very few who yearned for the levels of intimacy that I sought.

It was a beautiful afternoon when we met, and we decided to take a walk. As I practiced my meditation, we talked intimately about our respective divorces and the moments of illumination one grasps between the pain. Inwardly, my experiment was going well, but I wanted to push it further, to extend myself with this unknown woman by my side.

"Would you like to play a game?" I asked in a moment of courage.

"What do you have in mind?" she cautiously replied.

"Would you be willing to dialogue with me for a few minutes, sharing whatever thoughts and feelings you are having—without censorship of any kind?" I wasn't sure if I wanted to be so open, or if it was even wise for two strangers to play such a game, but she agreed.

It turned out to be one of the most remarkable experiences in my life. It was intense and exhilarating, for we were able to be profoundly open with each other, not in a matter of weeks or days, but in less than an hour. For that moment, my fears and tensions melted away, and a wonderful healing began. For the first time I realized how powerful certain therapeutic and spiritual exercises could be if they were brought into our conversations with our lovers and friends. That evening, a game of intimacy had been created, and the seeds for this book took root.

Love Games

I would like to invite you to play some games that will take you into the heart of intimacy and love. Games that can be played with your partner, your family, and your friends, or even played alone. Games that will expand your awareness of yourself and others. Games of imagination and trust, of communication and self-disclosure. Problem-solving games, relaxation games, sexual games, playful games, and a few that will take you into the shadows of the self, where the darkest secrets—and greatest potentials—reside.

These exercises incorporate the most current perspectives in psychology and communications theory, but they are not your typical relationship games, for they have been designed to give you an *experiential* sense of intimacy, involving your body as well as your mind. They make extensive use of the powers of your imagination and creativity, and they challenge you to take emotional risks. Some will entice you into reflective vulnerability, while others will touch on the spiritual realms, where the mysteries of the relational soul are found. And many are just plain fun.

"Games are for kids," a few may say, but the experts disagree, for games can teach one—young and old—how to get along with others: in school, in the workplace, and at home. Games improve cognitive development, stimulate effective parenting, and even ward off symptoms of disease. When carefully structured, games will challenge us to excel in virtually every activity in life.[1]

In my search for games of intimacy, I found myself exploring many fields: from psychoanalysis to family-systems therapy, from bodywork to theater and the spiritual arts. I was looking for the best of the best, games that were carefully researched but were easy to play at home. Of the thousands I reviewed, fewer than a hundred met the criteria I was looking for, which I arranged—along with several dozen that I created specifically for this book—into the following general groups:

Discovery Games

Who are we really, deep down inside? What secrets and fears lie hidden, and how might we help each other bring them into the light? These are the kinds of issues that discovery games illuminate by showing couples how to explore vulnerable feelings with sensitivity and care. Here you will find out what intimacy really means to your partner, how past relationships influence one's capacity to love, and how one's family dynamics can interfere with deepening emotional bonds.

Through the art of questioning, you will learn how to recognize the differences between your and your partner's values and belief systems concerning money, sex, and spirituality, and how you might heal your partner's emotional wounds. By exploring unconscious processes that interfere with intimacy, you can uncover potential problems before a conflict erupts, or even spend a romantic evening with an alluring alien beast!

Sensual Games

These games are designed to take you into the unexplored pleasures of the senses—of touch, taste, movement, sound, and sex—but in ways that are unexpectedly delightful and fun. Various techniques emphasize the subtleties of smiling, of gazing into your partner's eyes, and rediscovering the joys of kissing and melting fully into each other's arms. Treat your partner to a blindfolded banquet, a sensuous walk through nature, or a tantric embrace in which sensations and spirit converge.

Fire-Fighting Games

Many games can help couples build stronger bonds, but a single major conflict, if handled poorly, can make a relationship collapse. For this reason, I have given particular attention to anger, the most destructive emotion to express. Because anger is a slippery beast to tame, you will find eighteen original approaches to help you and your partner extinguish these fiery urges and fears—from meditation to blurting to painting the demons away—and to replace them with compassionate understanding and trust.

Problem-Solving Games

Once our emotions subside, we can begin the task of confronting the underlying problems within. In this section, you will learn how to implement many strategies for resolving both major and minor conflicts, redirecting disruptive forces into creative solutions and plans. Find out about the "referee" in a box, try the "Post-It" solution, and learn how to forgive the most difficult people in your life. Using cognitive and spiritual techniques, couples can initiate significant changes in behavior that will open the doors to greater intimacy, commitment, and love.

Romantic Writing Games

These creative games make use of paper and pen to touch your partner's heart: sending her an unexpected note, teasing him with an "envelope" trail, or designing a couple's journal to share intimate thoughts and dreams. These exercises will show you how to lure your partner into intimacy by practicing the poet's art, creating Zen telegrams, plagiarizing your favorite musical piece, and designing a couple's journal. Writing games bring you closer to your partner, whether you are a thousand miles away or lying together at home.

Playful Games

Having fun is an essential part of intimacy, thus you will find a chapter filled with games that are designed to tickle your partner's soul—sweet and silly ways to win an affectionate smile. From wrapping a present in an unusual way to playing with invisible balls, these imaginative treats will brighten anyone's afternoon or day.

Because most of these games depend upon our ability to dialogue openly with each other, I have devoted separate chapters to communication and the art of staying relaxed, two essential tools in the development of conscious intimacy. These exercises will show you how to become aware of your innermost feelings and thoughts and how to communicate them in unique and constructive ways. They will teach you how to listen effectively, not only to others but also to your own body and the subtle productions of your mind, and how to integrate contemplative dialogue into every part of your life. As a counselor, I have found these to be some of the most powerful and influential games for stimulating relational transformation.

In *Love Games,* there are other voices besides my own, all experts in the fields of psychology, medicine, education, and spiritual development. For example, you will have the opportunity to try out Nathaniel Branden's experiment with intimacy, take Aaron T. Beck's hostility quiz, teach your partner how to use Herbert Benson's relaxation response to deepen your intimate bond, and temper your anger with a meditation by The Dalai Lama. In all, nearly two dozen respected individuals will share their secrets for deepening intimacy, commitment, and trust.

A Global Vision of Love

The games in this book will stimulate many questions and issues that are often avoided or overlooked in relationships, and they will bring to the surface the hidden dimensions of your soul. This may evoke some anxiety, but ultimately these games (and the principles on which they are based) will make your relationship more meaningful and rich, whether

> From my perspective, intimacy requires mutuality, which means mutual valuing, mutual empowerment, mutual respect, and mutual empathy. A truly intimate relationship fosters the growth of both parties, not just one.
>
> HARRIET LERNER
> *The Dance of Intimacy*

you are in the beginning stages of dating or are long-term lovers or friends.

But intimacy is not a natural act. We must deliberately choose to go inward, beyond the point of comfort where most people tend to live. With conscious intimacy, we strive to ensure the emotional well-being of those we love. Conscious intimacy is filled with emotional risks, and we will sometimes stumble and fall. Feelings get unintentionally hurt. Old wounds get opened, and painful memories erupt. It is in these vulnerable moments of love that we need our partners the most.

The benefits of conscious intimacy extend far beyond our relationships at home, for intimacy brings understanding to the heart, where tolerance, compassion, and respect unfold. These qualities can, with time, transform the suffering of others throughout the world. This is the power of love.

Conscious intimacy is a difficult path to follow, for there are no set rules, no clearly delineated maps or signs, no mutually agreed-upon solution or plan. By choosing a path of consciousness, traditional values give way to a multiplicity of personal views, not because one loses touch with morality, but because there are simply more choices from which to select. In a world as culturally diverse as our own, there are many valid principles and beliefs; thus, in a global society, we can experience many styles of love, choosing for ourselves which level works best. But it is a decision that must grow from the intimate conversations we create with our lovers and friends.

As you play the games in this book, look for the hidden themes, the meanings behind the technique, and the wisdom that lies within. Then, when you turn to your partner for love, take a few minutes to listen and look, for there is so much more than our senses will ever discern. And when it comes to making love, remember: You have all the time in the world.

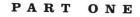

PART ONE

DEVELOPING CONSCIOUS INTIMACY

LISTEN

I do not understand where my words are coming from. They drive me, haunt me, and abandon me. I am at once a dry beach, lifeless, wordless, expressionless, when suddenly a wave breaks upon the shore of my thoughts, spilling words upon its surface where they struggle or die or return to the sea.

What do they mean? I listen but they are silent, empty of symbol and myth. Still, they are sacred. They guide my hand as my eyes follow. I utter them beneath my breath, hoping perchance to discover the secrets hidden behind the sounds, the syllables, the displaced comma, the period.

Listen to the silence of my pen. Listen to the ink as it seeps slowly into the paper beneath its touch. Listen, dear friend, to the silence that follows my love.

M. R. WALDMAN
Letter to an Unknown Woman

CHAPTER 1

The Art of Playing

ASK A CHILD if he would like to play a game and you will see his eyes light up, but ask a grown-up and you will probably see a look of surprise, uncertainty, and doubt. As experts have noted, too many adults have forgotten the value of play.

For a child, play is the essential tool for learning about life, "a bridge to reality," as Bruno Bettelheim once wrote.[2] Through play, a child experiments with different ways of constructing the world, for organizing feelings and thoughts, and making sense out of the complexities of social interaction. For an adult, it offers access to the unconscious processes within. And in science, imaginative play stimulates creative insight and discovery.

A game goes one step further by bringing fantasy and play into the world of relationships. In games, children learn how to get along with one another, and in many tribal communities, games continue to serve as a means for developing relational skills. They may even decide the political and economic future of a nation.

In our country, game theory has been applied to corporate management training, community development programs, and for strategic defense. Games show astronauts how to dock in space, and they are even used—for better or worse—to predict the outcome of thermonuclear war.

> *Today, many people suffer because, in their lives, the worlds of fantasy and reality, which for our greatest well-being must interpenetrate one another, remain apart.*
>
> BRUNO BETTELHEIM
> *A Good Enough Parent*

In therapy, games can be used to teach family members how to get along with one another. They illustrate how individuals interact, and they can help disputing couples resolve their differences in safe and effective ways. Even a game as simple as Pick-Up Sticks can highlight the psychodynamics of a family feud.

At home, a casual game of cards may help us unwind, while a recreational game like tennis can enhance our health. Complex games like chess can help us improve our concentration and cognitive skills, and if they are carefully constructed, they can even help us to achieve a state of mind that brings us into extraordinary states of consciousness and peak performance. In such a state, we are functioning at our best.

If games are so potent in developing childhood, adult, and therapeutic skills, why not employ them for the development of love? If we approached relationships as we would a complex game—with dedication, imagination, and a willingness to learn—we could, as professor Mihaly Csikszentmihalyi suggests, bring deeper meaning and enjoyment to our lives:

> [For relationships] to be enjoyable . . . the partners must discover new potentialities in themselves and in each other. To discover these, they must invest attention in each other—so that they can learn what thoughts and feelings, what dreams reside in their partner's mind. This in itself is a never-ending process, a lifetime's task. After one begins to really know another person, then many joint adventures become possible.[3]

Suggestions for Using This Book

Each game in this book is designed to exemplify a specific aspect of intimacy, to break down the complexities of relationships into understandable contexts, and to introduce practical ways in which we can develop our relational skills. In this sense, a love game becomes a metaphor for the work and courage it takes to develop conscious intimacy. The risks we take can be fun if we keep alive the imagination that a child brings forth in play. It is simply an invitation to go deeper into your soul.

Taken from a psychological viewpoint . . . play seems to be the essential feature in productive thought.

ALBERT EINSTEIN

Practicing Alone: At Play in the Fields of the Mind

As you read through the games in this book, take a moment and play them through in your mind, as if you were actually engaging a lover or a friend. How does each game make you feel? Does it intrigue you, or challenge an old assumption? Or does it strike you as silly or absurd? Does the idea of playing it with your partner make you nervous, excited, or both? The discomfort that a game can evoke may indicate unconscious barriers we have toward certain kinds of intimacy.

Just the simple act of reading about a game can change the way we see and feel, for intimacy is as much a part of our imagination as is the actual exchange we have with others. Our thoughts, as well as our experiences, shape our attitudes about every aspect of love, and a new idea may be all that it takes to find a new approach.

Journaling: Exploring the Powers of Ink

While you read, keep a special journal of your comments and impressions, noting how different games affect the way you think. In the act of writing, one learns to listen to one's self more carefully, an ideal tool for improving one's communication strategies and skills.

Experiment and play with your journal—color it, add a drawing or a poem, scribble gibberish—but make sure you write something every day. It doesn't matter whether it's a paragraph or a page, as long as you explore some aspect of intimacy and love. Make a list of the games that you would be willing to play with your partner and those that make you feel uncomfortable, along with your reasons why.

At various times, read passages from your journal to your mate; it is an intimate act of love. But knowing that your journal may be shared will affect your writing style. You may, for example, notice a greater hesitation to record certain feelings and thoughts. Instead of writing *from* yourself (which is a major key in the development of conscious intimacy), you may find yourself writing *for* someone else, censoring many personal reflections. If this happens, make a mental note of it and write about it if you can. Remember: You do not have to share anything you feel uncomfortable with, but, as time passes, you may find that it is easier to talk about it. With distance, emotional charges fade, and to share such a journey with someone you love can bring great satisfaction and joy.

Writing may also be a safer way to express vulnerable issues. By slowing down your thinking, it can interrupt destructive emotional states and give you time to better organize your thoughts. Over time, you can look back over your writing and see things that you could not grasp before.

Like intimacy, writing also requires commitment, for it can be quite challenging to express one's deeper feelings and moods. Writing, however, can help you communicate better because it forces you to translate emotional realms of experience into a language that others can grasp.

Wooing Companions to Play: Enticements and Pursuits

Now comes the difficult part: convincing another to play an intimate game. There are many ways to woo your partner, but the easiest is simply to read passages from this book. Tell your partner about a game that intrigues you, explain the reasons why, and then ask her if she would like to play. Encourage him to speak openly about his reactions, his curiosity, or fears and share as much as you can about yourself.

The invitation itself becomes a game, as does the conversation that unfolds. How do you entice her to play? What are the rewards, the dangers, and the rules? Every step of the invitation is a dialogical adventure, and even if the two of you never actually play the game, a movement into intimacy will have been made.

Pick two, three, or four games that you think your partner might like to play, and tell him or her how you made your choice. In so doing, you are showing your partner how you perceive his or her interests and concerns. If you want to be a little more

> *To be in love is to be in play, taken by illusions.*
>
> THOMAS MOORE
> *Soul Mates*

seductive, ask your partner to pick out several games that he or she believes would be interesting to you. Better yet, ask your partner to pick a game that he or she *doesn't* want to play. As you find out the reasons why, you will learn a great deal about each other's values, needs, and fears.

You can step even further into intimacy by talking about one of the games that you personally found intimidating. By showing your vulnerability, you demonstrate courage and strength, and doing so will also encourage your partner to do the same. You can experiment further by discussing one of the games that you think would make your partner uncomfortable to play. Then ask your partner to do the same, to select a game that he or she believes would be difficult for you to embrace. By doing so, you demonstrate to each other your capacity to recognize the other person's feelings—a powerful step toward intimacy that couples often overlook. Such conversations can prepare the way for exploring the more provocative games in this book—there are quite a few! But remember to respect the other's space. If your partner doesn't want to play a particular game, let it go without judgment or interpretation. At a later time, you may be able to reapproach the topic with greater ease.

But what if your partner doesn't want to play at all? There are several things to consider. Perhaps it isn't his way to work through issues of love, or perhaps she is preoccupied with other pressing concerns. Talk about it, focusing on your own feelings and desires but avoid expressing criticism or blame. As an alternative, you can write down your thoughts in your journal and then share them at another time. Or, you can play these games with a friend and then share your experience with your mate.

Other forces may also inhibit some people, for a game that promotes intimacy may bring to the surface unaddressed issues that seem too threatening to share or explore. For example, if a person feels fragile or insecure, openness can be perceived as a threat. If your partner reacts with discomfort but cannot tell you why, this may be what's happening inside. Usually, an affectionate embrace and a word of support are all that is needed to break the ice, but occasionally a therapeutic hand will help.

Love games, however, should not be used as ploy to change our partner's behaviors and beliefs, a task that some lovers attempt to embrace, but which usually ends in pain. An old Sufi story illustrates this point. There was once a young man who decided to bring wisdom and happiness to the world, but no matter how hard he tried, he could not enlighten a single soul. After many years, he realized he had failed, and so he prayed that he could at least have the power to influence those closest to him. Still, no one had changed. Finally, when he was humble and old, he realized a simple truth. "God," he now prayed, "please grant me the patience and the time so that I may begin to change myself."

In this spirit, it is my hope that *Love Games* will entice you to reflect more deeply upon yourself: to think about the underlying meaning of intimacy, to question your own behaviors and beliefs, to gently expose your weaknesses as well as your strengths, and to share your journey with those who are closest to your heart. If only one of these games were to help you become more compassionate and kind, then those who know you will benefit as well. You will be practicing the art of conscious intimacy and love.

Using a Friend for Support

With certain games, you may actually find it easier to practice with a special platonic friend, someone you can trust to support you through times of need. For example, a friend may be more willing to listen to your angers and fears, whereas your partner may feel somewhat overwhelmed. Lovers have more to risk, and they have less time or distance to absorb the impacts of a difficult exchange.

Friends also provide a different level of feedback. They may be more honest and direct for the simple reason that they do not have to share your bed. With a good support person, you have less chance of losing yourself in the intricacies of romance. Finally, by engaging a trusted friend, you may have an opportunity to explore new levels of dialogue, intimacy, and trust.

Creating a Game Plan

Let's assume that your partner or friend is willing to play some games and has made a commitment to join you in an exploration through this book. The next step is to decide what kind of commitment to make. How much time would you like to spend, and on which days? And how should you structure the games? You may use the following suggestions, altering them as you see fit, to create a plan that suits you and your partner the best:

- Sit down with your partner and make a list of the games you want to play, skimming through this book to see which issues attract you. Try to include as many of the recommended games that are described in the following section.

- Put a star by any game that your partner chose that makes you a little nervous to play, and talk about it in depth. Together, decide if or when that game should be played.

- Select one game that both of you think would be fun to play. The positive reinforcement will stimulate the desire to play more games.

- Place your game list where you can see it every day, and add to it as you read through the book. Place a checkmark by the ones that interest you the most and play them first, beginning with those that you consider nonthreatening and safe. Later, when deeper confidence and trust have been established, you can explore those games that seem a little more risky or make you feel vulnerable.

- Feel free to modify the games in any way you see fit, or create some new ones of your own. As relationships mature, we sometimes take our love for granted, forgetting the importance of spontaneity, playfulness, and romance.

- Try to play at least one game each week, setting aside an hour in a comfortable place where you will not be disturbed by people or phones. By creating a disciplined approach to intimacy, you enhance the power of these games.

- Think about one of the games the day before you play, and immerse yourself with loving thoughts about your mate. On the day you have set aside, check in with your partner to make sure that you are both in the right mood to play. If you are stressed out, consider one of the relaxation exercises in chapter 2.

- After you have completed a game, take some time to relax, together or alone, and reflect upon the effects of the exchange. Work with your journal, adding a few comments throughout the week.

- Some games can be emotionally intense, so on the following day, take a few minutes to talk with your partner about residual feelings and thoughts. It is always a tender act to inquire about your lover's psychological state.

Most important: Don't forget to have fun as you explore these relational games. Be playful and warm, take a few risks, and let your imagination soar.

Spending an Evening with Friends

For even greater excitement and intrigue, spend an afternoon or a day playing love games with other couples and guests. Call up your friends and invite them to a mystery evening of entertainment and prepare some special food and drink. Better yet, tell your friends to bring something wonderful to share, and when they arrive, blindfold them and give them samples of tasty treats as described in "Tangerine Love" (chapter 5, game 5). Then introduce them to "Two Thumbs Up" or one of the theater games outlined in chapter 9. Next, take your party on an imaginary journey into relaxation (chapter 2, game 5). Now you can shift to a more provocative game like "Confessions and Lies" (chapter 4, game 21) and conclude with the outrageously funny "Love, Asterian Style," in which you describe your ideal alien tryst.

Feel daring? Ask each person to pick one game at random. Even if you do not play it, the discussion will lead to a meaningful exchange and a deepening of intimacy among friends—more exciting than an evening of Trivial Pursuit and safer than a round of Truth or Dare!

Games People Should Play

As you experiment and read through this book, I encourage you to give your fullest attention to the following fifteen games, for they are essential to the development of conscious intimacy. The first three are also integral in bringing out the effectiveness of many other games.

The Relaxing Journey (chapter 2, game 5). This wonderful exercise, created by Josie Hadley and Carol Staudacher, incorporates the fundamental elements of relaxation—breathing, muscle relaxation, guided imagery—and will take you and your partner on a pleasant journey to inner peace. It should be used as a warm-up exercise every time you engage your partner in a serious discussion or game, for relaxation breaks down defensive barriers that interfere with the development of intimacy. This exercise also incorporates a posthypnotic suggestion to help you enter a state of relaxation whenever you choose.

The Intimate Yawn (chapter 2, game 3). This simple technique will show you the quickest route to becoming fully relaxed, but it is the most difficult one to convince people to do. If you can suspend your self-consciousness for a minute, you will see for yourself how effective this exercise can be.

Dialogical Meditation (chapter 3, game 1). This simple exercise is one of most challenging games in this book: while it promotes rapid intimacy, it can also bring up intense feelings of vulnerability. The game itself is a combination of three techniques: breathing and relaxation, free association, and a modified version of insight meditation. When two people sit down to play, they will enter an altered state in which they will find themselves, in a matter of minutes, talking about profoundly personal issues. Conversational defensives will be on hold, and the willingness to talk about vulnerable feelings and issues will be enhanced.

The Sentence-Completion Game (chapter 4, game 12). Popularized by psychologist Nathaniel Branden, this creative exercise provokes spontaneous dialogues on just about any topic you choose, and it will safely uncover feelings and thoughts that are often unconsciously repressed.

The Melting Hug and Hugging Meditation (chapter 5, games 1 and 2). These two exercises by Margo Anand and Thich Nhat Hanh are basic training for developing sensual conscious intimacy. In particular, they will show you how much one misses in one's everyday physical exchange. Indeed, all the games in chapter 5 will expose you to realms of sensual intimacy that couples can easily overlook.

Contemplative Love (chapter 5, game 17). More of an attitude than a game, this approach to sexuality suggests that you abandon all of what you have previously learned about making love and sink into the spontaneous joy of a mystical erotic embrace.

Checking In and The Friday-Night Solution (chapter 7, games 3 and 4). If couples would adapt these two weekly exercises, the majority of relational problems and destructive behaviors could be identified and defused. Because conflict and emotional turmoil are the two most difficult issues to handle in relationships, chapters 6 and 7 are devoted to managing anger and developing effective problem-solving strategies. Give the games in these chapters careful consideration, especially "Sitting with the Demons" (chapter 6, game 6) and "The Behavior Change Request" (chapter 7, game 11).

Forgiving Difficult People and The Seven-Day Cure (chapter 7, game 14, and chapter 6, game 12). These two exercises foster the development of compassion in everyday life, but they specifically focus on the task of expressing kindness in difficult situations and toward people you like the least.

The Couple's Journal (chapter 8, game 11). This is a very powerful way to maintain intimacy with your partner, even when you are physically separated from each other. You simply share a daily journal, but make sure you follow Jennifer Louden's suggestions and advice.

Role-Playing Each Other (chapter 9, game 16). In this intensely pleasurable game, you switch roles with your partner and spend part of the day acting out and mimicking each other's style. Although it is surprisingly funny, it often mirrors parts of ourselves that we have not acknowledged or become aware of, and thus it brings greater consciousness to the dynamic exchange of love.

When working with complex games such as these, it is important to include a dosage of playful and romantic games, which can be found in chapters 8 and 9. Some of my favorites involve paper, pen, and a touch of plagiaristic deceit: "The Envelope Trail," "Post Office," and "The Poet Thief" (games 2, 3, and 7 in chapter 8). And, for those who wish to venture into the vulnerable shadows of intimacy, where the greatest potential for growth can be found, consider an evening of "Sharing Secrets," "Confessions and Lies," and "Healing Each Other's Wounds" (games 20,

21, and 22 in chapter 4). Of course, there is always a game or two that blurs the line between light and shadow, fantasy and fact, as you will discover in "Love, Asterian Style" (chapter 4, game 10), where you will encounter some of the most alluring alien lovers your partner is yearning to meet!

But before you jump into these intimate corners of the soul, take a brief inventory of the following games people *shouldn't* play—the ones that quietly put distance between yourself and others and that can deal intimacy an emotionally fatal blow.

Games People Shouldn't Play

In his 1964 best-selling book, *Games People Play*, Eric Berne presented a dismal view of personal relationships. In our society, Berne wrote, people rarely seek out intimacy. Instead, they play games: games to pass the time away, games to avoid the feelings of hurt and despair inside, and games that are highly destructive to awareness and spontaneity. These people cannot handle deep intimacy—they are too much in pain—and so they hide behind a variety of behavioral masks or "games": *Alcoholic, Kick Me, Now I've Got You, If It Weren't for You,* and *Look How Hard I've Tried* are some of the labels Berne applied.

All these games have something in common: they're played *against* people's partners, not with them. They have hidden agendas, they aren't honest, and they pull a person, through conversation, into a false level of intimacy. Let's take a look at some the communication styles that Berne and others have described, games that can kill off intimacy like the plague.

The Empty Conversation

This is one of the most common games people play, and it goes by many names: "Chitchat," "Small Talk," "General Motors" (comparing cars or some other item of no particular interest), "Psychobabble," and so on. In all these games no real dialogue exists. They are simply conversations to pass the time, to relieve boredom, or to distract oneself from negative feelings or thoughts.

In the Empty Conversation, no one really listens. You'll recognize the style with the first few words that are spoken:

> *Starting tomorrow when you wake up, don't gossip. See what happens if you just give up making comments about anyone not present. Listen carefully to the voice in your mind as it is getting ready to make a comment, and think to yourself, "Why am I saying this?" Awareness of intention is the best clue for knowing whether the remark you are about to make is Right Speech. Is your intention whole-some, a desire to help? Or to show off? Or to denigrate?*
>
> SYLVIA BOORSTEIN
> *It's Easier Than You Think*

"Who won the football game last Sunday . . . ?"
"Have you ever been to . . . ?"
"Did you hear the one about . . . ?"
"Why don't they do something about . . . ?"
"Those damn politicians! Why, if I was . . ."

Such conversations aren't always destructive, for they can also give us breathing space between more intimate interactions. But many people spend their entire conversational lives at this level, without ever realizing how much intimacy has been excluded or lost.

Gossip

This game is potentially more destructive than the Empty Conversation, because it tends to generate suspicion and distrust: "Did you hear what So-and-so said?" "Guess what those kids did down the street?" "Isn't it awful what the neighbor did?" As secondhand information, gossip is often used to indirectly express anger, frustration, and personal unhappiness.

We all play this game at times, but it is always hurtful to the other. How does it feel, for example, if someone gossips about you? Gossip is an invasion of privacy and personal space, a substitute for intimacy by talking about someone else rather than yourself.

Here Comes the Judge

Gossip becomes more serious when it contains covert hostility and anger: "Guess what that idiot did?" "Those damn _____ (fill in the blank with your least favorite minority) . . . !" In its more subtle form, it may appear as an off-color joke, a sexist remark, or a racial slip-of-the-tongue.

Judges tend to take their internal problems and project them onto others. On the surface, they may appear friendly and sweet, but underneath they are angry and upset. They are blamers who think they are victims, and they feel deeply resentful, as if someone else were depriving them of their money, freedom, or security. They judge others but never themselves.

A variation of this game is Case Dismissed, where a person simply discredits or discounts another individual. "They have it better than they know" or "They're making a big deal out of nothing" are typical examples. Such statements are always hostile, and they certainly don't allow for the development of compassion, understanding, or tolerance.

U-Turns

In the previous games, conversational styles are usually focused on an invisible third person, but in U-Turns the opinions and judgments are directed toward the person one is talking with. He, she, and they suddenly become *you*: "If it weren't for *you*..." "You're always so _____ (fill in your favorite criticism)." Other remarks show a propensity to manipulate and control, and often begin with "You should" or "You can't." These kinds of statements assume that the problem is always someone else's and never theirs.

Often, the person who plays this kind of game hides behind a seemingly innocuous question or dismissal. For example, "Why did you bother to do *that*?" is really a disguised version of "I know better than you," and the person is really thinking, "You idiot." Vonda Olson Long, a communications professor at the University of New Mexico, calls these kinds of people One-Uppers and Discounters, because they always find a way to put you down as they try to take control. Their statements reflect judgmentalism rather than respect, and they assume that they can rescue you.[4]

A popular version of this game is called Psychology, where one person advises and diagnoses the other: "You're depressed," "You're overly reactive," "You ought to calm down," etc. My least favorite line is "You need to see a therapist," because when the person who uses such a phrase comes in for an evaluation, it often turns out that he or she is the one who is in serious psychological trouble. However, if I were to gently point this out, U-Turners can't agree. After all, they are too caught up in playing the game of Expert. They know better than anyone else.

War Games

If U-Turn remarks escalate, they may lead to other more threatening ones: "If you don't _____, I'm going to _____." People who make such remarks are about to engage in a simple game of war, posturing themselves defensively in order to overtake and control others. Often, in relationships where war games are frequently played, the marriage cannot be saved, for too much damage has been done to each party's self-esteem.

Help Me, Feed Me

These games are more benign, and in some ways more honest, because they reflect the underlying insecurities and fears of the person playing the game. "Poor me," "I'm no good," "Look how hard I've tried," "Honey, will you (help me, feed me, save me)?" and "If only I could . . ." are typical examples of childlike behavior that can be seen in the conversational styles of many insecure souls. Such people genuinely cry out for help, but they have little to give in return. They avoid going deeply into themselves, and although they invite other game players to participate (the Let-Me-Fix-You types), the dialogue usually ends on a note of disappointment. These people are hungry, and, like starving animals, they growl at anyone who comes too close.

"Psychologically, [such people] have never evolved beyond the pattern of a child-parent relationship," writes Nathaniel Branden. "If anything is troubling them, they want and expect their partner to be fully available to them, fully interested in what they have to say, unreservedly present and compassionate. They are oblivious to the fact that their partner desires the same of them, and oblivious also to how rarely they give it."[5]

Good Games

In Berne's view, the games people play are mostly hurtful, manipulative, and self-deceptive. But there are exceptions. Games like Helpful Servant, Teacher, or Nurse provide genuine value to others, even though they may have grown out of a childhood need to be loved. Players of these types of games often learn to embrace modesty, kindness, and generosity throughout their entire lives.

While most people, according to Berne, never free themselves from playing petty social games, there are a few who realize that autonomy can be found when they allow their deeper feelings to emerge:

> For certain fortunate people there is something which tran-
> scends all classifications of behavior, and that is awareness,
> something which rises above the programming of the past, and
> that is spontaneity; and something that is more rewarding than
> games, and that is intimacy. But all of these may be frighten-
> ing and even perilous to the unprepared.[6]

When we rediscover the spontaneity of the child, when we seek aware-ness in our acts of love, and when we expose the underbelly of our feel-ings to those we intimately know, we can begin the task of healing our partner's wounds. All that is needed is a little guidance to point the way—a simple suggestion, an experiment to try—and a willing lover and friend. These are the games that people should play: the ones you are about to en-counter in the chapters of this book. As you work through these exercises, watch carefully for the kinds of destructive interactions mentioned above, for they can unwittingly creep into conversation, particularly when one feels vulnerable or insecure. Sit down with your partner and go over these "anti-intimacy" ploys, exploring how often and how recently they have been used, either toward your partner, toward others you do not like, or even toward yourself in the silent dialogues within.

CHAPTER 2

Easing into Intimacy

This chapter includes nine relaxation techniques that are essential for build-
ing conscious intimacy with your mate. These methods include medita-
tion, guided imagery, and breathing techniques that can be used with your
partner to improve communication, increase sensuality, and refine your
problem–solving skills.

HERE IS A MODERN Zen story about the relationship among relaxation, enlightenment, and love:

Once upon a time, there was a young man who went in search
of the truth. He was seeking enlightenment and was willing to
travel to the ends of the earth to find it. He studied with many
gurus and saints, but he still felt empty inside.

One day, he fell in love with a beautiful young woman. They
married, and were happy, but he did not live in peace. His
adoring wife could not bear to see him suffer, and so she told
him about a sage who lived in the rugged mountains of the
north.

"Go seek the Master," she implored, and he did.

For three days he struggled up the slopes of the desolate
peaks, until he saw a cave with a very old man meditating at its
door. "Are you the famous guru of the north?" he asked.

"Perhaps," the old man replied. "What is it that you seek?"

"Oh, Master," the young man begged, "please show me the
essence of life, the key to intimacy, and the door to eternal

love." He waited patiently, with growing anticipation, knowing that sages will take a long time before they comment on something profound.

But the old man only smiled. He reached out and gently touched the seeker's arm, took a few deep breaths and yawned. "Now go," he suddenly said, "and practice what you have been shown."

The young man was deeply upset. After all, he had not risked his life climbing cliffs to be turned away with only a smile and a yawn, but there was nothing he could do. As he worked his way down the mountain, his anger turned to grief, and he sat upon a ledge and cried. All his life he had searched for enlightenment—for truth and happiness and love—but wherever he turned he felt lonely and empty and cold.

Exhausted, he took a deep breath and yawned, and suddenly all of the tensions melted away. For the first time in years he could relax, and in that moment he realized the simple wisdom of the old man's advice. His tears dried up, and as he looked across the mountain ledge to the valleys and streams below, he saw how beautiful it was. He thought about his wife, of her patience and kindness, and how much he yearned to be in her arms.

He smiled, and in that smile, enlightenment was his.

It doesn't sound sexy, but one of the best-kept secrets to intimacy and happiness lies hidden in our ability to relax. As the guru implied, a gentle touch, a smile, and a deepening of the breath may be all we need to open our hearts to love.

Stress, as we now know, is a leading contributor to disease, and relaxation is the key to reducing stress. As early as the 1930s, scientists observed the benefits that relaxation—be it through breathing, visualization, or meditation—could bring to the healing processes of the body. To date, over two thousand studies have demonstrated its effectiveness for treating heart disease, high blood pressure, chronic pain, cancer, diabetes, allergies, arthritis, and numerous other immune and stress-related diseases.[7]

In psychology, relaxation strategies are now used to alleviate anxiety and depression, interrupt addictive behaviors, increase visual sensitivity and auditory acuity, and improve memory, intelligence, and concentration.[8] By applying the principles of relaxation to relationships, couples can learn how to reduce the angers and fears that arise when emotional conflicts erupt, or use them to enhance empathic and sensual responsiveness. Indeed, a few deep breaths may be all that is needed to ease a troubled love, for when we are relaxed, problems are more easily identified and resolved. We are less defensive and more in touch with our deeper feelings and thoughts, and our ability to communicate improves.

Because many of the games in this book depend upon your ability to enter and remain in a relaxed state, the exercises that follow will show you how to develop this essential skill. As you experiment with each technique, find the one that takes you quickly and easily into relaxation, and use it as your warm-up exercise with every game you play. Then guide your partner through each game to establish which technique works best. Try to get into the habit of reminding each other to relax; not only is it pleasant and fun, but it will take you deeper into intimacy—one small breath at a time.

Choosing to Relax

When I lecture, I often ask the audience to try a little experiment. "But first," I say, "make yourselves as comfortable as you possibly can." It gets quite noisy as people readjust themselves.

"Why," I then ask, "was there so much movement and noise? Were you sitting *uncomfortably* before? Did you not want to be relaxed when you first came in? Did someone whisper, 'Please sit down, but stay tense'?" There is usually a lot of laughter in the group.

"Let's continue. Are you all relaxed now?"

"Yes," the audience responds.

"Are you absolutely sure?" More shifting and laughter is heard. "How about your shoulders? Are they as relaxed as they can be? Your arms, your hands, your neck, your jaw?" With each part named, a subtle readjustment takes place.

"Now take a really deep breath and see if you can relax some more. Better yet, yawn a couple of times." Within a few moments the entire group is stretching and yawning and moving about. And when I ask the members of the audience how they feel, smiles light up the room. They have all become the guru of the little Zen story that I opened this chapter with.

Dear reader: How much tension do *you* have right now as you hold this book in your hands? Can you let a little of that tension go, relaxing your shoulders and breathing just a little bit deeper as you soften the muscles around your eyes, in your fingers, your back, and your toes? Now take another deep breath and relax your body some more. How good it must feel to let extra tensions dissolve.

Relaxation, it seems, is not a natural act. In our society, we are told to stay alert, to hurry up, to sit up straight in our chairs. We are never told to relax, except in a pejorative way, when someone else is reminding us to calm down.

Rarely do we realize how much tension we hold. It has to be brought to our attention. To relax, we must consciously make a choice, taking an inventory of our body, mind, and breath. Once we get into the habit of relaxing, all we have to do is think about it, and our bodies will comply. But it is all too easy to slip back into our overly tense behaviors—negotiating rush-hour traffic, struggling with frustrating chores, and dealing with the irritability of others who are equally tense and rushed. There aren't any freeway signs or window posters reminding us to relax, but perhaps we can make up a few on our own.

Game #1
Red Light, Green Light (A Rush-Hour Meditation)

Do you remember the childhood game called Red Light, Green Light? One person calls out "green light" and everyone else runs toward the goal. When "red light" is called out, everyone has to freeze.

Here is a variation of that game, inspired by the Buddhist teacher Thich Nhat Hanh.[9] You play it while driving in a car. Every time you see a red light, a stop sign, or the red taillight of a car, use it as a reminder to relax, to *stop* and take a really deep breath of air. And with every green light you see, let it be a symbol to let *go* of the tensions in your body and your mind. Just imagine how relaxed you'll be the next time you are caught in a traffic jam—all those blinking red lights reminding you to relax, slow down, and breathe!

The object of this game is to take an unenjoyable daily activity—

washing dishes, doing laundry, vacuuming, etc.—and turn it around to benefit your health. If couples would regularly practice Red Light, Green Light, by the time they reached home, instead of being irritable, stressed-out, and beat, they would feel open and relaxed, capable of embracing each other with greater intimacy and care.

Game #2
Breathing into Intimacy

There are, of course, many ways to relax, but taking a deep breath is probably the easiest and the most powerful one of all. Slow, deep breathing triggers a series of physiological responses. Muscles expand, thinking slows down, and pleasure-enhancing endorphins are released. If we consciously deepen our breath when we interact with others, we will discover that our conversations flow easier. We can listen more attentively, respond with greater care, and heighten our sensitivity to sensual touch and play.

You may be surprised to know that most people do not fully breathe. They take half breaths in and barely exhale. Take a moment and notice how you are currently breathing. How shallow or deep is your breath? Does your belly rise and fall? Can you hear and feel the movement of air through your nose or mouth?

Now breathe in as fully as you can. Don't stop until your belly and chest expand as far as possible, then breath out slowly, squeezing out every ounce of air. When you think you've completely exhaled, push some more and you will see that a little more air comes out. Take another ten breaths, as deeply as you can, and notice how you feel. It will seem like a lot of work at first, and you may even start to cough and feel all sorts of aches, but unless something is seriously wrong, the discomfort will quickly disappear.

Now let your breathing ease. It will be fuller than before, and you'll feel tingly and calm. You should also notice an increased clarity of mind, an ideal state for processing information and resolving any relational problems of the day.

If you continue breathing deeply, even the simplest acts of pleasure will be enhanced. Just ask your partner to deeply breathe as you hold each other, and watch what happens next. You'll see firsthand how intimate breathing can be.

Game #3
The Intimate Yawn

I'm about to ask you to try something that you probably won't want to do, even though it is the fastest way I have found to promote deep relaxation. Stop reading for the moment and yawn ten times in a row, as deeply as you can, and watch what happens inside.

For twenty-five years, I have used this technique as a therapeutic tool, and I am always amazed at the resistance it provokes: "I don't feel like it," "I'm not tired," "I can't yawn," "It's not polite," "It's embarrassing," "You're not supposed to open your mouth in front of others. . . ." The excuses go on and on. I have to start yawning myself before the other person will reluctantly join in. "It's catching," they like to say. It's catching because yawning itself feels good.

Now, you'll probably have to fake the first few yawns, but after four or five imitations, a genuine yawn will emerge. When you are in the midst of a yawn, your breathing suddenly changes. Your mouth opens wide, you dilate your throat, and your diaphragm begins to move. All the muscles of your face, neck, and chest are stretched. Each successive yawn becomes easier, fuller, and more pleasurable, and by the time you reach ten, your ears may pop, your eyes may start watering, and your nose may begin to run. Everything is opening up as you flood your lungs with air. Distracting thoughts subside, your awareness sharpens, and your body and mind become calm. It is an ideal state to begin an intimate talk. In my counseling practice, when a client comes in who is exhausted, anxious, or distraught, five minutes of yawning will bring about an extraordinary change of mood.

Now I'm willing to bet that you haven't yet yawned ten times, so let me ask again: Yawn as many times as you can, but no less than ten. The pleasure you will discover will be worth your effort and time.

Consciously try to yawn throughout the day: at work, before giving a presentation or talk, and especially when a cop pulls you over for an infraction of the Red Light, Green Light game. Yawning when you wake up, and especially before going to bed, will diminish the remaining stressful vestiges of the day.

I want you to do one more thing. Pick up the phone, call several

friends, and ask them to yawn. Can you get them to overcome their resistance? Then see if you can get your partner to comply. You may have
to yawn a few dozen times yourself to get someone else to relax. If all else
fails, ask him to yawn as you give him a relaxing massage.

Game #4

Jack Kornfield's Meditation Practice

Breathing is also the key element in many forms of meditation, but meditation goes far beyond relaxation, offering the practitioner easy access to
deeper realms of awareness. Those who take the time to meditate just ten
minutes each day will find themselves profoundly alert and relaxed, an
ideal state in which to work through the daily problems of life. And for
those couples who choose to meditate together, research has shown that far
fewer conflicts emerge. For the person who chooses the path of conscious
intimacy, meditation becomes an integral part of life. With your partner
or alone, try out the following technique, presented by psychologist Jack
Kornfield, a teacher who was influential in bringing Eastern contemplative practices to the West:[10]

> First select a suitable space for your regular meditation. It can be
> wherever you can sit easily with minimal disturbance: a corner of
> your bedroom or any other quiet spot in your home. Place a
> meditation cushion or chair there for your use. Arrange what is
> around so that you are reminded of your meditative purpose, so
> that it feels like a sacred and peaceful space. You may wish to
> make a simple altar with a flower or sacred image, or place your
> favorite spiritual books there for a few moments of inspiring
> reading. Let yourself enjoy creating this space for yourself.
>
> Then select a regular time for practice that suits your sched-
> ule and temperament. If you are a morning person, experi-
> ment with a sitting before breakfast. If evening fits your
> temperament or schedule better, try that first. Begin with sit-
> ting ten or twenty minutes at a time. Later you can sit longer
> or more frequently. Daily meditation can become like bathing
> or toothbrushing. It can bring a regular cleansing and calm-
> ing to your heart and mind.

Find a posture on the chair or cushion in which you can easily sit erect without being rigid. Let your body be firmly planted on the earth, your hands resting easily, your heart soft, your eyes closed gently. At first feel your body and consciously soften any obvious tension. Let go of any habitual thoughts or plans. Bring your attention to feel the sensations of your breathing. Take a few deep breaths to sense where you can feel the breath most easily, as coolness or tingling in the nostrils or throat, as movement of the chest, or rise and fall of the belly. Then let your breath be natural. Feel the sensations of your natural breathing very carefully, relaxing into each breath as you feel it, noticing how the soft sensations of breathing come and go with the changing breath.

After a few breaths your mind will probably wander. When you notice this, no matter how long or short a time you have been away, simply come back to the next breath. Before you return, you can mindfully acknowledge where you have gone with a soft word in the back of your mind, such as "thinking," "wandering," "hearing," "itching." After softly and silently naming to yourself where your attention has been, gently and directly return to feel the next breath. Later on in your meditation you will be able to work with the places your mind wanders to, but for initial training, one word of acknowledgment and a simple return to the breath is best.

As you sit, let the breath change rhythms naturally, allowing it to be short, long, fast, slow, rough, or easy. Calm yourself by relaxing into the breath. When your breath becomes soft, let your attention become gentle and careful, as soft as the breath itself.

Like training a puppy, gently bring yourself back a thousand times. Over weeks and months of this practice you will gradually learn to calm and center yourself using the breath. There will be many cycles in this process, stormy days alternating with clear days. Just stay with it. As you do, listening deeply, you will find the breath helping to connect and quiet your whole body and mind. . . . You will discover how awareness of your breath can serve as a steady basis for all you do.

Game #5
The Relaxing Journey

The following relaxation exercise, created by hypnotherapists Josie Hadley and Carol Staudacher,[II] is one of my favorite games to play. It is a blend of many techniques—deep breathing, hypnotic suggestion, autogenic training, and visualization—that can be used to bring you and your partner into a wonderfully intimate space. You may record the exercise if you wish, but it is much more powerful to have it personally read out loud. First, read through it once alone, then guide your partner through the exercise while he or she rests comfortably in a chair, or on a couch or bed. If you wish, relaxing music can be quietly played. After you've finished, ask your partner to read the exercise to you so that you can both float gently in bliss.

Take a nice deep breath, close your eyes, and begin to relax. Just think about relaxing every muscle in your body from the top of your head to the tips of your toes. Just begin to relax. And begin to notice how very comfortable your body is beginning to feel. You are supported, so you can just let go and relax. Inhale and exhale. Notice your breathing; notice the rhythm of your breathing and relax your breathing for a moment. Be aware of normal sounds around you. These sounds are unimportant, discard them, whatever you hear from now on will only help to relax you. And as you exhale, release any tension, any stress from any part of your body, mind, and thought; just let that stress go. Just feel any stressful thoughts rushing through your mind, feel them begin to wind down, wind down, wind down, and relax. And begin with letting all the muscles in your face relax, especially your jaw; let your teeth part just a little bit and relax this area. This is a place where tension and stress gather so be sure and relax your jaw and feel that relaxation go into your temples and relax the muscles in your temples and as you think about relaxing these muscles they will relax. Feel them relax and as you relax you'll be able to just drift and float into a deeper and deeper level of total relaxation. You will continue to relax and now let all of the muscles in your forehead relax. Feel those muscles smooth, smooth and relaxed, and rest your eyes. Just imagine your eyelids feeling so comfortable, so heavy, so heavy, so relaxed and now let all of the muscles in the back of your neck and shoulders relax, feel a heavy, heavy weight being lifted off your shoulders and you feel relieved, lighter and more relaxed. And all of the muscles in the back of your neck and shoulders relax, and feel that soothing relaxation go down your back, down, down, down, to the lower part of your back, and those muscles let go and with every breath you inhale just feel your body drifting, floating, down deeper, down deeper, down deeper into total relaxation. Let your muscles go, relaxing more and more. Let all of the muscles in your shoulders, running down your arms to your fingertips, relax. And let your arms feel so heavy, so heavy, so heavy, so comfortable, so relaxed. You may have tingling in your fingertips. That's perfectly fine. You may have warmth in the palms of your hands, and that's fine. And you may feel that you can barely lift your arms, they are so relaxed, they are so heavy, so heavy, so relaxed. And now you inhale once again and relax your chest muscles. And now as you exhale, feel your stomach muscles relax. As you exhale, relax all of the muscles in your stomach, let them go, and all of the muscles in your legs, feel them relax and all the muscles in your legs, so completely relaxed right to the tips of your toes. Notice how very comfortable your body feels, just drifting and floating, deeper, deeper, deeper relaxed. And as you are relaxing deeper and deeper, imagine a beautiful staircase. There are ten steps, and the steps lead you to a special and peaceful and beautiful place. In a moment you can begin to imagine taking a safe and gentle and easy step down, down, down on the staircase, leading you to a very peaceful, a very special place for you. You can imagine it to be any place you choose. Perhaps you would enjoy a beach or ocean with clean, fresh air, or the mountains with a stream; any place is perfectly fine. In a moment I'm going to count backwards from ten to one and you can imagine taking the steps down and as you take each step, feel your body relax, more and more, feel it just drift down,

down each step, and relax even deeper, ten, relax even deeper, nine . . . eight . . . seven . . . six . . . five . . . four . . . three . . . two . . . one . . . deeper, deeper, deeper, relaxed. And now imagine a peaceful and special place. You can imagine this special place and perhaps you can even feel it. You are in a [INSERT SPECIAL PLACE]. You are alone and there is no one to disturb you. This is the most peaceful place in the world for you. Imagine yourself there and feel that sense of peace flow through you and sense of well-being and enjoy these positive feelings and keep them with you long after this session is completed, for the rest of this day and evening, tomorrow. Allow these positive feelings to grow stronger and stronger, feeling at peace with a sense of well-being, and each and every time that you choose to do this kind of relaxation you will be able to relax deeper and deeper. Regardless of the stress and tension that may surround your life, you may now remain more at peace, more calm, more relaxed, and allow the tension and stresses to bounce off and away from you, just bounce off and away from you. And these positive feelings will stay with you and grow stronger and stronger throughout the day as you continue to relax deeper and deeper.

Enjoy your special place for another moment and then I will begin to count from one to ten and as I count from one to ten you can begin coming back to full consciousness, and will come back feeling refreshed as if you had a long rest. Come back feeling alert and relaxed. Begin to come back now. One . . . two . . . coming up, three . . . four . . . five . . . six . . . seven . . . eight . . . nine, begin to open your eyes, and ten, open your eyes and come all the way back, feeling great.

Game #6
The Inner Vacation

Once you have become familiar with the structure of the previous game, The Relaxing Journey, construct a personal fantasy for your mate. First, ask your partner for a list of favorite experiences—vacation spots, relaxing activities, enjoyable activities—and then ask him to lie down as you take him on a relaxing inner vacation. Take your time, and exaggerate the soothing qualities of your voice, for it will lull your partner into a dream-like world. Begin the journey on a plane or a boat that is about to land at the most wonderful place in the world, filled with every pleasurable experience that you can think up. Use the images and activities that your partner gave you, for they will stimulate pleasurable memories and thoughts.

Remind your partner to breathe deeply and relax, yawning, stretching, feeling warm and heavy, and so on. When you have succeeded in creating a state of bliss, switch places and let your partner guide you to your innermost place of joy. Of course, if he or she is too blissed out to respond, make a date for a more convenient time.

Game #7
Couples Breathing

This little technique is a delightful way to integrate breathing with the intimacy of love. Tonight, when you go to bed, lie next to your partner and notice how she breathes. Let yourself melt into her breath—synchronizing yours to hers—as you quietly drift into sleep.

It is even more enchanting if your partner joins in. As the two of you lie there, your awareness will move gently back and forth as a variety of feelings, thoughts, and images flow through your mind. You will find yourself floating in a semi-conscious world of dreams, and when you wake up in the morning, you will feel particularly refreshed.

If you wish, you may also sit facing each other, at a table or on the floor, and consciously breathe together. You can do this within your natural rhythm of breath, or you can be more structured, breathing *in* as your partner breathes *out,* and then breathing out as she breathes in. In the tantric traditions of the East, this is considered by many to be a spiritually erotic high. In chapter 5, this exercise will be expanded to include a variety of ways to sensually touch, taste, and gaze upon your partner's body and soul.

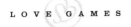

Game #8
Heavy Artillery—Progressive Muscle Relaxation

Some people may have difficulty using the previous exercises to relax; still others may prefer a different approach. The following technique, developed in the 1920s by the American physiologist Edmund Jacobson, is the "heavy artillery" of relaxation training and is quite effective when working with people who are unusually tense or who have muscles that feel like steel. It is a basic stress-reduction technique used in clinics throughout the world and is presented here by Herbert Benson, founding president of Harvard's Mind/Body Medical Institute.[12]

> In progressive muscle relaxation, you methodically sweep through your body, tensing and then relaxing each major muscle group. This attunes you to the difference in feeling when your muscles are tensed or relaxed and is another way to elicit the relaxation response.
>
> This technique can be done in any large chair that supports your head and neck, but is best done lying on your back on a firm but soft surface, such as a thick carpet or workout mat. (A bed is too soft—you're more likely to glide off to sleep.) Lie on your back with your arms along your sides. Loosen any clothing that's uncomfortably tight, and take off your shoes.
>
> You can have someone read you the instructions, or make a tape for yourself. These should be read at a slow, easygoing pace:
>
> First, tense the muscles throughout your body, from head to toe. Tighten your feet and legs, tense your arms and hands, clench your jaw, and contract your stomach. Hold the tension while you sense the feelings of strain and tightness. Study the tension and notice the difference between how the muscle feels when it is tensed and when it is relaxed. Then take a deep breath, hold it, and exhale long and slowly as you relax all your muscles, letting go of the tension. Notice the sense of relief as you relax.
>
> Now you're going to tense and relax individual groups of muscles, keeping the rest of your body as relaxed as you can.

You'll hold the tension for a few seconds in each part of your body while you get a clear sense of what the tension feels like; then breathe deeply, hold the breath for a moment, and let go of the tension as you exhale.

Start by making your hands into tight fists. Feel the tension through your hands and arms. Relax and let go of the tension. Now press your arms down against the surface they're resting on. Feel the tension. Hold it . . . and let go. Let your arms and hands go limp.

Shrug your shoulders tight, up toward your head, feeling the tension through your neck and shoulders. Hold . . . then release, letting go. Drop your shoulders down, free of tension.

Now wrinkle your forehead, sensing the tightness. Hold . . . release, letting your forehead be smooth and relaxed. Shut your eyes as tight as you can. Hold . . . and let go. Now open your mouth as wide as you can. Hold it . . . and gently relax, letting your lips touch softly. Then clench your jaw, teeth tight together. Hold . . . and relax. Let the muscles of your face be soft and relaxed, at ease.

Take a few moments to sense the relaxation throughout your arms and shoulders, up through your face. Now take a deep breath, filling your lungs down through your abdomen. Hold your breath while you feel the tension through your chest. Then exhale and let your chest relax, your breath natural and easy. Suck in your stomach, holding the muscles tight . . . and relax. Arch your back . . . hold . . . and ease your back down gently, letting it relax. Feel the relaxation spreading through your whole upper body.

Now tense your hips and buttocks, pressing your legs and heels against the surface beneath you . . . hold . . . and relax. Curl your toes down, so they point away from your knees . . . hold . . . and let go of the tension, relaxing your legs and feet. Then bend your toes back up toward your knees . . . hold . . . and relax.

Now feel your whole body at rest, letting go of more tension with each breath . . . your face relaxed and soft . . . your arms and shoulders easy . . . stomach, chest, and back soft and relaxed . . . your legs and feet resting at ease . . . your whole body soft and relaxed.

Take time to enjoy this state of relaxation for several minutes, feeling the deep calm and peace. When you're ready to get up, move slowly, first sitting, and then gradually standing up.

Game #9
Herbert Benson's Relaxation Response

In this final game, I would like to show you how to experience Herbert Benson's famous Relaxation Response, an exercise that shows how relaxation is integral to the spiritual traditions of every culture throughout the world.

In the early 1970s, Benson discovered that a group of meditation students could substantially alter their body's metabolism, creating a state of relaxation that was effective in the treatment of headaches, pain, insomnia, stress, anxiety, depression, and other related ailments. Later, he discovered that the same benefits could be elicited by virtually any other meditative technique, be it Eastern or Western in origin. Yoga, Zen, hypnosis, autogenic training (cultivating feelings of heaviness and warmth in the body), and progressive relaxation were found to be equally effective in triggering the relaxation response.[13]

Benson and his associates identified two basic components that create this special state. The first was the use of a repetitious word or phrase, which helped to minimize distracting thoughts. The second was the deliberate ignoring of those thoughts that did intrude. Benson then discovered that nearly every religious tradition throughout history used some form of repetition—a word or phrase or prayer, or a muscular activity—that served as a point of focus for spiritual contemplation. When tested in the laboratory, all these forms of repetition were effective in soothing the body and mind.

Any sound will work. When I was a preschool teacher, I discovered that humming could calm down an entire class of five-year-olds. One long *Mmm* was all I had to say. I didn't have to explain anything, and I never explained my intentions, but the kids would automatically join in and form a line. A *neat* line, with no pushing or crowding or interruption. I could walk them around the entire school, humming away in an exquisitely organized way, which is no small feat if you have ever worked with kids.

Imagine what could happen if we were to bring these universal principles of relaxation into our homes, our schools, and places of work. If we were to practice this version of Benson's technique with our family and colleagues and friends, we could, perhaps, bring greater tolerance and peace to the world. Guide your partner through the following steps and see how it affects your life:

1. Find a word, a phrase, a prayer, or a sound that has great meaning for you, one that feels particularly peaceful or calm. Then ask your partner to do the same. It may be a simple sound like *aum* or *aahhh* or *mmmmm,* or a familiar word like *thanks* or *shalom* or *peace.* If you prefer, you may use part of a favorite prayer or chant.

2. Sit comfortably and close your eyes. Take several deep breaths, and as you exhale, silently make your sound. You may, if you wish, say it out loud, which dramatically transforms the experience. If you want to try this in a group, use the same word or sound, speaking in unison as you all breathe out.

3. Stay with your breathing and the repetition of sound. When thoughts or feelings intrude, acknowledge them and let them go. Don't try to achieve a particular goal or state; just keep practicing for ten to twenty minutes. When you finish, sit quietly for a few moments and then open your eyes. If you are with others, make contact with their eyes. Stand up and stretch, then share your experiences with each other.

If you practice this exercise once or twice a day, you will notice, in just a few weeks, significant shifts in your awareness and behavior. You'll feel calmer, less anxious, and receptive. You may even lose your desire to smoke or drink or overeat, for the simplest meditations can cause tremendous change. It happens all the time.

In the next chapter, we will apply these relaxation techniques to the art of communication. By bringing our breathing and awareness into our intimate dialogues, we can more easily explore sensitive and difficult issues in meaningful and creative ways.

CHAPTER 3

The Art of Communication

The exercises in this chapter are essential for playing many of the games in this book, helping you to enhance your communication skills in creative and unusual ways. Learn how to use imaginary conversations for processing anger and fear, discover the "felt" sense of listening to your partner's speech, and experiment with dialogical meditation, the ultimate conversational game.

IN MY COUNSELING OFFICE, there hangs a little card, a reminder to help me stay focused and calm:

> I *think* about what I say, *before* I say it.
> I *listen* to what I say, *as* I say it.
> And I *reflect* upon what I say, *after* I say it.

If couples were to follow these three simple rules, the majority of relational conflicts, I believe, would subside. How often do we really pay attention to what we say? How carefully do we consider the effects of our words upon others? And do we really try to understand what our friends and lovers are trying to say? To think, to listen, and to carefully reflect upon what we say is the key for having meaningful dialogues with others.

Relationships thrive upon communication. Without communication, we couldn't survive, for the way we use language influences every part of life: from shaping personal identity to governing the social, cultural, and political structures of the world. We express ourselves not only through reason but also with emotions, through the tone of our voice, and the ways in which our bodies move. An extended silence, a quiet glance, or a gesture of the hand are as significant as the words we choose to speak. If we really want to know our partners, then we must give attention to the many levels of communication that exist: to the hidden meanings, covert desires, the indirect concerns, and to the ways we listen and respond.

But communication, by itself, is not an intimate act. It is simply a structure for getting along with others, for working out the rules of interaction, and for negotiating survival needs. If we truly desire intimacy,

> *Most of the time, in order to know and be known, we have to communicate or disclose something about our inner states or experiences. . . . Intimacy—the penetration of barriers—implies the capacity to let down defensive walls that keep us from revealing ourselves. . . . Once we know another and that person knows us, we are bonded in an incomparable way.*
>
> RUTHELLEN JOSSELSON
> *The Space Between Us*

then we must use our words to probe deeper into each other's lives.

There is a difference between everyday conversation and intimate dialogue. In our day-to-day communications our feelings are often concealed. Beginning in the first few years of life, we learn to be cautious about sharing feelings and thoughts. In contrast, an intimate dialogue is personally revealing. We learn to talk not only *to* the other person but also *from* ourselves, sharing what we internally think and feel.

But it takes courage to expose this inner life. Will we really be listened to and understood, or will we be criticized and judged? Or worse, will we simply be ignored? One false move, an off-color remark, a laugh that is interpreted as a scoff, and the intimate moment is lost. We may even discover a hidden personality, a shadow self filled with forbidden fantasies, urges, and fears.

In a conscious relationship, couples work together to create a satisfying exchange, cultivating a flexible style of interaction that is unique and specific to each person's developmental needs. With time, an intimacy can be constructed in which we learn to tolerate the occasional callous remark. But there are many people who don't know where to begin.

The Ultimate Communication Game

In 1994, my psychology colleagues and I developed a game that could, in a matter of minutes, propel two people into a profoundly intimate conversation. We called it *dialogical meditation,* a technique that integrated psychoanalytic principles with contemplative practices from the East.

Two people begin by facing each other and closing their eyes, breathing deeply and guiding themselves into a state of relaxation. Then they gaze at each other, paying attention to whatever feelings and thoughts emerge, and sharing them, in turn, with each other. Between each commentary, they return to their breathing as they let the previous feelings and thoughts dissolve.

In this free-associative dialogue, no objective or goal is sought; one simply observes where the conversation leads. Here is an example of what transpired once between a doctor and his colleague who were first introduced to the technique:

> *"Mmm,* I feel very relaxed," Tom began, after breathing deeply for about three minutes.
>
> "Ah, yes. It feels so strange, like I'm onstage or something," Barry replied.
>
> "My thoughts are breaking up. All I can do is sit and look at you. You look so incredibly relaxed." Tom closed his eyes and took another deep breath.
>
> "Your voice reminds me of the therapist Carl Rogers," Barry said.
>
> Tom smiled. "Why thank you. I don't think I've ever been so complimented."
>
> Barry suddenly turned sad. "You know, it's been very painful for me recently. Since my marriage ended, I haven't been able to focus well on my work. My mind keeps drifting away."
>
> Tom took a very deep breath; tears were welling up in his eyes. "My first impression was to reach out and touch you, and then a voice inside said, 'No, let him sit with his feelings for a bit.' "

"It's hard, really hard, but if I let these feelings go, I actually feel very happy and warm." Barry smiled and then added, "You know, it just occurred to me that I don't have to *try* to heal my clients. I can just be there with them as we are being with each other now."

Tom laughed. "Right before you said that, I had the very same thought about my patients! We try so hard to do our jobs, when all we have to do is open up."

The game soon ended, and the two men glowed with satisfaction. They were astonished at how easy it was to reach such an intimate place.

Each time this game is played, something new comes up. In this free-flowing state, a conversation can quickly shift from subject to subject or fall into extended periods of silence. Long-forgotten memories come suddenly into consciousness, but vulnerable feelings also erupt, bringing with them potent waves of anxiety. But as soon as the person returns to his or her breathing, the anxiety subsides. If a particularly uncomfortable thought arises, one may choose to note it in silence and explore it privately at a later time. Of course, because both participants are in relaxed and open states, it usually feels safe to share such thoughts. Rarely does this happen in personal dialogues and talks.

In dialogical meditation, a conversation can end at any time. Even if the game begins with a specific topic to explore, no conclusion is consciously strived for. Instead, one watches for a natural pause, or a moment when the flow of dialogue subsides. Sometimes, one partner may feel tired, or overwhelmed by a feeling of irritability that just won't go away. When this occurs, it helps to take a break and reschedule another time to talk.

With a little practice, dialogical meditation will naturally become part of one's conversational flow. The essence of this game is not just in the communication of words but also in the space we share together. In dialogical meditation, we are practicing how to *be* with another person, in conversation *and* in silence. In such a state, relationships can take on a numinous quality—a heightened sense of awareness where one's surroundings seem to come alive. It is a transcendent quality, hard to describe with words, but similar to how one might feel when watching a spectacular sunset or dawn.

I once gave a demonstration of dialogical meditation at a local bookstore. There were twelve women present in the audience, with two men sitting in the back. First, I guided the participants through a simple relaxation exercise, and then I asked for volunteers. Two women responded, and they sat down in front of the group, facing each other. They breathed deeply, as instructed, and shared the first thought that arose, which, in this case, was the degree of discomfort they felt.

"It feels embarrassing," said the one, pausing to take a breath.

"It doesn't feel natural," replied the other. "I don't know a thing about you."

After several pauses, comments, and breaths, they each acknowledged the other's courage in volunteering. Taking turns, they shared their reasons for coming. For one, it was a question of divorce and, for the other, the loneliness of her life. They were from different cultures, a generation apart, and yet it took only a few minutes before they were embracing each other's dilemma. When the game concluded, the women gave each other a hug. I asked the audience how long it usually took for an intimate conversation to unfold, and everyone laughed, responding with "an hour," "a week," or "forever."

I then asked if there was anyone in the audience who did *not* want to play the game, and the hands of the two men shot up. "Why not?" I questioned, and one responded, "I'm only here because my wife told me to come." The other man nodded in agreement. Knowing their reluctance, I invited them to play, and to my surprise they both came forward. I asked them to breathe and relax, and when they began to speak, a very different conversation took place. They confided how pressured they felt by their wives, who wanted them to be more communicative, and then they each

> *I feel a sense of satisfaction when I can dare to communicate the realness in me to another. This is far from easy, partly because what I am experiencing keeps changing every moment. Usually there is a lag, sometimes of moments, sometimes of days, weeks, or months, between the experiencing and the communication: I experience something; I feel something, but only later do I dare to communicate, when it has become cool enough to risk sharing it with another. But when I can communicate what is real in me at the moment that it occurs, I feel genuine, spontaneous, and alive.*
>
> CARL ROGERS
> *A Way of Being*

shared an intimate story about their feelings. I looked at the audience, and every woman, without exception, was smiling. By the time we ended the game, the men acknowledged an intimacy they rarely felt. For the moment, they were friends, looking forward to sharing the evening with their wives.

Expressing Vulnerabilities and Fears

In the therapeutic setting, dialogical meditation is particularly effective with couples who are striving for a more intimate union in life. But both partners must be willing to expose their vulnerabilities and fears. The following story, taken from a couple's therapy session, demonstrates the healing power of sharing one's deeper feelings and thoughts.

Karen and Jim had been together for close to twenty years and were high-school sweethearts when they married. They had wanted a family of their own, but after many years of trying, no pregnancy emerged. Karen grew distant, Jim withdrew into himself, and their communication fell apart. Karen would try to initiate a conversation, but she would always come away with a feeling of disappointment, and if the topic of children came up, she would get particularly upset. Therapy was a last resort.

"I can't get him to open up," she said. "I see something going on inside, but he just says that things are going fine." Jim looked down at the floor and confirmed his belief that everything was okay, but complained that he often felt pressured by his wife.

"Perhaps there's a little truth in what both of you are saying," I replied. "But I don't think that either one of you is expressing how you really feel."

They both disagreed, saying that they had gone over the same issues again and again. You could feel the tension in the air.

"Let's try a little experiment," I suggested. "I want you to close your eyes and breathe deeply for a few minutes, relaxing as much as you possibly can. Then, when you open your eyes, I want you to say whatever comes to mind, without censorship. Okay?"

They agreed, and I led them through a basic relaxation exercise. Jim was the first to speak. "I really feel uncomfortable being here," he volunteered. "I knew I'd be put down."

"Good," I said. "Now just let that feeling go and return to your

breathing and relaxation. Karen, what is the first thought or feeling that comes to you right now?"

"I'm angry," she replied. "And frustrated." They both felt trapped in silence.

Normally, when such a dialogue took place at home, communication between Karen and Jim would quickly come to an end or turn into a fight as they became enmeshed in their postures of defense. But I knew that the breathing and relaxation would allow them to go a little farther.

"Jim," I prodded. "I want you to take another deep breath and tell us what you're really feeling inside."

Jim sat quietly for a moment, weighing the risks of completely opening up. "It makes me feel like a failure," he finally said, covering part of his face.

Karen did not respond. She was hanging on to her anger as a defense, and I knew that too much silence could shut things down. If she truly wanted intimacy, she had to open up.

"Karen," I asked carefully, "how do you feel when Jim exposes his feelings of failure?"

"It hurts," she said, holding back her tears, "and I want to run and hide." She turned away from Jim.

"What else, Karen?" I say, reminding her to breathe. "What are you feeling now?"

With tears streaming down her face, she breaks. "I want to be there for him, but I don't know how. He won't tell me what he's feeling inside. I think he's really upset, but he always wears a smile."

"It's really hard," he replies. "I'm trying to do everything I can. I'm working around the clock, I'm exhausted, and I just didn't want to burden you with all this stress. That's why I try to act like everything is fine. I feel so torn up, I don't know what to do."

"Karen, how does it feel to hear what Jim just said?"

"It feels great. I really need to hear what's going on inside. I didn't know you felt so bad. I was feeling like a failure, too, but I didn't want to admit it. It's just too painful at times. I'm thirty-nine, I want a child, but I need to know that you're there." They smiled and cried and held each other as they talked about their lives.

Therapy, like any relationship, depends upon our willingness to communicate our *inner feeling states*—the subtle fears and anxieties, the nuances of our joys and pains—for these are the cues that alert our partners to how we experience life. If we do not talk about feelings, and if we do not talk *from* them, our friends and lovers will not be able to respond.

Intimacy requires risk, and if we begin our relationships by sharing our deeper fears and concerns, we may not need professional help, as did Karen and Jim, to save a valuable love. The following exercise will show you and your partner how to use dialogical meditation to deepen your emotional ties.

Game #1
Dialogical Meditation

Although dialogical meditation was originally designed to promote effective therapy, its value lies in its application to many levels of intimacy: improving communication, encouraging self-disclosure, exploring issues of trust, exposing unconscious processes, and creating an environment in which emotionally laden problems can be easily resolved. Using dialogical meditation, you can speak more directly and listen more carefully to what your partner says. Even your sensuality will increase, for when you enter this contemplative state, all of your senses come alive: physically, emotionally, and spiritually.

There's really no secret to these remarkable claims, for the key lies in your ability to relax and to allow your thoughts and feelings to flow. When you integrate dialogical meditation with the other games in this book, the experience is greatly enhanced, and it will take you more deeply into the subtle meanings and values that are embedded in each game.

The rules are simple, for all you need is a willing partner or friend. With a little practice, you can even integrate the technique with others who do not know that you are playing a sophisticated game; yet they will unconsciously respond with greater openness themselves.

1. Find a comfortable place where you will not be interrupted, and sit facing your partner—on a couch, at a table, or on the floor.

2. Close your eyes and breathe deeply for several minutes, calming your mind and relaxing every part of your body. When you feel

ready, open your eyes and gaze at your partner, breathing slowly in and out.

3. When a thought or feeling occurs, voice it to your partner in a sentence or two, then take a deep breath and let the thought and feeling go. Do not censor anything to yourself, but if it feels too uncomfortable to share, just note it silently and see what comes up next.

4. Your partner, who has been listening, will now take a breath and say the first thing that crosses his or her mind in response to what you have said. When finished, he or she will take another deep breath, which is your signal to respond with another feeling or thought.

5. As you keep taking turns, a spontaneous dialogue will emerge. Do not speak too long, and always return to your breath, reminding each other if one forgets. If you lose the contemplative flow, close your eyes and focus on your bodily state.

6. When either one of you feels ready to stop, even if the urge seems to occur in the middle of an important topic, let the other person know, hold each other's hands, and close with a compassionate acknowledgment. Take a break or go for a walk together, and when you feel refreshed, talk about your experiences. If an important conversation was interrupted, schedule a time to play the game again.

A friend of mine, a respected psychoanalyst and author, read about dialogical meditation in my book *The Art of Staying Together* and told me that it was fascinating to play in his imagination, but he wasn't sure if he had the courage to do it with his wife. It is a paradox worth pondering: we ask our partners to disclose their most intimate thoughts, but we hesitate when it comes to ourselves. Yet in every situation I've seen, when both partners risk emotional intimacy, a deeper bond unfolds.

What, then, might we do to encourage a more open exchange? We can begin by testing the waters with a fantasy relationship or two.

Game #2
The Imaginary Dialogue

Let's take a moment to experiment with dialogical meditation, using your imagination instead of playing with someone real. First, take a few minutes to breathe deeply and relax, for this will enhance your ability to visualize a dialogue between yourself and another. Close your eyes, and as you are breathing, think about three or four people from your past who elicit fond memories, and then pick the one who holds the most emotional impact for you right now. It could be an old flame, your first love, or a favorite teacher or a friend. Take out a sheet of paper and write down his or her name.

Visualize this person sitting in front of you, and then take another deep breath. How does it feel to think of this person again? As you gaze at your make-believe friend, notice what kinds of thoughts come to mind. Do not try to control, direct, or censor anything; just let your feelings and thoughts go. Jot them down on the paper you took out.

How does your imaginary friend respond? Write down the response, then spend the next few minutes letting an intimate conversation take place. What would you really like to say to this person after so many years, and how might he or she respond? Is there anything you wanted to say that you couldn't say before? If given a second chance, what would you say or do differently?

Now push your imagination further and express something you never shared before. Be daring: say something risky and vulnerable, and then fantasize about how your friend reacts. See where your unconscious processes go, be it pleasant, surprising, or uncomfortable. It's only a fantasy, but it can show you layers of feelings and thoughts that may have been buried for years. When the imaginary dialogue concludes, notice your state of mind. You should feel calm, alert, even euphoric.

> It seems to me that a confidential verbal relationship may be more intimate than a sexual relationship, which we tend to regard as the epitome of intimacy. . . . It takes a lot more effort—and existential commitment and trust—to have significant and satisfying verbal intercourse than to have sexual intercourse.
>
> THOMAS SZASZ, M.D.
> *The Evolution of Psychotherapy*

Now, if your real-life partner is willing, guide yourselves through several imaginary scenarios with people you have known from the past. Not only will you learn a great deal about significant people in your partner's life, but you will also be encouraging each other to speak more openly about deeper feelings and thoughts. With a little imaginative help, you can explore many intimate realms that have been overlooked or blocked.

Game #3

Shadow Play

There is also a shadow side to intimacy, a place where one's feelings and thoughts are not so romantic or nice. These are the more difficult parts to expose: the angers, hurts, and fears that lovers tend to hide.

In relationships, these darker emotions appear when problems and conflicts flare up. Some may feel unsafe to express, but they are important to expose, for they often provide clues to underlying feelings and concerns. A surface anger may connect to a deeper hurt from the past, a shame may hide an inner talent, and a nervous anxiety may point to a secret desire or wish. Other shadows may have to be tamed—a hidden addiction, a destructive impulse, an incapacitating fear—before a healthy relationship can bloom.

An imaginary conversation can also be used to provide a meaningful emotional release. According to psychoanalyst Roberto Assagioli, some people need to reexperience their unconscious fears and hostile feelings before they can truly feel safe in expressing affection and warmth toward others. When one of Assagioli's patients expressed difficulty in forming intimate attachments with men, he asked her to relive scenes from her childhood, visualizing the difficulties she had with her parents. The more she could allow herself to feel her hatred and rage, the freer she became in expressing her yearnings for greater intimacy and love.[14]

Try the following experiment: Think of someone from the past who has caused you anger and pain, a person who still irritates you somewhere deep inside. Jot down the name on a piece of paper.

As you visualize this person, let your anger and hurt increase. Breathing rapidly (pumping the air in and out of your lungs), tighten your jaw and the muscles in your shoulders and neck. Turn your hands into fists and exaggerate your emotional state. Notice what kinds of thoughts come to mind, and let this person have both barrels of your rage. Then write down the feelings and thoughts that come up.

Now, slow your breathing down and relax all the muscles in your body: your arms and shoulders, your neck and jaw and face. Think about how this imaginary person might respond. Does he listen or apologize, or does she simply walk away? Play out several scenarios and watch where your imagination goes, and when the fantasy comes to an end, notice your reaction and bodily state. You will probably feel relieved, as if you have let go of a cumbersome weight that you have carried around for years.

This technique can also be used to process emotional feelings that are stirred up when someone in the present hurts and angers you. If you take a few minutes to fantasize a dialogue or a fight, you may find not only relief but also a variety of solutions with which to approach an antagonistic friend.

> ### CHALLENGING THE PERCEPTIONS OF THE MIND
>
> *Imagine three people sitting in front of you: a friend, an enemy, and a stranger. . . . Settle the mind on the breath, then consider each person in turn, noticing how the image you have of them provokes a certain mood. . . . Are you able, even for a moment, to witness these people in all their autonomy, mystery, majesty, tragedy? . . . Can you notice the restrictive and selective nature of the image you have formed of them? Can you let go of the craving to embrace the friend and banish the enemy? Can you love the stranger?*
>
> STEPHEN BATCHELOR
> *Buddhism Without Beliefs*

Ask your partner if she would be willing to describe a painful conversation with someone from the past, then guide her through a fantasy scenario or two. Just by listening and being there, we can greatly assist others who may be struggling with anger and hurt. Through fantasies like these we can learn about our partner's vulnerabilities and fears—information that can direct us toward more caring dialogues and acts.

Game #4
The Imaginary Fight

Imaginary dialogues can also be used to expose potential vulnerabilities that could arise between you and your partner when you bring up a sensitive issue or complaint. Let's say, for example, that you need to talk

> *There are three simple steps toward the handling of neurotic fear. Each of these steps should be preceded by a deep breath and calm abiding within an image that appeals to you and can relax you. First, admit you feel fear. . . . Second, feel the fear fully, i.e., defenselessly, with no escape, with no attempts to get rid of it. . . . Third, and most difficult, act as if fear could not stop you.*
>
> D A V I D   R I C H O
> *When Love Meets Fear*

about a sexual or monetary problem (the two most common topics of dispute) with your spouse. Using your imagination, visualize a most unpleasant encounter: a terrible fight, a screaming fit, or a cold, demeaning stare-down. Then think about the kinds of things that you might actually say to each other in a moment of anger or rage.

Now, visualize the ideal encounter between you and your mate. How does the conversation begin? How do you avoid a conflict, what do you say, and how does your imaginary spouse respond? This type of exercise not only helps you to prepare for a real encounter, but it will also often provide you with useful strategies that you had not considered before. By using their imaginations, couples can resolve many conflicts before they actually occur.

Finally, take a sheet of paper and make a list of all the topics that you or your partner might find disturbing to talk about. Think about the problems that could emerge if you talked about the darker emotions concerning money, sex, fantasies, politics, religion, old age, family history, personal secrets, and lies. If you do not find the courage to broach these topics with your mate, you can create an imaginary dialogue to sort through most of your fears. When you have completed the visualization, ask yourself if your concerns were irrational or real. Often, it is only in one's imagination that fears can prosper and grow.

Real People, Real Conversations

Dialogical meditation teaches couples how to follow the flow of their feelings and thoughts without censorship. It is a difficult task to accomplish, but there are some people who seem to have no trouble expressing what they feel. They spew out everything—anger, hurt, rage, disappointment, ecstatic joy, etc.—believing that it is a healthy thing to do. Nothing could be farther from the truth. Such people often feel inordinately insecure, and because they have little sense of personal boundaries, they often broach intimate issues without preparation or agreement from their mates. Such behavior seriously damages the relationships they are in.

In real life, no matter how intimate you may be with a lover or friend, you cannot carelessly express whatever you think and feel. Even within the boundaries of dialogical meditation, certain thoughts may come to mind that could deeply hurt your mate if you blurted them out.

THE SIXTY-SECOND RULE

Any time a person asks a question, the respondent needs to pause sixty seconds before answering. Since the pause is obligatory, the likelihood is that the answer will include reflection, examination of intention, preview of tone—all the things that make for a wise response.

SYLVIA BOORSTEIN
It's Easier Than You Think

One must first pause and reflect upon the other person's ability to respond in a meaningful and constructive way. It may take dozens of internal conversations before you can successfully address your mate. The first step, then, is to develop an appropriate emotional state, one that promotes compassion, intimacy, and trust.

Game #5
Creating Serenity

Before engaging in a deep conversation, it is helpful to evoke a state of serenity for meeting face-to-face. The more relaxed you are, the more you will be open to the deeper feelings inside, and the easier it will be to respond with sensitivity.

One of the most important moments in relating is when couples first see each other after being away, yet many people come home preoccupied with other affairs. In such a state, you cannot acknowledge your spouse with the tenderness that she needs.

Before you arrive home and greet your mate, spend fifteen minutes creating a serene internal space. You can do this while preparing dinner, or before you leave the office, or even in the car when driving conditions are safe. Breathe deeply and relax, then visualize your partner in your mind—her beautiful smile, his open arms—and imagine a romantic embrace when the two of you first meet. Like a first date, such thoughts can rekindle those important moments of love.

> Think *about serenity; realize its value, its use, especially in our agitated modern life.* Praise *serenity in your mind;* de-sire *it. . . . Pledge yourself to remain serene throughout the day whatever happens; to be a living example of seren-ity; to radiate serenity.*
>
> ROBERTO ASSAGIOLI
> *Psychosynthesis*

Think about what your partner would like from you when you meet—a gentle hug, a five-minute massage, the reading of a poem, a simple gift—and surprise her with it when you arrive. And if your partner is filled with tension, your own serenity will melt the stress away. Who would not cherish being met in such a way? The more loving thoughts we hold about our mates throughout the day, the more satisfaction we will feel with every aspect of life.

Game #6

The Observing Self

Sometimes, however, we just can't seem to enter into serenity. Our minds are filled with distractions and worries, and no matter how hard we try to calm ourselves, our thoughts will not turn off. The easiest thing to do when such occasions arise is simply to sit back and watch.

As anyone who has practiced meditation knows, the mind does not like being quiet. In fact, the more we try to calm it, the busier it seems to get. Swami Vivekananda called it the "monkey mind" because it jumps around incessantly from thought to thought:

> There was a monkey, restless by his own nature, as all monkeys are. As if that were not enough, someone made him drink freely of wine, so that he became still more restless. Then a scorpion stung him. . . . To complete his misery, a demon en-tered into him. What language can describe the uncontrol-lable restlessness of that monkey? The human mind is like that monkey; incessantly active by its own nature; then it becomes drunk with the wine of desire, thus increasing its turbulence. After desire takes possession . . . the demon of pride enters the mind, making it think itself of all importance. How hard to control such a mind! The first lesson, then, is to sit for some

time and let the mind run on. The mind is bubbling up all the time. It is like that monkey jumping about. . . . Give it the rein; many hideous thoughts may come into it; you may be astonished that it was possible for you to think such thoughts. But you will find that each day the mind's vagaries are becoming less and less violent, that each day it is becoming calmer.[15]

There is great benefit in simply watching what the mind produces, for it provides an entry into the deeper labyrinths of your soul. As you watch, stay focused on your breathing and relaxation, for soon you will develop an awareness that is separate from a normal state of consciousness. This is your *observing self*, a separate awareness that is less judgmental and reactive. It's almost like being of two minds: the familiar one that is so often caught up in itself and another one that is simply quiet, relaxed, and aware. This observing self also *thinks* differently, often providing deeper insights about yourself.

Developing an observing self greatly benefits relationships because you are capable of remaining detached from emotional issues and reactions that might distance you from your partner. In an intimate conversation, you can speak from your observing self as you silently follow the ramblings of your everyday mind. The more you practice this meditative technique (which will be enhanced by reviewing Jack Kornfield's suggestions in chapter 2, game 4), the easier it becomes to talk about difficult issues with your mate. It also improves your listening skills by showing you how to listen to yourself.

Game #7
Talking about Intimacy

Since intimacy is not a natural act, each couple must create a meaningful plan for closeness that suits their respective needs. Ask your partner what her intimate desires are, and talk about how each of your needs can be met. If communication ranks high on the list, decide how often an intimate dialogue should take place. Research suggests that a minimum of ten minutes each day is necessary, but many couples need and want more. If work separates you during the week, a two-hour weekend chat can reestablish a bond.

> When the two of you have something important to discuss, I suggest that you sit facing each other and hold or touch each other's hands while you talk. Why? Because when you maintain physical touch and eye contact, there is much less chance of garbled messages and misunderstanding.
>
> LORI GORDON
> *Passage to Intimacy*

Because intimacy itself can mean many things to different people, ask your partner the following questions. By asking questions about your partner's desires, rather than stating your own, you demonstrate a willingness to listen and respond to his or her deeper needs:

What does intimacy mean to you?

What forms of intimacy do you desire from me?

What kind of intimate exchange would you like in the morning, the evening, and the afternoon?

What would be your fantasy of the ideal intimate weekend?

What fears or problems have you had, or do you now have, with intimacy?

After carefully listening to what your partner says, you can then share your own concerns and ideals. As you discuss these issues, notice how your definition of intimacy evolves, for when people talk about such feelings, they often discover more avenues for expressing feelings of love. They feel more open, receptive, and responsive to those they care for and respect.

Take a sheet of paper and write down a summary of your and your partner's definition of intimacy. Post it where it can be seen by both of you, and make a note on your calendar to look at it again in a month. Intimacy is a vast and complex subject, and its meaning will continue to mature.

Game #8
The Traveling Conversation

Most of the games in this chapter formalize the dialogical process: you make an arrangement to sit down with your partner and you carry out a specific task. Even dialogical meditation, which encourages a spontaneous flow of thoughts and feelings, is structured around a formal contemplative process. But there is a more informal way to stimulate constructive dialogues: walking. It automatically takes you into your breathing, connecting you with your body and the environment in which you walk.

Whenever I have a difficult situation to discuss with my partner or friends, I invite them to take a walk, and the more complex the problem is, the longer the hike will be. I personally prefer to walk in nature: in a park, or in the mountains, or along a beautifully landscaped street. Nature grounds me in my senses, and the colors and textures and smells help clear my mind of excess thoughts. It is part of my spiritual essence and practice. Walking keeps me focused, and I will hike for as long it takes to work through the problem at hand. In a "traveling" conversation, the destination is the space in which a dialogue best flows, where a strong connection is felt between you and the person you are with.

When I am dealing with particularly stressful issues, I take a strenuous hike, for the exercise can interrupt emotions that might otherwise interfere with an intimate conversation. Sometimes, before I broach a sensitive issue, I will just keep walking until my emotional state collapses from exhaustion. When this occurs, I know that I can more easily relate my feelings and thoughts to the person I am with.

The relationship between walking and insightful dialogue is well known to philosophers and poets. Einstein, for example, would use his walks to clarify his theories of relativity, and Emerson, Thoreau, and Hawthorne all drew inspiration from their walks. So the next time an important issue comes up with your spouse, take a long walk and open your heart to the powers of the natural world.

> *I was walking through the woods and I noticed that the green things were nodding to me; they were affirming me; they were, in effect, saying yes, we appreciate you and you appreciate us.*
>
> RALPH WALDO EMERSON
> *Essay on Nature*

> *Walking inspires and promotes conversation that is grounded in the body, and so it gives the soul a place where it can thrive.*
>
> THOMAS MOORE
> *Soul Mates*

Game #9
Nathaniel Branden's Experiment with Intimacy

Nathaniel Branden, a leading relationship expert who emphasizes the importance of consciousness for developing lasting love, devised a daring experiment for establishing intimacy in a single day. Branden uses his technique with couples who are distant or estranged, but I have found it to be a valuable exercise for anyone who is intimately involved. All it requires is to spend twelve hours with your partner, without interruption. By the end of the day, you will have created a template for intimacy that can be used for many years to come. Here is Branden's description of the game:

> Sometimes, when working with a man and woman who have become estranged from each other or whose relationship appears to have become lifeless and mechanical, I will propose a certain "homework assignment." They are asked to spend a day together, entirely alone. No books, no television, no telephone calls. If they have children they make arrangements for someone to take care of them. No distractions of any kind are allowed. They are committed to remaining in the same room with each other for twelve hours. They further agree that no matter what the other might say, neither will leave the room refusing to talk. And of course there must under no circumstances be any physical violence. They can sit for several hours in total and absolute silence if they like, but they must remain together.
>
> Typically, in the first hour or two there is some stiffness, there is self-consciousness; there may be joking or sparks of irritation. But almost always, after a while, communication begins. Perhaps one partner talks about something that has angered him or her. Perhaps a quarrel develops. But then, within another hour or two, the situation begins to reverse itself; there is growing closeness, a new intimacy. Very often they make love. Afterward they are generally cheerful and, although it may be only three o'clock in the afternoon, one of them, out

of nervousness, frequently proposes that the experiment has "worked" so it is all right now to go off to the movies or take a drive or visit friends or *do something*. But if they stay with their original commitment, which of course they are urged to do, they soon move down to a much deeper level of contact and intimacy than the earlier one, and the area of communication begins to expand. Often they share feelings they have never discussed before—talk of dreams and longings that they have never revealed before. They discover things in themselves and their partner that they have never realized before. They are free during this twelve-hour session to talk about anything, *providing it is personal,* as opposed to discussions of business, problems concerning the children's schoolwork, domestic details, and so forth. They must talk about themselves or each other or the relationship. Having placed themselves in a situation where all other sources of stimulation are absent, they have only their own selves and each other, and then they begin to learn the meaning of intimacy. There is almost always a gradual deepening feeling, a deepening emotional involvement, an expanding experience of aliveness.

More often than not the day ends happily. But sometimes it ends with the realization that the relationship may no longer serve the needs of either and that they may not wish to remain together. This is not a failure of the experiment, but a success. It is a success because the waste of two lives in an empty marriage or relationship is a tragedy.

When I first propose this experiment to couples I receive one of two reactions, generally speaking: anticipatory excitement—or anxiety. Either reaction is informative. If the thought of spending twelve hours in the presence of "only my mate" fills one with apprehension, that is a fact worth knowing.

I have found that for two people who love each other but who do not know how to make their relationship work, or do not seem to know how to communicate effectively, a twelve-hour session of this kind, participated in at least once a month, can produce the most radical changes in the quality of the relationship. One of the changes is the unexpected discovery of

communication skills they did not even dream they could possess.

The Art of Listening

Branden's experiment emphasizes the importance of setting aside time for talking about intimacy, but there is another part—a silent dimension—that is equally important yet often overlooked: the ability to listen well.

When we are talking *to* others, there are many things to consider. How, for example, do I communicate what I really want to say? Does the tone of my voice illuminate or hide my feelings? Am I talking defensively? Am I being too vague? Is the other person understanding what I say, or am I talking too long or abstractly? Listening, too, requires equal attention and skill:

> *Each one of us has a responsibility in a relationship for knowing what we are receiving and what we are giving. . . . [and] the simplest way to find out is to ask—and be willing to listen undefensively, with an interest in learning rather than in justifying our own behavior.*
>
> NATHANIEL BRANDEN
> *The Art of Living Consciously*

Am I *really* paying attention to what the other person says?

Do I interrupt or respond too soon?

Do I fully understand what the other person *means*?

Can I clearly identify what the core issues are?

Can I grasp what the unspoken issues are?

Am I listening to the person's tone, mood, and body language?

Am I judging what the other person is saying?

Can I suspend my own beliefs and see things through the eyes of the other?

These are just some of the questions an active listener must ask. In your relationships with others, how well do you think you listen, and how often to you feel that others have carefully listened to you? Most people will respond by saying that it doesn't happen often enough.

Game #10

True Listening

Think about a recent conversation you had. How clearly do you remember what the other person said? Did you really pay attention, and did you really understand what he or she was trying to convey? Or did you only half-listen, waiting for the opportunity to focus upon your own issues and concerns?

"True listening," says psychologist Scott Peck, "no matter how brief, requires tremendous effort. First of all, it requires total concentration. . . . If you are not willing to put aside everything, including your own worries and preoccupations for such a time, then you are not willing to truly listen."[16] Peck, in his therapeutic work, often requires that his clients talk to each other *by appointment,* with one person focusing entirely upon what the other person says. It is one of the best ways to bring into consciousness the subtle aspects of listening.

Think of an important question or issue that you would like your partner to discuss, and then invite him or her to talk. Your goal is to keep your partner talking for twenty minutes or more, but do not disclose your plan. Using as few words as possible, you must show your partner that you are genuinely interested and listening as fully as you possibly can. Instead of sharing your own views, direct your partner into his or her own thoughts. Ask questions, and when something seems vague, ask for clarification. If your attention wanders, ask your mate to repeat what was said.

If you can make it last twenty minutes without arousing suspicion, paraphrase and reflect back to your mate—*without judgment*—what he or she

If you set aside a period of time when you only listen, and indicate only whether you follow or not, you will discover a surprising fact. People can tell you much more and also find more inside themselves than can ever happen in ordinary interchanges. . . . In ordinary social interchange we nearly always stop each other from getting very far inside. Our advice, reactions, encouragements, reassurances, and well-intentioned comments actually prevent people from feeling understood. Try following someone carefully without putting anything of your own in. You will be amazed.

EUGENE GENDLIN
Focusing

> [The third ear] can catch what other people do not say, but only feel and think; and it can also be turned inward. It can hear voices from within the self that are otherwise not audible because they are drowned out by the noise of our conscious thought processes. . . . Trust these messages, [and] be ready to participate in all flights and flings of one's imagination.
>
> THEODOR REIK
> *Listening with the Third Ear*

has said. This shows your partner that you were listening carefully, one of the most therapeutic gifts you can give.

Tell your partner about the experiment, and discuss the experience together. Ask your partner how often he or she truly feels listened to, and talk about what each of you can do to listen more fully to the other. After every intimate talk, make a habit of asking your partner for an evaluation of your listening and communicating skills.

Dialogical meditation can offer specific help in the development of listening skills, for the exercise is designed to help us become less attached to what we say and hear. We communicate something to our partners, then consciously let go of the thought, returning to our breathing as our partners speak to us. In this brief silence, where our thoughts are put aside, we develop a different kind of listening and attention. We literally don't do anything with what we hear. We don't interpret or analyze. We simply allow the other person's words to flow through us like a stream.

When we listen to the sounds of a stream, we do not try to understand it. We feel it, we enjoy it, we take it in, and for a very brief moment we become one with the trickle and flow. The same is true in relationships: when we allow ourselves to resonate with the other person's experience, a closer bond is felt. We are listening with the third ear, as Theodor Reik would say, where one mind speaks openly to the other, in silence.[17] Only then can we come to appreciate all that lies beneath the surface of our words.

The following two exercises will help you to develop these special listening skills:

Game #11
The Felt Sense of Listening

Imagine, for a moment, that you are sitting on a boat, floating on the ocean or a lake. Can you *feel* what it is like as the boat bobs up and down? Now imagine that you are at the top of a giant roller coaster. Can you re-capture the *bodily sense* of falling or spinning around?

These are not intellectual memories; rather, they are memories of a *felt sense* of the experience. But what is the felt sense of a relationship? What do trust, intimacy, and compassion *feel* like? These sensations, when recognized, can open you up to fuller expressions of love.

Sit down with your partner and face each other, breathing deeply to relax. Using the dialogical meditation technique, begin a conversation, but instead of focusing on what you say, turn your attention to listening. Don't try to make sense out of the words; just focus on the tone of your two voices—the softness, the peaks and valleys of the conversational flow. Notice what happens in your body. How do certain statements affect your mood? Experiment with each other by expressing yourselves in different ways. Say something soothing and notice how it feels; then notice the difference when your partner responds in a soothing way. Then, speak force-fully, with agitation, with fear, with anger, excitement, and surprise, paying close attention to the bodily feeling sense.

As you listen, you will then begin to perceive an inner sensation—a gut-level response—that is clearly separate from your emotions and thoughts. This is the felt sense of listening, and with a little bit of practice, you can bring this quality into every intimate talk. When dealing with complex emotional issues, you will find it eas-ier to focus on your partner's needs; you will not be pulled into a defensive reaction or response.

If you have trouble identifying

> *Our minds are incapable of listening as long as they are translating, justify-ing, condemning, accepting, or rejecting something. . . . If you listen partially, with a particular prejudice or bias, if you listen as a capitalist, as a communist, as a socialist, as a member of any partic-ular religion, or God knows what else, obviously you are only listening to what you want, and therefore there is no lib-eration, no understanding of the new.*
>
> KRISHNAMURTI
> *The Collected Works*, vol. 8

this subtle bodily response, try the exercise again using only sounds: *aahhh, mmmmmm, oohhh*. Once the vibrational quality is felt, you should be able to feel a similar response to spoken phrases and words.

The felt sense of listening exemplifies an important point: that communication contains much more than words and the meanings we attach to them. "Words strain, crack and sometimes break, under the burden, under the tension, slip, slide, perish, decay with imprecision, will not stay in place," T. S. Eliot once wrote, for all great poets have known the limitations of speech. When we listen to another's words, we need to remember that they often mean something different from what we may think, that words are vague and can only partially describe one's feelings and thoughts. Thus, it is wise to assume that we can, at best, only catch a glimmer of what our partners think and feel. Only with time—and I believe it takes years—will we truly understand.

Game #12
Listening with Your Body

Listening is more than an intellectual process, but it is often difficult to step outside of the analytic style of thought. To help people past this barrier, transpersonal psychologist Charles Tart uses an innovative technique, one that integrates psychology with esoteric teachings from the East:

Try a little experiment. I would like you to hear me talking to you *in* your lower legs. I would like you to feel my voice in your legs. Are you hearing me in your legs?

STUDENT: *No.*

Are you feeling your legs now?

STUDENT: *Yes. Somewhere there.*

Are you hearing my voice and feeling your legs simultaneously?

STUDENT: *Yes, now I'm getting it.*

See, that's it. It sounds pretty good. Judging from the quality of your voice and posture, it sounds like you are sensing, looking, and listening. I can't be sure, of course, you could be doing it in a purely passive way. But I think you're doing it well now.

Close your eyes for a second. Just listen to the sound of my voice and open your attention to your whole body, your body in general. Are there any places in your body in which you feel my voice more than other places? It might be a moving pattern or it might be a static pattern. Now compare that sound to loud clapping. [*Claps several times.*] Is there a difference?

STUDENT: *I can hear the clapping with more vibration. Your voice I hear more in my ears.*

How conventional to hear sounds with your ears! We are taught that it is our ears that we hear with. All the authorities tell us that. Did anybody else try this while I was talking with her? Did you hear me in your legs?

STUDENT: *I heard your voice more in my body and the clapping more in my ears.*

ANOTHER STUDENT: *I felt your voice most in my solar plexus area.*

I would suggest you all get a little practice with the following meditation exercise.

Once in a while sit down for ten minutes, close your eyes, and listen to whatever sounds there are. Simultaneously, sense whatever sensations there are in your body. Don't force a connection between sounds and body sensations, but notice when there is one. I think success at this is primarily a matter of sensitization. As far as I know, everybody can do this, but you have to be sensitized. . . .

You can do this meditation in three ways, all of which are useful. One is to formally decide where in your body you want to experience sounds, in your arm, say, or your knee or your solar plexus, whatever. Or you could systematically scan your whole body in a regular pattern, and notice whatever sensations occur as you try to hear whatever sounds are occurring there. The third is to simply follow whatever sensation is strong in your body at any given moment and notice how sounds register there, too. Try it various ways, over several different sessions.

This is a good meditation for noisy environments: the sounds become a necessary part of your technique, instead of being treated as a distraction.

Beyond Words: The Silence of Intimacy

Often, when couples sink deeply into intimacy, they arrive at a place of inner mutual silence. Although no words are spoken, communication is still taking place in one's being. We hear the language of the body in the breath. We see the expressions of the face change from one moment to the next: a smile, a gentle sigh, a softening in the eyes, a nod of admiration. Every nuance and gesture bespeaks the intimacy we hold. This is the intimacy of silence, and the beauty that lies within.

Within this fleeting silence, something different occurs: our sense of identity falls away. When thoughts come to an end, there is no "self," no concept of "I" or "you," only the experience of now, and in this wordless intimacy, a glimmer of truth may be found.

As you explore the body of games that follow, try to practice the tools you have learned in this chapter to foster intimacy with your mate. Prepare yourself before each encounter, calming your body and your mind, generating compassionate thoughts, listening carefully, and following the wisdom of your observing self. Use each game as an opportunity to expose the deeper, more vulnerable parts of yourself. By consciously going within, you will touch your partner's soul.

PART TWO

LOVE
GAMES

Who is this Beautiful One,
This One who stays up all night
teaching love games to Venus and the Moon?
This One
whose enchanting gaze
seals up the two eyes of heaven?
O seekers, it is your own heart!

RUMI

CHAPTER 4

Discovery Games: Exploring Your Partner's Inner World

These games will help you and your partner know each other better, show-ing you how to examine each other's underlying values and beliefs con-cerning love, sex, family, money, and spirituality. By creating a safe environment in which to expose vulnerable issues, we can deepen our in-timate bonds and help each other to heal relational wounds.

IT WAS A LONG, long time ago when Eve took an apple from the for-bidden tree. But when she bit into the fruit, she saw that it was good, and so she gave one to her man.

"I cannot," said Adam, "for God has warned me that I will die."

A serpent appeared and whispered in Adam's ear: "You will not die, but your eyes will be opened and you shall be like a god, knowing evil from good."

And so they ate from the Tree of Knowledge and saw themselves for the very first time, with all their vulnerabilities and shame. Standing face-to-face and stripped of their ignorance, they became frightened and hid amongst the leaves.[18]

Discovering Who We Are

When it comes to issues of intimacy, we are all like Adam and Eve. First we fall in love, roaming through Edens of romance, blissful but naive. Eventually we stumble upon something hidden, a secret that portends a deeper meaning or truth. Then we are enticed by the serpent of con-sciousness to discover ourselves. Having tasted of this wonderful fruit, we invite our partners to open up their souls. But they, like Adam, are frightened and hesitant to expose the more vulnerable parts of their souls. Childhood fears emerge, feelings get hurt, and they retreat into the safety of themselves. Communication and intimacy recede.

Intimacy is a conscious act in which we agree to share our hidden selves, our weaknesses as well as our strengths. If we really want to know who our partners are and explore the deeper realms of intimacy, we must risk the loss of innocence. But it takes courage to look within and share what we might find, for we often fear how our partners might respond.

The games in this chapter are designed to gently open unconscious doors, taking you into the places that are often overlooked during the early months of romance and insufficiently dealt with in the later years of love: issues concerning money, values, friendship, family secrets, and childhood lies. By playfully exploring such issues through the metaphor of a game you will see how the patterns of the past influence and possibly interfere with current relational events. These games will teach you how to approach complex issues with sensitivity, and they will show you how to encourage your partner to expose more of the inner world that lies hidden within the soul.

> Children come into the world with a sense of celebration and delight in the awesomeness of life. Then we eat of that wonderful, terrible fruit depicted in the story of the Garden of Eden, and our lives become divided. In childhood we have innocent wholeness, which then is transformed into informed separateness. If one is lucky, a second transformation occurs later in life, a transformation into informed wholeness.
>
> ROBERT A. JOHNSON
> *Balancing Heaven and Earth*

Questions are at the core of discovery games, for questions encourage our partners to talk more fully about themselves. But questions, if carelessly put, can also feel invasive, and so we often push them aside. When dating, we sweep them under the table because they interrupt romance. And if by chance we fall in love, we may fail to ask deep questions for fear of disrupting the flow. Questions, too, can burst the bubbles of fantasy that underlie romantic beliefs, and thus there are many who enter marriage without really knowing who their partners are.

Even after we are married, essential questions go unasked because we do not want to stir up conflict, for questions can uncover differences we did not see before. On the other hand, the asking of questions implies that a person is genuinely interested in what we think and feel. As long as we are not met with a critical or judgmental reply, we will often share our vulnerabilities in the interest of deepening understanding and love.

This first exercise is designed to help you establish a healthy questioning dialogue with your mate.

Game #1
What, Where, When, and How?

Pick a time, once each week (on a Friday evening, for example), to play the following game with your partner, and continue it for the next three months. On a sheet of paper, write down a question that you would like to ask your partner, and then write down a second question that you have never thought about asking him or her before. It can be simple, silly, or deep, as long as it is somewhat different from the questions you have asked before. Ask your partner to do the same, and then read them to each other. If a question bewilders you or

> *I want to unfold.*
> *I don't want to stay folded anywhere,*
> *because where I am folded, there I am a lie.*
>
> RAINER MARIA RILKE

puts you on the defensive, you do not have to answer it, but if you can, talk about the reaction it caused. If your partner doesn't want to answer a question, let the issue go, trusting that he or she will think about it privately. At a later time, you may find that you can reapproach the topic with ease.

One of the most important questions to ask, however, is almost always overlooked, and so I have made it the focus of the next game. It is a simple question about love.

Game #2

A Question of Love

Take two blank sheets of paper, and at the top of each one, write, "What is your definition of love?" On the back, write, "What is my partner's definition of love?" Give one sheet to your partner and, for the next few minutes, write down every thought that comes to mind, continuing until the pages are full. When you have finished, read your definitions to each other, but be prepared for a surprise, for each of you may embrace very different notions about love.

How do I love thee? Let me count the ways.
I love thee to the depth and breadth and height
My soul can reach, when feeling out of sight
For the ends of Being and ideal Grace.
I love thee to the level of everyday's
Most quiet need, by sun and candle-light.
I love thee freely, as men strive for Right;
I love thee purely, as they turn from Praise.
I love thee with the passion put to use
In my old griefs, and with my childhood's faith.
I love thee with a love I seemed to lose
With my lost saints,—I love thee with the breath,
Smiles, tears, of all my life!—and, if God choose,
I shall but love thee better after death.

ELIZABETH BARRETT
BROWNING

I discovered this game by accident, when a client and her fiancé came in to discuss their marital plans. They were very excited and constantly talked about their love, so I asked them to define what they meant. She spoke, and then the trouble began, for as her boyfriend talked, she could do little more than stare with disbelief. "I had no idea you thought *that* way," she finally exclaimed, and for a moment their future seemed to dim. But as they conversed, they slowly came to realize what the other person meant. The differences were hard to accept at first, for their fantasies did not match, but they found the courage to honor each other's commitment and vision of love. Many years later, they told me how important the conversation had been, for it helped them to appreciate the complexities of love. They no longer took each other's feelings for granted, and they often sat down to reexamine their values and beliefs.

Couples often say "I love you," but they rarely tell each other what it personally means, partly because it is difficult to put into words. But when the effort is made, we become more sensitive to what our partners desire and need.

Game #3
The Ten-Minute Intimacy Test

Like love, intimacy also means different things to different people, and if we want to have our intimate desires come true, we must discuss what these feelings and beliefs are about. This test will help you to step outside of yourself so that you can discover how your partner feels about the quality of intimacy that exists in your current relationship. It is especially useful in relationships in which communication skills are weak.

Mark down your answers to the following questions, which encourage you to think about the relationship through your partner's eyes:

1. How satisfied is your partner with the intimacy in your relationship?

   never ≺ 0 1 2 3 4 5 6 7 8 9 10 ≻ always

   How satisfied are you with the intimacy in your relationship?

   never ≺ 0 1 2 3 4 5 6 7 8 9 10 ≻ always

2. Does your partner trust you?

   never ≺ 0 1 2 3 4 5 6 7 8 9 10 ≻ always

   Do you trust your partner?

   never ≺ 0 1 2 3 4 5 6 7 8 9 10 ≻ always

3. Does your partner get enough physical (nonsexual) affection from you?

   never ≺ 0 1 2 3 4 5 6 7 8 9 10 ≻ always

   Do you get enough physical (nonsexual) affection from your partner?

   never ≺ 0 1 2 3 4 5 6 7 8 9 10 ≻ always

4. Does your partner feel sexually satisfied?

   never ≺ 0 1 2 3 4 5 6 7 8 9 10 ≻ always

Do you feel sexually satisfied?

never ◄ 0 1 2 3 4 5 6 7 8 9 10 ➤ always

5. Are you as romantic as your partner desires?

never ◄ 0 1 2 3 4 5 6 7 8 9 10 ➤ always

Is your partner as romantic as you desire?

neverr ◄ 0 1 2 3 4 5 6 7 8 9 10 ➤ always

6. Are you as communicative as your partner desires?

never ◄ 0 1 2 3 4 5 6 7 8 9 10 ➤ always

Is your partner as communicative as you desire?

never ◄ 0 1 2 3 4 5 6 7 8 9 10 ➤ always

7. Are you sensitive to your partner's feelings, moods, and
emotional states?

never ◄ 0 1 2 3 4 5 6 7 8 9 10 ➤ always

Is your partner sensitive to your feelings, moods, and
emotional states?

never ◄ 0 1 2 3 4 5 6 7 8 9 10 ➤ always

8. Do you share, to your partner's satisfaction, your private
feelings and thoughts?

never ◄ 0 1 2 3 4 5 6 7 8 9 10 ➤ always

Does your partner share, to your satisfaction, his or her private
feelings and thoughts?

never ◄ 0 1 2 3 4 5 6 7 8 9 10 ➤ always

9. Does your partner find you helpful and supportive?

never ◄ 0 1 2 3 4 5 6 7 8 9 10 ➤ always

Do you find your partner helpful and supportive?

never ◄ 0 1 2 3 4 5 6 7 8 9 10 ➤ always

10. Does your partner think that you are generally happy and
satisfied about life?

never ◄ 0 1 2 3 4 5 6 7 8 9 10 ➤ always

Do you think that your partner is generally happy and satisfied
about life?

never ◄ 0 1 2 3 4 5 6 7 8 9 10 ➤ always

When you have finished, read these questions to your partner and,
using a different-colored pen, mark down his or her responses. Then talk

about the differences in how each of you responded, exploring what each of you can do to improve the quality of your love (the problem-solving games in chapter 7 will help you to develop such skills). Then take this test again in several months and note what improvements have been made.

Game #4
Exploring Family Love

Many of the ways in which we interact with our partners are shaped by the values, beliefs, and experiences we encountered with our parents, and thus the more we know about our partner's past, the easier it will be to understand some of the conflicts that sometimes emerge. A person, for example, who comes from a family where touch is restricted may feel quite uncomfortable with a partner who is accustomed to a lot of physical closeness. Others, who grew up in environments where feelings were suppressed, may experience difficulty when expressing themselves to their mates.

For this conversational game, set aside an hour to discuss the following questions of intimacy with your mate. When we listen to such stories of the past, we often feel more compassion toward our partners, and we can better understand the issues they struggled with growing up. Through such conversations you can begin to transform historical behaviors that may continue to hamper your intimacy and love.

> *When you feel stuck and do not know how to proceed, go back into your memory and remember family interactions. . . . In the family, patterns of behavior are learned as ways of coping with stresses. In marriage, scenes from the family are reenacted over and over in an effort to resolve or complete what was left unfinished from childhood.*
>
> LIBERTY KOVACS
> *Journal of Couples Therapy*

1. How did your parents express their love toward each other, and do you express your love in similar ways?

2. Did you feel adequately loved by your parents, and, if not, what would you have wished them to do?

3. What were your parents' values, and what did they value the most about you?

4. What were your parents' moral and spiritual values, and how are they similar to or different from yours?

5. Did your parents trust and respect each other, and did they trust and respect you? Has your ability to trust and respect others been influenced by your parents?

6. How well did your parents communicate to each other and with you? Do you communicate in similar or different ways?

7. How well did your parents express their feelings of love, sadness, anger, or fear? Were you allowed to express yours, and how did they react when you did?

8. How often did your parents fight, and how did you react when they did? Do you fight in similar or different ways with your partner and children, or do you suppress the feelings that come up?

9. How did your parents discipline or punish you? Do you think they were fair, and, if not, how do you wish you were treated? Do you discipline or punish others in similar or different ways?

10. What did you love the most about your mother and your father, and do you find similar qualities in your partner's behavior and beliefs?

11. What did you hate the most about your mother and your father, and do you find similar qualities in your partner's behavior and beliefs?

Game #5
"Past-Wife" Regressions

Many relationship problems can also be traced to previous affairs of the heart. For example, people who have experienced a traumatic divorce may automatically distance themselves when a situation arises that mirrors a painful moment from the past. Often one's partner is in the dark, for he or she does not know that a disturbing memory has been evoked.

For this exercise, it is best to set aside a special time—an afternoon in the park, a relaxing fireside date, etc.—to explore the lovers of your and your partner's past. On a sheet of paper, write down the names of the three most important relationships that each of you had, and then take turns explaining how those moments of intimacy affected you. But do not judge or interpret what you hear. Just listen with your fullest attention as your partner's story unfolds:

How did each significant relationship in your life begin, and why did it end?

What kinds of problems did you encounter, and how were they resolved?

How did each relationship influence your notions about love, trust, and marriage?

What did you learn about yourself?

What were the most beautiful parts of those early relationships?

What were the most painful aspects of your past relationships?

As you listen to your partner's account, see if you can identify similar patterns in your current relationship, behaviors that may be presently interfering with the development of intimacy and trust.

Game #6
Love Story

Using the questions from the previous game, have a conversation with your mate about the very first time you fell in love, for this is one of the most significant events in a person's life. For most people, nothing is more bittersweet, for it embraces all our fantasies and fears.

Some individuals find it difficult to listen to their partner's romantic highs, but if you can talk about the feelings of jealousy or envy that are stirred up, you may be able to bring greater intimacy into your life. Such storytelling can even alert you to subtle forms of love that your partner desires but has never put into words.

When you talk about your first love, add drama to your story. Give your partner the feeling of what you went through: the excitement, the

emotional struggles, and disappointments that ensued. Describe, if you can, what that first kiss was like, and how you felt when you first made love. What were your hopes and fantasies, and (assuming that the relationship ended) how did you recover from the loss? The sharing of such stories is a task that may leave us feeling vulnerable, but if we want to learn the deeper secrets in our partner's heart, exploring first loves will help.

Game #7
The Dating Tree

In this exercise, you will creating a visual chart of how your patterns of intimacy have developed. First, list the most important love relationships in your life. If there are fewer than six people on your list, you can include significant relatives, teachers, or friends who have influenced your views about love. Then take a large sheet of drawing paper (or tape two eight-by-ten-inch sheets together) and draw an outline of a tree—like the example on the following page—with branches coming off the trunk for each significant relationship on your list. At the end of each branch, and at the top, draw a circle for each relationship on your list (make it large enough to include the qualitative highlights of that relationship). The circle at the top will be for your present or most recent relationship.

Now make a similar drawing for your partner, and together, fill in the following information: At the base of the trunk, put the name of your first love and then list three or four aspects that capture the essence of that affair. Work your way up the tree, adding the important relationships, and ending at the top with your partner's name and qualities. Work together, as fast as you can, putting down the first thoughts that come to mind, and when you are done, share your dating-tree history with each other.

Analyze your chart. Do the previous lovers share similar characteristics with one another? Can you see any patterns in terms of how you or your partner selects potential mates? Do certain emotional themes repeat themselves, and have they been met or thwarted in the past? By charting your relationships, you will discover subtle elements that shape your behavior and beliefs. For example, with the dating tree that Peter (a client of mine) created, he and his wife were able to see how he repeatedly turned to women for a sense of security and acknowledgment, and thus they were able to talk about the fears that continued to come up in the present. By

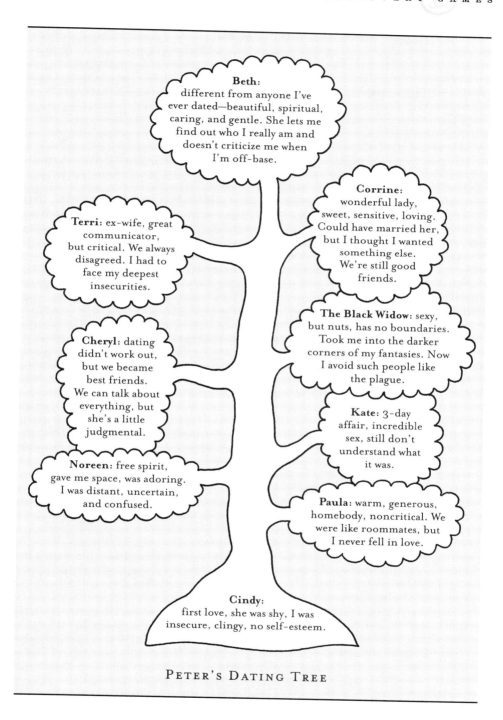

Beth: different from anyone I've ever dated—beautiful, spiritual, caring, and gentle. She lets me find out who I really am and doesn't criticize me when I'm off-base.

Corrine: wonderful lady, sweet, sensitive, loving. Could have married her, but I thought I wanted something else. We're still good friends.

Terri: ex-wife, great communicator, but critical. We always disagreed. I had to face my deepest insecurities.

The Black Widow: sexy, but nuts, has no boundaries. Took me into the darker corners of my fantasies. Now I avoid such people like the plague.

Cheryl: dating didn't work out, but we became best friends. We can talk about everything, but she's a little judgmental.

Kate: 3-day affair, incredible sex, still don't understand what it was.

Noreen: free spirit, gave me space, was adoring. I was distant, uncertain, and confused.

Paula: warm, generous, homebody, noncritical. We were like roommates, but I never fell in love.

Cindy: first love, she was shy, I was insecure, clingy, no self-esteem.

PETER'S DATING TREE

sharing his chart with his wife, Peter deepened his appreciation for the kindness she bestowed upon him, and his feelings of insecurity diminished.

Game #8
Priorities

A common problem that occurs in relationships deals with how we prioritize our involvements concerning the amount of time that we devote to work, to developing intimacy with our mates, and to spending time with our kids. Because we live in a world where men and women assume different roles and hold different expectations, conflicts emerge when we do not talk about them. Professors Judith and Erich Coché developed a simple, yet powerful, game that can help couples address priorities that enhance or interfere with love:

> The choice of whether or not to have children and at what point in the development of the marriage is a task which represents a major hurdle for many couples. Once the choice has been made and children are there, differing expectations of who-is-responsible-for-what produce marital dilemmas. As the children get older, issues of triangulation and playing parents against each other become new tests of marital strength. When one is designing an exercise for couples around children, it is frequently difficult to find something that touches each couple. . . .
>
> One of the most powerful exercises is deceptively simple. Each person ranks the importance of three issues: financial stability, children, marriage. No ties are allowed and ranking must be done quickly. After each has written down his/her ranking, partners take turns in reading out their hierarchy. The discrepancies between two marriage partners are usually quite remarkable and present an excellent stimulus for discussion. It is important in the discussion to clarify that no superiority of one answer over the other is implied in the question, but that differences in rankings may be giving a couple trouble and are deserving of further attention.

One night, as we were doing this exercise, Ellis came up with a ranking of (1) financial stability, (2) children, (3) marriage, while his wife, Jaime, chose (1) children, (2) marriage, and (3) financial stability. In the discussion, Ellis at first maintained that by placing such high priority on the financial security for his family he was, in fact, doing what was best for his family and deserved praise for it. Jaime expressed sadness and concern that for Ellis the children were only second and the marriage third. The recognition of this shocked the couple into exploring their fear of intimacy in the marriage by being so involved in career and raising of children.

It turned out that attendance in [a family therapy] group was the *only* activity the couple were doing together without the involvement of the children. It was this discovery that prompted Ellis and Jaime to decide to pay more attention to their marriage outside of the group, to set more time aside to be with each other, and to explore the substantial blocks to marital intimacy.

Game #9
Exploring Sexuality

For many individuals, sex is a difficult topic to discuss, yet it is an essential issue to explore. When we do not talk about our sexual desires and fears, we cannot adequately respond to our partner's feelings and needs.

"I often work with couples who do not understand why they no longer feel sexually attracted to each other, even though they profess to love each other," writes author Margo Anand. "They feel emotionally choked and consequently sexually turned off. They are afraid to tell the truth about their feelings because they fear they will hurt the other person, or that the relationship will suffer as a result."[19]

The easiest way to undo this conditioning, the experts say, is to talk about the fantasies and fears we have. Make an appointment with your mate and, using the following questions as a guide, see what you can discover about your partner's sexuality that you did not know before. The first set of questions will illuminate how your parents' sexuality may have shaped your current behaviors and views:

Sexuality can be an attitude, an openness to the world, to the cosmos beyond. . . . Sex, in other words, puts us in touch with the center of existence, makes us see the dance of molecules, makes us feel truly alive.

ERICA JONG
The Devil at Large

What were your parents' attitudes about sex? Were they open or secretive?

Did you ever discuss sexuality with one or both parents? How did that feel?

How did your parents make you feel about your sexuality?

How did your religious upbringing influence your sexual views?

What were your earliest sexual experiences and thoughts?

How did your sexual views change when you were a teenager?

What kinds of fantasies did you have between the ages of five and ten?

What kinds of fantasies did you have in high school?

After you have discussed these questions, talk about the difference that you see between your and your partner's past. Might any of your current sexual problems relate to these differences and the ways that you were influenced by parents, religion, or peers? By understanding your partner's history, you can often improve the sexual responsiveness in your relationship.

Now take a few minutes to discuss the following questions, which look more closely at one's personal fantasies and fears. If a question seems too intimidating to discuss, talk about the reasons why and then move on. At a later time, after you have practiced other games in this book, you will be able to return to and address these critical issues of love.

What fears do you have about being sexually rejected?

Have you ever felt sexually unattractive, embarrassed, or unskilled?

Does your partner sexually touch you the way you really want to be touched?

Do you have questions or fears concerning orgasms or ejaculations?

Which forms of sexual activity make you feel uncomfortable?

Do you ever have sexual fantasies that you would be anxious to share with your mate?

Could you tell your partner about a sexual fantasy involving someone else?

If you dreamed of having sex with someone else, could you share such a dream with your mate?

Would you be comfortable talking about masturbation with your lover?

> You may discover that sharing sexual fantasies is a healing experience and even something that can be actively enjoyed, bringing more excitement into your sex life. Give yourself permission to accept your sexual fantasies and to share at least one of them. . . . and don't be afraid to go into elaborate detail when your turn comes. There is great feeling of relief—and often humor—that comes with sharing the most bizarre and explicit fantasies and dreams. Besides, it is often an indirect way of teaching your partner how you would like to be loved.
>
> MARGO ANAND
> *The Art of Sexual Ecstasy*

Would you be able to discuss in detail a sexually abusive incident from your past?

Finally, take two pieces of paper and fold them both in half. At the top of column one, write "The three most difficult issues I have with sex," and at the top of column two, write "The three most difficult issues my partner has with sex." Hand one of the pages to your partner and fill them out together. When you have finished, read your papers to each other, listening carefully and accepting what the other has to say, without criticism or defense. Then talk about potential solutions that either of you may have.

> Are you ready to take a small first step toward a great sex life? Are ten seconds a day too much to devote to this glorious end? Here is a simple suggestion: From now on, when you see your mate after a day's work or any extended absence, make the first act between you a kiss that lasts at least ten seconds.
>
> FELICE DUNAS
> *Passion Play*

If this exercise feels too intimidating, then have an *imaginary* conversation with your lover about the difficult issues you may have with sex. How do you think he or she would react and respond? An imaginary dialogue can help to lessen your sexual fears, which will then allow you to approach your partner with greater openness.

Game #10

Love, Asterian Style

Intimate discussions of love and sex need not be serious, for a playful fantasy can also illuminate our desires and needs. In this game, you will share with your partner the most romantic and wild sexual encounter you can dream up, not with someone of the opposite sex, but with an alien creature from a planet far, far away. This may sound outrageous, but it will actually expose many dimensions about your deepest notions of love. So fasten your seat belt and prepare to take a journey into the stars, where your ideal "lover" awaits.

Imagine that you are traveling to a famous romantic retreat, somewhere in the Galaxy of X. It is the hot spot of the universe, and you are promised that you will find the partner of your dreams. When you first arrive, you literally bump into one of the local Asterians. You feel strongly attracted, and so you extend your hand in a gesture of friendship. The Asterian suddenly pulls back, waves its arms, and abruptly turns to leave. A guide rushes over and informs you that you just communicated something vulgar! "It happens all the time," he says, explaining that Asterians have an unusually erotic effect on humans. Nothing personal, he assures you—it's just a chemical reaction of sorts. He takes you to your hotel and you retire, gratefully, to your room.

In the evening, your guide announces that your ideal companion has just arrived and that the two of you will be brought to the Hall of Intimacy, where you will be left alone to figure things out. On these mating grounds, there are no rules to break. Enter Olin—O for short—a Plaedian Hesperite. You can tell that O is a creature of exquisite stature and grace, but your first impression is disappointing, compared with your experience with the Asterian. With O, you feel a mild curiosity, but nothing more. You certainly won't stick out your hand, for with all those armlike things, the possibility of embarrassment looms large.

Olin sits down on the floor and looks away; perhaps she or he (gender has no meaning on Asteria) is disappointed too. It will take some time to get to know each other, and so you decide to relax and let the process unfold. You think about all the corny things that people used to

say in the movies to create a conversation with an unknown soul, such as putting your hand to your chest and saying your name à la Tarzan and Jane, but you let such silliness go. Still, you are deluged by a battalion of thoughts about intimacy, romance, and love—ideas that were based upon meeting all the people you knew on Earth but which have little value here. As these thoughts dissolve, other feelings emerge—interest, boredom, anxiety, frustration, fear—but after a while, they too fall away.

Finally you reach a quiet place and begin to gaze at O. Olin is doing the same, and when both of your eyes meet, something special opens up. Such eyes! Your body tingles as you lose yourself in those mesmerizing orbs of light. You spend hours just taking each other in.

Olin breaks the silence by whistling softly and stretching several arms across the floor. You gaze, enjoying O's movements and sounds—raspy, strange, but inviting—and you let yourself join in, humming and brushing the floor with your hands. You have begun to dance—a dialogue of body and sound and eyes—and as you watch and respond, you begin to feel a subtle attraction that is growing out of your exploration of time and space and touch. You are sharing the experience of discovery, and in that moment you realize how much you missed in those adolescent rushes to embrace, so many galaxies ago.

Be it Venus or Mars, on Galaxy X or Earth, this is how genuine intimacy begins: with a temporary suspension of our fantasies, hopes, and dreams. Only then can we gaze into the depths of our partner's heart and soul.

In preparation for this game, share the story above with your partner, and then ask your mate to create a similar imaginative plot, using the following questions as a guide:

Describe what it would feel like to fall in love with an alien being from another planet.

What fantasy emerges? What does the creature look like, and how do you first react?

How do you approach each other, what do you do or say, and how does the romance unfold?

What desires and fears can you imagine, and how does your fantasy conclude?

Encourage your partner to be creative, playing with all the possible scenarios that might occur and saying anything that comes to mind. You may also guide the person by posing descriptive questions such as: What color is your lover? What kind of clothing does he or she wear? Is your lover tall, or is he or she without form?

When I asked Susan, my partner, what her fantasy would be, she had trouble at first, but with a little encouragement, she began: "First I would look for a connectedness in the eyes, for a feeling of familiarity or comfort. But I would also look for something that transcended space and time, as if I had known that person before. I would be filled with an expansive feeling, and his essence, if he were to die, would remain. It would be a connection beyond the physical."

I could have asked her about the psychospiritual dimensions of her fantasy, but instead I inquired about the sexual details of their embrace. Ignoring my request, she sagely replied, "It would be very intense, like an out-of-body experience, expansive and floaty and light."

"And what would this alien creature look like?" I implored.

"Well, I hate to admit it, but it would be certainly much easier if he was handsome. I thought about your image of Olin, with all those arms, and that would really be hard for me. I would want a more human-looking alien. But then I think how important it is to get beyond the physical looks, to touch upon the other person's thoughts and feelings and values. If he weren't kind or loving, it wouldn't be interesting, and I would have to feel a sense of strength and respect—that's very important to me. Communication would also be essential, whether it was through telepathy or some other form."

Fantasy games like these help to open up deeper channels of communication, for they can bring us face-to-face with unexpressed feelings, values, and dreams. In Susan's fantasy, for example, we can see how much she values the spiritual dimensions of intimacy. And in the fantasy I created about Olin, one may discern a struggle between body and mind—of sensuality and exchange—an issue that many men confront throughout their relational lives. When such fantasies are exposed, realistic intimacy can blossom and grow.

Now let's return from the outer realms of the universe to the inner realms of the unconscious, where fantasy and reality blur every night in our dreams.

FIRST LOVE

When Julie, age ten, was asked what her alien boyfriend would look like, she replied with childhood innocence: "He would be green and look like an octopus, with many testicles and eyes!" Ah, love—how much we are influenced by those childhood memories and thoughts.

Game #11
Sharing Intimate Dreams

One of the most effective ways to explore the unconscious dynamics of love is to share your actual dreams with your partner. Dreams contain symbols of the most important aspects of life, reflecting wishes, fears, and partially resolved conflicts through visual metaphor—particularly those issues that you are struggling with inside. But you do not need a therapist or a book to decode the meaning of dreams. By simply listening to your partner's dreams and sharing your impressions and thoughts, you will often be able to pick up clues and help each other to work through personal and relational issues.

When working in a dream-sharing context, you must be very careful about interpreting your partner's dreams, for interpretation can feel like an imposition, judgment, or criticism. When your partner tells you a dream, first sit with your thoughts and take it in, knowing that the dream will influence your own unconscious realms. Encourage your partner to explore the different feelings and meanings that the dream evokes for him or her: Does it have any connection to the past, to family, to spirituality or work, or to a current relational issue? When a dream feels incomplete, you can ask your partner to fantasize various endings, exploring different scenarios and outcomes. Here are a few questions with which you can guide your partner:

Describe the content of the dream, even if it is fragmentary or obscure.

What are the main themes that you see in the dream?

How might this dream reflect issues and events from the previous day?

What are the feeling and tone of the dream?

How did you feel after the dream when you woke up?

What associations can you make to each element of the dream?

What memories does the dream bring back?

What message or advice might the dream offer?

If the dream feels incomplete, what ending could you give it?

If the dream is disturbing, what could you do to bring about a resolution?

Wait until your partner asks you for your impressions of the dream, and as you share them, pay close attention to the reactions they evoke. Such reactions could signal a misunderstanding or alert you to a vulnerable topic that the person is not ready to address, for one of the functions of dreaming is to work with issues that are too difficult to approach consciously.

It is also less imposing to talk about your partner's dream in terms of what it brings up for you. For example, let's say that your partner had a dream in which she got angry at her boss and threatened to quit. Many people might jump to an obvious interpretation and say something like "I think you are unhappy with your job." But it would be less imposing and more helpful if you were to talk about the situation as if it were happening to you: "If I had a boss like that, it would really be hard. Part of me would want to quit, part of me would want to knock out his teeth, and another part of me would be terrified of losing my job and being unemployed." When your partner hears such a response, she can decide if any of your feelings are similar to hers, and she can also gain insight into how you would handle a similar conflict of your own.

By sharing the bulk of your dreams with your partner, you provide each other with a sophisticated road map to how you internally process important emotional issues. And because everyone dreams, this avenue of exchange becomes one of the simplest and most powerful forms of exposing inner truths.

But what if sharing your dream makes you feel too vulnerable, or your partner's dream stirs up disturbing feelings and thoughts? If this happens, work with them privately for a few days, write them down in a journal, or discuss them with a friend. At a later date, you can share your reactions with your mate.

> *[One] technique I have found helpful in working on my own dreams is to tell my dream to someone else and have him or her relate it back to me as if it were his or her dream. Seeing it as another person's dream will often unblock my consciousness long enough for me to get the insight.*
>
> BRUGH JOY
> *Joy's Way*

Sexual dreams are the most difficult ones to share because we often fear how our partners may react. The following exercise will help you work with such dreams, either alone or with your partner's help. It has been adapted from Jenny Davidow's excellent book, *Embracing Your Subconscious*:

Many people get very worried if they have a dream, fantasy, or impulse in which they are attracted to someone other than their partner. In a dream, if they make love with an exciting new person (who may or may not resemble someone they actually know), these people may feel guilty, as though they have been unfaithful to their partner. Or they may take their attraction as clear evidence that they are no longer interested in staying in their relationship. None of these interpretations may be true. Your new attraction may be a symbol for a valuable part of you that is seeking expression.

> *Fantasy is innate to human beings, as irrepressible as our other instincts. As such it is more than a private luxury, more than a basic necessity. Fantasy is as well a collectively human responsibility, calling for the conscientious, courageous and joyful participation by the citizen in lustful imagination.*
>
> JAMES HILLMAN
> *Pink Madness*

Dreams, fantasies, impulses, and real experiences in which you are attracted to or sexually involved with someone other than your partner have much to say about the subconscious influences at work in you—and in your relationships. If your subconscious is bringing a problem in your real-life relationship to your attention, you will be in a better position to deal with it effectively after you have done an Inner Dialogue.

WHAT TO DO: Choose a dream, fantasy, or real-life experience in which you are attracted to someone who is not your partner. In this exercise, you will speak not only as yourself but also as the other two parts of the love triangle: the new person to whom you are attracted and your partner. You will speak to each of them about what you like and don't like about them, and then let them respond. You may discover attractive aspects of yourself that you will want to reclaim. You are also likely to gain insight into how your subconscious influences feelings of attraction to certain people in your life.

Find a quiet place for fifteen minutes to do an Inner Dialogue, a process that lets you give a voice to the people and feelings you need to explore. Inner Dialogue enables you to shift from your normal conscious perspective into a state of mind that includes the perspective and wisdom of your subconscious. You may wish to write your Inner Dialogue in your journal as it unfolds, so you will have a record of it to reflect on later. After you have completed this process, you may want to share part or all of it with your partner. In your imagination:

- Speak as the person you are attracted to, describing yourself as him or her.

- Speak as your partner, describing yourself as him or her.

- Speak as yourself: Dialogue with the one you are attracted to, and then with your partner.

- Tell the person you are attracted to, and then your partner, what you like and don't like about each of them. Let each of them respond.

- Notice in what ways the two people are different, and in what ways they're the same.

- Think about the qualities of both people as qualities— both positive and negative—that you need to be more aware of in yourself.

- Negotiate an agreement between you and your partner, as well as between you and the one you are attracted to. Think about each pairing and the ways in which the qualities or energy belonging to you and the other are complementary, two parts of a whole. Enter into an alliance with each that gives both of you room to express a little more of yourselves.

- Consider some ways in which you could benefit from using the qualities each person represents (even to a small degree). Imagine expressing those qualities with good results in a particular situation in your life.

To deepen your dream-sharing skills with your partner, I highly rec-ommend the following two books: *Where People Fly and Water Runs Uphill,* by Jeremy Taylor, and *Dreamscaping,* a collection of essays for working with your dreams, which I edited with Stanley Krippner.

Game #12
The Sentence-Completion Game

This is one of my favorite games—a nineteenth-century parlor game that later become a therapeutic technique[20]—for it encourages spontaneous and humorous conversations, dialogues that often lead to a deeper un-derstanding of our partner's issues and concerns. Sentence completion is a simple tool for probing underlying feelings and thoughts and is par-ticularly helpful for couples who have difficulty initiating intimate levels of exchange.

Ask your partner to pick a topic: it could be money, sex, childhood memories, politics, feelings, vulnerabilities, anger, self-image, God— wherever your imagination wants to go. Using that topic as a focus, you then create a partial sentence—a sentence *stem*—that your partner is to complete. For example, you might say, "The thing I like most about money is _____." Your partner then says the first thing that comes to mind, *as fast as he or she possibly can,* without censoring or worrying about the result. It doesn't even matter if the sentence makes logical sense.

After your partner has responded, you create another sentence stem or repeat the same one again. If you do use the same sentence stem, your partner must say something new. By asking the same question three or four times, you can guide your mate deeper into his or her self. Give your partner about ten or twelve sentence stems and then switch roles, having your partner make up stems based upon the topic you first chose. Then pick a new topic and play a second round.

Here's an example of how the sentence-completion game works: John and Lisa decided upon the topic of intimacy, and he began by asking her to complete the following stem: *"The thing I fear most about intimacy is _____."* *"Being hurt,"* she replied.

John repeated his question: *"The thing I fear most about intimacy is _____."* Lisa paused, then said, *"That you might reject me if I open up too deeply."*

Lisa's response prompted John to probe more deeply, saying the following sentence stem four times: *"The ways that I reject you and hurt your feelings are _____."*

Lisa: *"By not listening."* . . . *"By becoming defensive."* . . . *"By failing to be my mother.". . . "Wanting to have sex all the time."*

With each repetition, Lisa went further into her feelings, which she normally kept to herself. Then she and John switched, with Lisa giving similar sentence stems. John's feelings, they discovered, were similar to Lisa's. He too feared rejection, particularly in regard to his desire to have sex. By playing the sentence-completion game, Lisa and John had given each other a panoramic description of their feelings and fears about intimacy, free from the judgmental and defensive traps one so often falls into when vulnerable issues are addressed. It took them just a few minutes to probe into a issue they had struggled with for months.

This game provides an excellent way to explore sensitive relational issues, but almost any topic you choose will uncover aspects about your partner's personality and preferences that you had not known about before.

The following examples of sentence stems will help to get you started, but the real fun comes when you can create new ones as you go along. Feel free to ask about the past ("*As a child, I dreamed about _____.*"), to speculate about the future ("*When I'm ninety years old, I want to _____.*"), or explore a wild fantasy or fear. As with other communication games, take a few moments to breathe and relax to calm your body and mind.

My most important quality is _____.

If I allowed people to really see me, _____.

My deepest fears are _____.

My deepest longings are _____.

My favorite way of being touched is _____.

When I look into your eyes, _____.

The strangest thought I've ever had is _____.

The most difficult issue I face in marriage is _____.

If I could have one fantasy come true, it would be _____.

Life seems most fulfilling when _____.

Life seems most painful when _____.

After you have read these sentence stems to your partner and listened to the response, have your partner read them to you. Then create some sentence stems of your own, exploring the issues that have meaning and value in your life.

Game #13
"If I Were"

If you had difficulty with the sentence-completion game, this playful version will help to liven things up. It's a wonderful game to play with family or friends, and it helps to break the ice when couples have difficulty opening up to each other.

Take turns with your partner completing the following sentence stems as fast as you can. Don't *think* about your answers; just trust your intuition and say whatever comes to mind. Create new sentence stems as you go

along, and, if you want to, ask the same stem several times in a row to elicit deeper, more imaginative feelings. Those sentences with an asterisk are ideal for repeating.

If I were a color, I would be ———————————— .

If I were a dinosaur, I would be a ———————————— .

If I were a stone or a gem, I would be a ———————————— .

If I were a food, I would be a ———————————— .

If I were a flower, I would be a ———————————— .

If I were a wild animal, I would be a ———— so that I could ———— .

If I were a mythical creature, I would look like ———— and do ———— .

If I were a tool, I would be a ———————————— .

If I were a planet or star or galaxy, I would be ———————————— .

*If I were a famous person, I would be ———————————— .

*If I were an inventor, I'd create ———————————— .

*If I could be anyone else in the world, I would be ———————— .

*If I were turned into the opposite sex, I would ———————— .

*If I were rich, I would ———————————— .

*If I were poor, I would ———————————— .

*If I were the president, I would ———————————— .

*If I could become invisible, I would ———————————— .

If I could ——————, I would ———————————— .

If I were a ——————, I would ———————————— .

After you have finished, talk with your partner about the feelings the game brought up. Which answers did you find the most intriguing? Which ones surprised you? What memories did it stir up? Allow for an intimate conversation to unfold as you talk about these issues and feelings.

Game #14
"If YOU Were"

When you have completed the previous exercise, go through the list above, only this time, substitute the word "you" for "I" and complete the sentences *for your partner.* For example: "If *you* were a wild animal, *you* would be . . . an enormous bear."

This is a far more intimate and revealing game because it gives your partner access to the *different* ways in which you view each other. As you play this game, pay attention to any discomfort that it may cause and talk about that with your partner. Be prepared for a certain degree of discomfort when your partner completes the sentences for you, and make sure you explore, with the greatest sensitivity, the reactions you have to each sentence completion. Ask your partner what she or he thought about your choice, and tell your partner how you came to your selection and what it means to you.

When Toni responded to her husband's stem, "If *you* were a wild animal, *you* would be a _____," she described him as an enormous bear. But Ed seemed somewhat perturbed. "Are you telling me that I'm too pushy and overbearing?" he suspiciously replied. Toni smiled. "No, honey, I was thinking of a great big teddy bear, like the one I used to cuddle up with as a kid." After a moment's reflection she added, "Sometimes, though, you do seem a little over-Bear-ing!" They both laughed, even though they had uncovered a sensitive relational spot.

Sometimes feelings of inadequacy or insecurity can be intuited from a person's response. When I played this game with the neighborhood kids, one little girl said she wished she were a turtle so that she could hide under rocks. I asked her why she wanted to hide, and she replied, "So I won't have to hear my mom and dad yelling at each other."

Game #15
"I Love It When"

This variation of the sentence-completion game, inspired by author and therapist Lori Gordon,[21] is designed to help couples explore the ways they need to be nurtured when they are feeling down and out. Take

a few minutes to read these sentence stems to your partner, and then reflect upon how he or she replied. Switch roles, with you completing the sentences, and then talk about the differences in your responses and needs.

When I am sick, I love it when   _____ .

When I am tired, I love it when you   _____ .

When I am worried, I love it when you   _____ .

When I am afraid, I love it when you   _____ .

When I am unhappy, I love it when you   _____ .

When I celebrate, I love it when you   _____ .

Game #16
The $64,000 Question

Issues concerning money are the most commonly cited reasons for divorce, and thus it is essential for couples to fully discuss their views. But money is a difficult topic to address, for we have been taught to be secretive about our financial values and fears. The following experiment demonstrates how deeply invested we are with irrational ideas about money.

Ask your spouse to hand you a twenty-dollar bill. As soon as you get it, tear it in half. Most people will jump. "Are you *crazy*?" they might scream. "You can't do THAT! It's money!" If someone tore your twenty-dollar bill in half, you would probably respond in kind. This little experiment simply shows how emotionally volatile issues of money can be.

> *Money may be the husk of many things, but not the kernel. It brings you food, but not appetite; medicine, but not health; acquaintances, but not friends; servants, but not faithfulness; days of joy, but not peace and happiness.*
>
> HENRIK IBSEN

The following four games will help you examine the differences between your and your partner's monetary values—your fantasies, your fears, your family's financial histories—and they will help you to refine your financial goals and dreams.

We'll begin with a sentence-completion game. Sit down with your partner and ask him or her to complete the following stems, saying whatever comes to mind without censoring one's feelings or thoughts. With each question, let your partner respond and then complete the sentence for yourself.

If I made an extra thousand dollars today, I would _____ .

If I made an extra hundred thousand dollars, I would _____ .

If I had a billion dollars, I would _____ .

If I woke up tomorrow and found that I was broke, I would _____ .

Talking about money makes me feel _____ .

One of the worst experiences I've had with money was _____ .

One of the best experiences I've had with money was _____ .

My biggest hangup about money is _____ .

My partner's biggest hangup about money is _____ .

After you have completed this exercise, discuss the following questions with your partner. You will need about an hour to explore them, but if discussing a question makes you feel too vulnerable, postpone its discussion for another time.

How much money do you need to feel secure?

How often do you worry about money, and why?

How has money caused problems in previous relationships?

In your relationship, who directs or controls the money, and how does it make you feel?

How do you feel about your partner's income and savings? Your own?

How does it feel to make less (or more) money than your partner?

Do you deal with money differently than your partner, and do you have different values?

How have money issues interfered in your present relationship?

What do you think your partner's greatest difficulty with money is?

These questions can open the doors for better communication, but they can only serve as a starting point for further dialogue and exchange. And remember: Money issues are best discussed when you and your partner are in a calm and loving mood.

Game #17
The Money Tree

Many of our notions about money have been shaped by our parents' beliefs. Because our partners come from different backgrounds than our own, conflict and confusion can easily erupt, especially when a financial crisis occurs. By exploring the roots of our monetary ideals, we can more easily find solutions that are based upon our current desires and needs.

The Money Tree maps each significant relationship in your life. Take two sheets of paper and draw a chart using the model on the following page as a guide. In each box, briefly describe the ways in which each family member relates to money, putting down descriptive words and phrases to describe their financial frames of mind: generous, stingy, obsessed with making money, rich, poor, puts high value on possessions, worries all the time, spendthrift, etc. In addition to parents, siblings, and grandparents, include on your chart other relatives or friends who left an impression upon you concerning money.

When you and your partner have finished, place your charts next to each other to see how your family values compare. Then discuss the following questions about your past:

How did your parents relate to each other concerning money matters?

Did your parents fight about finances?

Did you get an allowance, and how did you feel about it?

How did you feel about your parents' monetary ethics when you were a child? How do you feel about them now?

YOUR FAMILY "MONEY TREE" CHART

MOTHER	FATHER
Handles family budget *A coupon bargain hunter*	*Conservative, cheap, doesn't spend money on self*

BROTHER	SISTER
Workaholic	*Spendthrift*

GRANDMOTHER	GRANDFATHER	GRANDMOTHER	GRANDFATHER
Wealthy family	*Generous with gifts*	*Financially successful*	*I never knew him*

How do other family members (siblings, grandparents, etc.) deal with money?

How much are your current money values shaped by your family and your past?

Does comparing your answers and chart with your partner's shed light on any of the financial conflicts that you may currently have?

Game #18
A Penny for Your Thoughts

Now let's take a look at how you think about your monetary future. What are your long-term financial goals? How do they compare with your partner's concerns, and how might the two of you forge a mutually satisfactory plan?

Take two sheets of paper and divide each one into three sections, labeling them as follows: *Immediate Financial Goals, Financial Goals for the Next Ten Years,* and *Long-Term and Retirement Goals.* Give one sheet to your partner and, working as fast as you can, jot down all the key words and phrases that

come to mind. What kind of possessions do you want? Where do you want to live? What kind of security do you seek? What do you want to accomplish for your children? Do you need or want to provide for your parents or other family members?

Share your chart and discuss these issues with your mate. Take out another sheet of paper and outline a mutually agreed-upon financial plan, to be reviewed and revised every six months. To comprehensively address this task, I would suggest that you and your partner make an appointment with a financial counselor who can advise you about the many problematic issues that can occur.

Game #19

Heavenly Thoughts

Spiritual beliefs hold the key to many relational values, but couples often take such values for granted and thus do not talk in depth to each other about what they mean. By exploring your partner's spiritual beliefs, you can help each other to live more closely to the values you honor and respect. This sentence-completion game will help you to initiate a heavenly conversation or two. Just take turns responding to the following sentence stems, and then talk about the feelings they bring up:

As a child, what I loved most about religion was ——————.

As a child, what I disliked most about religion was ——————.

The way my parents dealt with religion and spirituality was ———.

When growing up, my favorite religious stories were ——————.

When growing up, my least favorite biblical stories were ———.

If I could change one thing about the religion I was raised in, I would ——————————.

My current spiritual beliefs are ——————————.

My beliefs about God are ——————————.

The most difficult issue for me concerning spirituality and religion is ——————————.

The spiritual values I would like to develop more fully are _____ .

The religious values I find most restrictive are _____ .

For me, heaven (be it reality or metaphor) is _____ .

Hell, be it real or imaginary, symbolizes _____ .

If I were God, I would _____ .

If I could add three new Commandments, they would be _____ .

When dealing with values, ethics, and morals, the question may arise: How honest should you be with your partner about shameful events in the past? Should couples disclose all, and risk being rejected, embarrassed, and hurt, or should some things remain secret that, if discovered, could damage one's trust and the integrity of the relationship itself? The following two games, whether they are played with your partner or privately contemplated, will help you to develop a more ethical intimacy with those you cherish and love. The first game deals with secrets, and the second one deals with lies. Both can stir up feelings of vulnerability, so if you choose to include your partner, pick a time when the two of you are feeling exceptionally loving and close. As an alternative, you might consider discussing these games with a trusted colleague or friend.

Game #20
Sharing Secrets

Secrets are the thoughts we yearn to share with some people but feel obliged to hide from others, but almost always they contain the seeds of important aspects of our selves. Secrets have their roots in the past when, as children, we learned to hide those behaviors and thoughts that others objected to.

Secrets also come in different sizes and shapes. Hiding an affair is a big secret, whereas hiding a few extra dollars in your sock for that "special occasion" is a little one. But the problem with secrets—big or small— is that they are difficult to hide completely, and our partners, on some level, always seem to know. Consciously or unconsciously, they feel that something is hidden, and this sense of secrecy can interfere with the de-

> *Sharing secrets with your partner builds intimacy. As you and your partner reveal your secrets, you can be for each other a bulwark against the judgments of the world.*
>
> HARVILLE HENDRIX
> AND HELEN HUNT
> *The Couples Companion*

velopment of intimacy and trust. Worse, when a secret is suspected, one's internal fantasies go to work: "What is she hiding?" "Did he have an affair?" "Something must have happened at the office." The uncertainty of not knowing can drive many people nuts. But if we take the risk to share *some* of the secrets from our past, we can begin a process that can lessen childhood guilt and shame and open the doors for greater honesty, truthfulness, and respect in our adult relational lives.

Take a few minutes alone to think about the secrets you had growing up and see how vulnerable they make you feel today. On a sheet of paper, make a list of these events, particularly the ones that caused you embarrassment or shame. Do these things still cause you pain, and can you share these stories with your mate?

Now make a list of all the secrets you currently have. What behaviors, thoughts, and attitudes do you hide from your friends, from your neighbors, or from the people at work? What do you feel you should keep hidden from your partner, and why? In your imagination, fantasize how your partner would respond if he or she found out your secrets. Take the fantasy as far as possible: Would you be forgiven and understood, or would the relationship collapse?

Pick one or two secrets from your list that you would be willing to share with your mate, and make an appointment to talk. Since feelings of vulnerability may arise, you may find it helpful to discuss these issues using the dialogical meditation technique (chapter 3, game 1). When you have finished, ask your partner if he or she would be willing to share one small secret from the past. Over time, you and your partner will be able to explore all the intimate secrets from the past.

Game #21
Confessions and Lies

People lie for many reasons. It may be out of fear or guilt, or for reasons that are sometimes difficult to grasp: to hide an inner wound, to maintain power and control, or to protect a friend in need. But truth is a virtue that many consider absolute, and, for some, a single violation can bring a relationship to its knees.

The question of lying itself is often difficult to broach, but when couples talk about this virtue in general terms, they can learn how to better respond to and respect each other's needs. *Confessions and Lies* is a simple exercise that will help you to explore this complex ethical issue.

Make a list of the ten most significant lies you have told in childhood and adulthood. Date each one with your age and make a brief comment next to it about why you chose to lie. Next, make a list of the kinds of lies that you feel might be justified to tell

> *Truth–telling is, on the one hand, closely linked to whatever is most essential in our lives. It is the foundation of authenticity, self–regard, intimacy, integrity, and joy. We know that closeness requires honesty, that lying erodes trust, that the cruelest lies are often "told" in silence.*
>
> *Yet this perspective is only part of the overall view. In the name of "truth," we may hurt friends and family members, escalate anxiety nonproductively, disregard the different reality of the other person, and generally move the situation from bad to worse.*
>
> HARRIET LERNER
> *The Dance of Deception*

at some future time (for example, would you ever tell a child that he or she is unattractive, or tell a hostile neighbor how you really feel?). Again, make a brief note about why you feel that way. Which type of lies do you think are unjustified, and why? And how would you feel if your partner lied about a similar issue or event?

Pick three items from your list that you would be willing to share with your mate, and set up a time to talk. You may want to test the waters by first confessing something from childhood. Then ask your partner if he or she would be willing to share a similar story from the past.

Questions about truth and lying, when gently explored in this way, contribute to the development of marital values, for even a generalized discussion can strengthen relational trust.

Game #22
Healing Each Other's Wounds

"Your love relationship has a hidden purpose—the healing of childhood wounds," wrote Harville Hendrix in his best-selling book, *Getting the Love*

You Want. To consciously embrace such a notion takes courage and time, but if we give it a try, we can help our partners to heal many of the wounds that hold one back from reaching the deepest levels of intimacy and love. Ask your partner to complete the following sentence stems, and write down his or her responses on a separate sheet of paper.

1. *What I really wanted from my parents was* _____ .

   One thing my partner can do to help me heal this wound is
   _____ .

2. *One thing that my mother did that hurt me deeply was* _____ .

   One thing my partner can do to help me heal this wound is
   _____ .

3. *My father once hurt me by* _____ .

   One thing my partner can do to help me heal this wound is
   _____ .

4. *The worst thing that happened to me at school was* _____ .

   One thing my partner can do to help me heal this wound is
   _____ .

5. *The most painful thing a friend ever did to me was* _____ .

   One thing my partner can do to help me heal this wound is
   _____ .

6. *The most painful thing that happened to me in a love relationship was* _____ .

   One thing my partner can do to help me heal this wound is
   _____ .

7. *One thing about my past that I would most like to forget is* _____ .

   One thing my partner can do to help me heal this wound is
   _____ .

8. *In my present relationship, the most painful experience was* _____ .

   One thing my partner can do to help me heal this wound is
   _____ .

9. *The things that cause me embarrassment now are* _____.

One thing my partner can do to help me heal this wound is

_____.

10. *The things that cause me shame are* _____.

One thing my partner can do to help me heal this wound is

_____.

When your partner has finished answering, switch roles and have your partner, who will write down your responses, read each question to you. Then compare your answers and talk about the things that you are willing to do to help heal each other's wounds. Remember that you and your partner are there to support each other, to listen without judgment or interpretation, and to respond as best one can from the heart.

Over the next few days, think about your responses to this game, and arrange a follow-up time to talk. Sitting face-to-face, enter a relaxed and contemplative state and share with each other your feelings, reactions, and thoughts. Talk about how you understood each other's wounds, but don't feel disappointed if your partner seemed to miss the point, for it may take many discussions before your partner can fully grasp your needs.

> *The advice we offer to couples is for partners to "bleed" when they are psychologically hurt. We say, "Show your wounds to your partner, and just as if you were physically bleeding, more often than not you will receive the care taking you desire." . . . We find it useful to have the bleeding partner focus primarily on his or her own wound rather than on blaming the other for the injury.*
>
> CLIFFORD NOTARIUS,
> SAMUEL LASHLEY, AND
> DEBRA SULLIVAN
> *Satisfaction in Close Relationships*

Game #23
A Final Question of Love

Discovery games, as you have seen, emphasize the importance of asking questions, for questions infer that we are not taking our partner's love for granted. Questions open the door for discovering who we really are be-

> *If we always see and hear things as we are accustomed to, then we will miss, neither see nor hear, that which is different and unique. A not-knowing position . . . allows possibilities that knowing does not. One of those possibilities is dialogue.*
>
> HARLENE ANDERSON
> *Conversation, Language, and Possibilities*

neath the surface of social image and pride. Questions are the key to maintaining a comprehensive connection to the soul, to the hidden aspects of self that make relationships exciting, mysterious, and new.

The questions you have explored in this chapter will make it easier to fully enjoy the games of sensuality that follow in chapter 5. But before we proceed, take a few minutes and ask yourself once more: "With all that I have learned, how do I define *love* now?" Put it in a note and give it to your partner with smile and a hug, thanking him or her for all that has been given and shared.

CHAPTER 5

Sensual Games: Awakening Your Pleasure Zones

The games in this chapter are designed to take you and your partner into the subtle realms of the senses: of touching and holding and kissing, of gazing and tasting and smelling, and of exploring the world of intimacy through sights and sounds and blindfolded walks through nature. These pleasurable techniques will show you how to reach deep into your partner's soul with imagination, gentleness, and a touch of spiritual joy.

"TO LOVE IS TO LIVE TO THE FULLEST. . . . One must not only be in love with what one does, one must also know how to make love. . . . One must be in it and of it wholly." Thus wrote Henry Miller as he reflected, toward the end of his life, upon his literary and artistic career.

Miller lived in the world of the senses, breaking the rules of society by writing openly about his sexual fantasies and loves. His goal was to live life passionately by immersing himself in the *sensual* nature of the world. For Miller, what truly mattered was the freedom to be internally alive, to write, to draw, and to love—freedom to savor the body in every possible way. In order to embrace such freedom—to appreciate that special form of intimacy that only the body can grasp—we must heighten our physical awareness of the self.

Couples who enter therapy often complain about the quality of their physical intimacy. "He doesn't hold me enough," she might say. "But she rarely feels like making love," he replies. Both partners desire more physical intimacy, but they haven't taken the time to carefully explore each other's needs. And when they do talk, the topic of conversation may be limited to the most superficial layers of sex. If we really want to know how to please our partners and experience the joys of sensuality, we need to question each other about every nuance of touch.

With your partner, set aside an afternoon or an evening to talk about the following issues and concerns:

Kissing: Since the beginning of history, kissing has been regarded as an art. But what do we really know about our partner's desires? Ask your partner about how he or she would like to be kissed. What forms of kissing turn her off? Does he like to be kissed firmly or gently? How long do you like to kiss? Where do you like—and dislike—to be kissed? Talk about your first kiss, your most erotic kiss, and the worst and funniest experience you've had when kissing someone else. Then kiss your partner and reappraise your skill.

Holding and Hugging: Have a conversation with your partner about being hugged and held. How much do you like to be held, in what ways, and for how long? What are the best and worst times of the day or night to be held? If holding or hugging feels uncomfortable, talk about your feelings and concerns. At the conclusion of your dialogue, ask your partner how he or she would like to be held tonight.

Touching: There are many ways to touch. Find out what your partner's likes and dislikes are. Does she like to be lightly tickled and stroked? Does he like to be massaged? What parts of your body do you enjoy—and not enjoy—having touched? What are the best times to be touched, and when does touch feel like an intrusion? When you have finished this conversation, make an appointment with your partner to spend an hour exploring each other's body with touch.

Sex: Ask your partner what you can do to make sex more enjoyable and meaningful. Talk about your sexual histories: how you felt about sex when you were young, the negative experiences you may have had, and how you felt about sex when you and your partner first met. What were your childhood fantasies and fears? Share with your partner your best sexual experience together and talk about what made it so special for you. Finally, ask your partner what he or she would like to explore the next time you sexually embrace.

In the art of physical intimacy, talking can help to set the mood for future embraces and forewarn you of areas that might displease your mate.

But there are also numerous experiments and exercises that can teach you how to become more sensitive and aware of each other's desires and needs. The following games will help you to use your creativity and imagination to enrich each physical embrace.

Game #1
The Melting Hug

The Melting Hug is a wonderful exercise created by Margo Anand, renowned for her techniques that integrate physical, spiritual, and tantric love. Hugging, she suggests, is one of the most intimate acts of love, but in order to appreciate its power, we must fully surrender ourselves into our partner's arms. With such an embrace, many tensions and fears can dissolve, and a profound emotional connection can be made. As Margo Anand writes:

> Although it may be natural and easy for you, I find that many people are self-conscious about hugging. Being held close is such a simple, deeply longed-for experience, yet it can evoke initial shyness and sometimes emotional responses. Who has not been asked by a partner, "Please, just hold me," and known that the loved one has spoken from a profound need to be reassured and comforted?
>
> Hugging matters. Good hugs are therapeutic. They can restore the feeling of being cherished and protected—that primal, wordless sense of security and well-being that we innocently demanded as children but rarely allow ourselves to experience as adults. Instead, we usually surround ourselves with defenses and resistance that shield us against experiencing things too intensely. The more we enter into the practices and explorations of High Sex, the more such resistance may appear. Hugging provides us with a simple opening of the door to trust. And because it feels so good, it can also remind us that bliss is our true nature. It is always there within us as a most precious resource.
>
> When I introduce people to hugging in my trainings, they say they often learn more about each other in those few moments of close embrace than they normally do in days or

months of verbal interaction. Some typical responses after this exercise are:

"I felt as if you wanted to grab me. It was too strong."

"You were gentle and receptive. I felt I could trust you."

"You felt tense, so I couldn't relax myself."

"You enveloped me like a gentle cloud, and I melted away."

As you enter this practice, be open to anything that may happen, and be prepared to share honestly what you experience with your partner.

Allow fifteen minutes for this exercise.

Do this practice with your partner.

Start by exploring your feelings about an ordinary hug by going to your partner and exchanging a hug. Just be natural about it—don't try to make it anything special. Do it for three minutes. It may feel like a long time because hugs are usually about as quick as a handshake, but this will give you time to explore your responses.

Then gently separate yourself, close your eyes, and check how it felt. Note whether resistance came up. This resistance may signal limits you have set for yourself, either conscious or unconscious. Did you feel guarded or uneasy? Did you feel that any part of your body remained stiff? Did you hold your breath part of the time? If so, why? Does that express some fear of intimacy that you may want to explore?

What about your partner? Check how you felt about him or her, in the same way that you reviewed your own feelings.

Then sit down, facing each other.

Partner A, honestly share what you felt, both about yourself and your partner. Partner B, listen attentively, in a receptive frame of mind.

When Partner A has finished, Partner B should say how he or she felt about the hug.

Some partners begin by giving what I call the "Donald Duck Hug"—coming together like two cartoon ducks, with their pelvises tilted back and only the upper parts of their bodies touching. The exchange conveys the feeling, "Okay, let's be friendly, but let's not get too close."

In High Sex we want to have a delicious whole-body, whole-hearted hug. I call it the Melting Hug. Here's how you do it:

Stand across the room from your partner. . . . Then slowly walk toward each other, maintaining eye contact and remaining as relaxed as possible. Let your breathing be deep and full, yet effortless. When you come near each other, open your arms in a welcoming gesture, with the palms of your hands open to each other.

Touching, nest against each other's chests, and slowly wrap your arms gently around each other. Let your hands feel they are really holding flesh, bones, and muscles, without exerting pressure. The aim is not to squeeze each other—love is not measured in pounds per square inch—but to embrace the whole body fully.

Allow your pelvis to relax and move forward, touching the pelvis of your partner. Allow your thighs and your bellies to meet. Try keeping your knees slightly bent to enhance your sense of balance and groundedness. Let your bodies relax so that you can melt into each other, giving yourselves over to a trusting embrace, secure in the kind of letting-go that you felt as a child when your mother held you.

After a minute or two, notice your partner's breathing pattern. Let your own breathing harmonize with your partner's so that you softly inhale and exhale together. If this harmonized breathing comes easily, do it now for a few minutes; otherwise, you can wait until you have a little more experience and it comes naturally. You need not make any effort. This exercise is about welcoming, receiving, enjoying, and dissolving into each other. That is why I call it the Melting Hug.

Game #2
Hugging Meditation

Hugging can also be used to deepen our spiritual connection with others, for within a loving embrace, our busy minds slow down. We can relax and

breathe more deeply, and as we hold each other in our arms, we become more focused and aware of our bodily presence and love. Thich Nhat Hanh, a highly respected Buddhist teacher, created this meditative technique to show how a simple act of affection can be used to deepen one's awareness of life and love:

> Hugging meditation is a combination of East and West. According to the practice, you have to really hug the person you are hugging. You have to make him or her very real in your arms, not just for the sake of appearances, patting him on the back to pretend you are there, but breathing consciously and hugging with all your body, spirit, and heart. Hugging meditation is a practice of mindfulness. "Breathing in, I know my dear one is in my arms, alive. Breathing out, she is so precious to me." If you breathe deeply like that, holding the person you love, the energy of care, love, and mindfulness will penetrate into that person and she will be nourished and bloom like a flower. . . . To be really there, you only need to breathe mindfully, and suddenly both of you become real. It may be one of the best moments in your life.[22]

To practice hugging meditation, take your partner in your arms, and focus on your breathing. In the previous exercise, The Melting Hug, your goal was to sink deeply into the sensual awareness of the experience, but in hugging meditation, the purpose is to become aware of your emotional and mental condition as well. As you hold each other, simply follow your thoughts and feelings as they rise and fall away. When your body and mind become calm, turn your attention to the love you feel toward your partner and observe the thoughts that travel through your mind.

There are some people, though,

> *When you let yourself be hugged, you are letting the other person have some of the control and some of the power, another road to fearlessness. . . . To work on that fear, you let yourself stay in the embrace for one more minute than you can stand. . . . Next time you add another minute. And before you know it you can hug as long as you like.*
>
> DAVID RICHO
> *When Love Meets Fear*

who feel uneasy hugging and being hugged. Their bodies become stiff as they unconsciously try to distance themselves. Such people may have received little affection from their parents or associate touching with a traumatic event. Others may feel that a hug implies sexual intimacy and thus withdraw from a friendly embrace. A person who may be used to hiding his or feelings will also pull away because a hug can bring forth deeper feelings and emotions. All these people are missing out on an essential form of touch.

If you find yourself tensing up when you get an affectionate hug, take a deep breath and focus on relaxing your body. But do not let go of your partner. It may take a minute or two, but your fears and tensions will begin to disappear.

Game #3
The Healing Smile

Smiling is a communication tool, but it is also sensual act: it feels good when we are smiled upon, and it relaxes our muscles when we smile. It also releases a bevy of hormones and neurotransmitters that help you to eliminate internal tension and stress. Smiling also heals others: it can soften your partner's heart and bring a moment of joy, even if you are in the midst of a heated debate.

For a truly healing smile, you must first relax all the muscles of your face, softening your eyes and releasing the tension in your jaw. Only then will a warmer, fuller smile spread across your face.

Thich Nhat Hanh recommends that we do "smiling meditation" throughout the day, taking a few minutes whenever we can simply to smile and breathe: in the elevator, while driving, while waiting in the supermarket line, wherever—whenever you have a spare moment or two. With this technique, you are simply igniting and remembering the happiness inside.

Each week, take a few moments to smile and gaze upon your partner—in the morning upon waking, when your

> Smiling means that we are ourselves, that we are not drowned into forgetfulness. . . . If we are not able to smile, then the world will not have peace.
>
> THICH NHAT HANH
> Being Peace

NATURAL HIGHS

Just as the hunter has to keep hunting to prove that he is still the best catch in the community, so the modern male has to keep his partner smiling. What makes this idea particularly appealing is a property of smiling and laughter that few people know about: they are both particularly good at stimulating the production of endogenous opiates. . . . Being morose and down-at-the-mouth makes you unhappier. So the best recipe for happiness in life is to smile as much as possible—thanks to the surge of opiates flooding through your veins, it makes you feel warm and contented. By the same token, making a prospective mate laugh lulls them into a sense of narcotic security.

ROBIN DUNBAR
Grooming, Gossip, and the Evolution of Language

---

mate comes home from work, and during the meals you share. You will see how easy it is to deepen your affection and love.

Game #4
Laughing Your Way to Intimacy

Like smiling, laughing pumps volumes of pleasure-enhancing opiates through our bodies, making us feel happy, contented, and warm. Laughter breaks the ice in a conversation and takes the edge off an uneasy dialogue. It can even be used to open up someone who is shy or withdrawn. As Norman Cousins once said, laughter may be the best medicine of all, alleviating depression and anxiety, and prolonging the quality and length of life.

But how do we make our partners laugh? We can tell a joke or act silly, but my favorite technique is to tickle my partner every now and then. Physiologically speaking, tickling has been shown to be an excellent way to stimulate the body's immune response. It is erotic, seductive, amusing, and stimulating, but it must be tactfully applied, for tickling is a game that balances precariously between intimacy and invasion.

Begin by stroking your partner's body with the tips of your fingers, experimenting with varying degrees of pressure and speed, but stay beneath the threshold of the tickle response (when your partner protectively defends his or her body by pulling in the arms and legs). Then ask your partner to relax and breathe deeply, for this will intensify the sensual feelings. As you continue to experiment and play, a nonverbal dialogue begins—a contest in which you both anticipate and avoid the overwhelming urge to withdraw. In a sense, you, the instigator, are plotting how to touch the most forbidden sensual parts while your partner tries to let go.

With adults, tickling can lead to unexpected sexual highs. But if you really want to cross some neurological wires of intimacy, try tickling each other simultaneously. Let yourself lose control, surrender to the eros of the moment, and your happiness is guaranteed.

Game #5
Tangerine Love

In keeping with our hectic schedules, we often forgo the pleasures of a simple meal. We rush to eat and run out the door, never realizing that we have missed an important moment to make contact with our mates. Make an effort to actually sit down with your partner for breakfast, dinner, or lunch, and use that time to acknowledge your love. Then try the following experiment—a game that transforms eating into a sensual and erotic embrace—for it will teach you how to savor love's many textures and tastes.

Slice three different fruits, arrange them on a plate, and put them in the refrigerator to chill. Bring your partner (a woman, in this example) to the dinner table and place a blindfold over her eyes. Kiss her and assure her that she will be pleasantly surprised. Place the plate of fruit on the table and pour a glass of her favorite liquid: juice or water or wine.

What does it mean to eat a tangerine in awareness? When you are eating the tangerine, you are aware that you are eating the tangerine. You fully experience its lovely fragrance and sweet taste. . . . An aware person can see the tangerine tree, the tangerine blossom in the spring, the sunlight and rain which nourished the tangerine. Looking deeply, one can see ten thousand things which have made the tangerine possible. Looking at a tangerine, a person who practices awareness can see all the wonders of the universe and how all things interact with one another.

THICH NHAT HANH
Old Path White Clouds

Hold one slice of fruit in your open palm, then take your partner's hand and guide it slowly across the fruit's surface. Place the fruit beneath her nose and ask her to breathe in deeply. Encourage her to savor the smell. Now brush the fruit across her lips, and let her touch it with her tongue. Ask her to take a small bite, chewing as slowly as she can, and remind her to savor the fragrance and texture before she swallows her treat. By slowing down the process of eating, the fruit will taste more flavorful and sweet.

Kiss her gently on the lips, and tell her to linger upon the texture and taste of your mouth. Then hand her the glass of liquid, and tell her to hold it in her mouth for a moment or two before swallowing. Kiss her again, select a different piece of fruit, and start the ritual over from the beginning.

When you have come to the final slice, hold it between your teeth and press it to her lips. Join her in the ritual and hold your lips to hers until the ceremony is done. May your future meals be blessed!

Game #6
Stolen Glances, Secret Strokes

To simply gaze at our partners with openness—without expectation or desire—can be a powerful expression of love. Not only does it bring us into the present, but we can also reconnect with the feelings that were stirred when our eyes first met, so many years ago.

It is said that the eyes are the gateways to the soul, but some couples experience discomfort when they are asked to gaze at each other. "It doesn't feel natural," one says. "And it's somewhat impolite," another adds. A dozen reasons may come to mind to interrupt such a gaze, but if we take a few minutes to silence such thoughts, we can appreciate the benefits that a loving gaze can bring: dissolving tension, shyness, and the defensiveness we hold within.

Begin this exercise by gazing at your partner when he or she is asleep. Study the features of her face, the curve of his body, and the shape of the palm of her hand. Gaze at this person as if you were looking at him for the very first time, paying close attention to the smallest details. Study the texture of her hair, the creases in his face, and the angles of her cheek.

Pay particular attention to the parts that you look at or touch the

least, and then touch them with your
hand (most people love to be gently
touched while they sleep, but there
are some who don't, so use your judgment for this part). Place your hand
against the nape of her neck and softly
give a squeeze, but be careful not to
wake her. Slowly run your hand across
his shoulder and upper arm. Pause
for a moment at her elbow and feel it

> In the heavens I see your eyes,
> In your eyes I see the heavens.
> Why look for another Moon
>   Or another Sun?—
> What I see will always be enough for me.
>   RUMI

resting against your palm. Continue to stroke the rest of his arm, lingering at the knuckles and exploring the texture of his nails. Remember,
though, that these are affectionate touches and not designed to stimulate
a sexual response.

By touching and gazing in these ways, we are taking a few minutes to
deepen our emotional bonds. In the morning, when your partner awak-
ens, ask what he or she recalls, and then repeat the ritual once more, gazing at her body, holding his arm, and running your fingers through her
hair. You can even try to steal an extra kiss!

Game #7
Gazing into Intimacy

Invite your partner to try the following experiment: Sitting face-to-face,
gaze into your partner's eyes and allow your feelings and thoughts to flow
spontaneously. Do this for a minimum of five minutes. In this exercise,
there is no touching, for you are learning how to develop intimacy
through your eyes alone.

At first you will notice a variety of reactions ranging from discomfort
to joy, but eventually, as your thoughts begin to settle down, you may feel
a pleasant tingly sensation throughout your limbs. Try deepening your
breathing, for it will reduce anxiety as it heightens the intensity of the act.
Colors become brighter, sounds seem richer, and the intensity of your
gazing will increase. You might even experience a vibrant energy, like a
quiet, orgasmic flow.

As you continue to gaze at your partner in silence, you may begin to
feel distracted or overwhelmed. If this happens, just close your eyes for a

> *Eye contact is one of the strongest and most intimate forms of contact between two people. It involves the communication of feeling on a level deeper than verbal because eye contact is a form of touching. For this reason it can be very exciting. When, for example, the eyes of a man and a woman meet, the excitation can be so strong that it runs through the body to the pit of the belly and into the genitals. Such an experience is described as "love at first sight." The eyes are open and inviting, and the look has an erotic quality. Whatever the feeling conveyed between two pairs of eyes, the effect of their meeting is the development of an understanding between two people.*
>
> ALEXANDER LOWEN
> *Bioenergetics*

moment and take several relaxing breaths. Continue gazing for a minimum of five minutes (some people have reported profound experiences by continuing for twenty minutes or more), and when the two of you decide to stop, share your experiences and thoughts. Then try the following exercise when you go to bed that night.

Game #8
The Dreamer's Gaze

This is my favorite gazing exercise, for it allows you to drift into a dreaming state filled with affection toward your mate. Climb into bed with your partner, and as you lie next to each other, gently gaze into each other's eyes. As you gaze, breathe deeply, going through each part of your body—your hands, arms legs, feet, back, neck, face, etc.—and let all the tensions go. As you do so, feel yourself sinking deeply into the bed.

Continue to gaze at your partner and, using your hands, gently touch each other's face—hair, eyes, lips, ears, the sloping of the nose—but don't lose contact with your eyes. If you sense a lot of tension in your partner's face, ask her or him to take a deep breath and let it go. When you begin to tire, kiss your partner and say good night, and drift quietly into sleep. In the morning, you will feel a deeper sense of connection to your mate.

Game #9
Tantric Visions of Love

In Buddhism, the tantras are special teachings given to advanced students of the contemplative arts. The highest yoga tantras were powerful meditations upon the most sublime and exotic dimensions of the soul, and the ultimate goal was to directly experience the powers of the gods. However, these deities don't actually exist; they simply represent various emotions, values, and spiritual ideals. Vajrayogini, for example, dances in a ring of fire, symbolizing untamable clarity and freedom, whereas Tara sits tranquilly on her lotus, offering spiritual liberation and well-being.[23] When you visualize such deities, you are attempting to bring those qualities into your relational life. You are, metaphorically speaking, gazing upon your partner with divine compassion as he or she makes godly love to you.

> *Tantric Buddhists eulogized the body as an "abode of bliss" and boldly affirmed that desire, sexuality, and pleasure can be embraced on the path to enlightenment. In keeping with this life-affirming orientation, the movement upheld the possibility of liberating relationships between men and women.*
>
> MIRANDA SHAW
> *Passionate Enlightenment*

To practice this tantric art, you can begin by visualizing your lover as a perfect human being, recognizing that he holds within his nature the seeds of compassion and contentment. Close your eyes and imagine your lover close to you, filled with happiness and joy. See the smile on her face, the softness in his eyes, and use your imagination to see this person growing happier and happier, radiating with joy. Then imagine this energy, this radiance, pouring back into your heart and soul as your partner gazes into your eyes.

If you are away from your partner for an extended period of time, this exercise will help to keep the flames of love alive, and, when you later meet and embrace, your sensual pleasures will increase.

Game #10
Developing the Artist's Eye

Here is a more complex exercise that artists use to enhance their visionary experience. When applied to relationships, it can help us to appreciate our mates in a deeper, more physically aesthetic way.

Let's begin by using an example from nature. Most of the time, when we look at a tree, we focus on the parts: the leaves, the branch, and the

> *Awareness means the capacity to see a coffeepot and hear the birds sing in one's own way, and not the way one was taught. . . . The aware person is alive because he knows how he feels, where he is and when it is. He knows that after he dies the trees will still be there, but he will not be there to look at them again, so he wants to see them now with as much poignancy as possible.*
>
> ERIC BERNE
> *Games People Play*

trunk. But the artist learns how to look at the spaces between the leaves, where different patterns and shapes emerge. Try it out yourself: take a moment and stare at a tree or bush, but focus your vision entirely on the spaces and shadows that are cast. Take a pen and draw these shapes—called negative space—on a sheet of paper. When you are done, you will see a picture that is vibrantly alive. And although you did not draw a single part of the tree, you will have captured a hidden essence of its life.

Now study your partner's shadows from as many angles as you can. Lie down on the floor and gaze up at his or her body, then look down upon your partner from above. Walk slowly around your mate, noting the subtle qualities of form: her posture, the way he tilts his head, the space between her body and her arms. If you do this for just five minutes, you will discover many new qualities that can deepen your appreciation of your partner's form. It is a compliment and a gift to pay such loving attention to the subtleties of our mates.

Game #11
Soundscaping

This playful game, designed to heighten your listening sense, was introduced to me over thirty years ago. Each time you play it, it will help you become more sensitive to places and people that surround you.

Begin by having your partner sit in a comfortable chair and ask him (for this example, we'll assume your partner is a male) to listen to the following instructions. Read slowly, in your softest and warmest voice, pausing at each comma and period to give him time to absorb the experience of the game. Since it is easy to go too fast, I have put in brackets to remind you to pause at crucial points; when you reach one in the text, wait until you see that your partner has completed the task:

I would like you to close your eyes and take several deep breaths, sinking deeply into your chair and relaxing every muscle in your body: your arms [pause], your hands [pause], your legs and your feet [pause], your back [pause], your neck [pause], and your head [pause]. Relax your eyes and the muscles of your face.

Now listen to the sounds around you: your breathing [long pause], the creak of the chair [long pause], the vibration of the house [long pause], the sounds outside [long pause]. The more you focus, the more sounds you can hear. But do not think about them; just notice them and let them pass.

Stomp your feet [pause], slide them across the floor [pause], and tap them against your chair, listening to the different qualities and tones. Now turn your listening inward to the pounding of your heart against your chest [long pause]. Make a few sounds [pause], hum [pause], and say some words out loud [pause]. Pick one long word and say it slowly, listening to the nuance of each consonant and syllable [pause], then try another word.

Keeping your eyes closed, rise to your feet [pause], and slowly turn your head from side to side [pause]. Like an antenna, listen to the changing sounds and tones [long pause].

Now I'm going to take your hand and guide you carefully through the rooms of the house. As you move, notice the sound of your footsteps against the floor, and the rustle of your clothing against your body. As we move from room to room, listen for the subtle changes around you. Each sound has its own unique quality, and the more you focus, the richer the experience becomes. You can even hear the pressure of the air.

Here is where the fun begins. Guide your partner (with his eyes closed) through each room of your house. As you go, create different sounds for him to hear. Move a chair across the floor. Open a creaky door and slam it. When you are in the kitchen, turn on the faucet in the sink, fill a glass with water, and pour it out over the dishes and pans. Pick up an apple or a carrot and bite into it with your mouth close to your partner's ear. Rustle some papers. Fill a glass with water and gargle. Tap against various parts of the house: a table, a door, the walls, the stove—everything creates a different sound.

Encourage your partner *not* to identify the sounds. Rather, he is to attempt to suspend his intellectual process so that he can be carried away by the sounds (for example, when we listen to music, we hear it as a whole—we rarely try to isolate and identify the individual instruments). Use your imagination, and try to create sounds that your partner can't figure out. It's really wonderful to hear unidentifiable noises, for it generates curiosity and surprise.

The game is so much fun to play that you may find an hour or more might pass. When the time feels right, switch with your partner, sit back in a chair, and enjoy your soundscaping treat.

Soundscaping is more than just an enjoyable game, for underneath its surface, many intimate exchanges take place: you are guiding your partner into greater sensuality, he is surrendering himself to you (an act of trust), and you are sharing a new experience with each other. These are the little things that stimulate long-term love and romance.

Game #12
Keeping in Touch

One way to deepen your physical intimacy is simply to touch your partner when you are having a conversation. Just rest your fingers on her shoulder as you talk, or take his hand into your palm. These little acts not only demonstrate empathy and concern; they also trigger the body's relaxation response. And, of course, when you are more relaxed, conversations become more loving and intimate.

Try the following experiment for one week, gently touching your partner as often as you can. In the morning, before getting out of bed, touch your partner's cheek with your fin-

To help sustain your high-touch relationship, talk about how touch was used in the homes you grew up in. Was your family "high contact" or "low contact"? . . . You could discuss how to become more touch-oriented, even if you grew up in a family that shunned physical contact. You might also explore each other's comfort zones. Both of you probably prefer different amounts and kinds of touching. For one of you a soft touch on the hand may mean as much as a lingering embrace to another.

LES AND LESLIE PARROTT
Saving Your Marriage Before It Starts

gertips. At breakfast, stand for a moment beside your mate and rest your hand upon his or her shoulder, and when you pass each other in the hall, brush each other's fingertips. Touch your lover's arm when you want to interject a thought and use your eyes to make contact as often as you can.

Research confirms that these simple acts of kindness improve the quality of communication, lessen the possibilities of conflict, and increase the degree of relational satisfaction that couples experience in their lives.

Game #13
Plotting for Kisses

From infancy on, we are plotting for kisses, says analyst Adam Phillips, "not only as foreplay but also as ends in themselves. . . . a threat and a promise. . . our most furtive, our most reticent sexual act, the mouth's elegy to itself."[24] Why then, do we spend so little time past adolescence exploring the intimacy of lips?

Kissing is an essential act of love, yet it seems to me that couples rarely talk about or show each other how they want to be kissed. Some couples, for example, only peck. Their lips stay frozen, and they do not let themselves melt into their partner's embrace. But even the fervent kisser can be faulted if he has forgotten to linger with her lips.

Ask your partner to give you a lesson in kissing. Find out how he or she wants to be embraced. Ask for an affectionate kiss, a passionate kiss, an intimate kiss, and then surrender your mouth to the experience. Then take your partner on an "adolescent" date, making out in the car as you apply your accumulated years of skill. Kiss for as many hours as you can.

One may amuse oneself by playing a little game of who can seize the other's lips first. If the woman loses she must sulk, push her lover away, turn her back on him and try to quarrel by saying, "I want revenge." If she loses a second time, she must pretend to be twice as upset. Later, when her lover is preoccupied or asleep, she must seize his lower lip between her teeth so that he cannot pull away. Then she can burst out laughing, make a great deal of noise, make fun of him, dance around him and, raising her eyebrows and rolling her eyes roguishly, say whatever comes into her head. The same kind of game may also be played with scratches, bites, caresses and palpitation.

THE KAMA SUTRA
Third century, A.D.

Spend the night exploring the wonders of the skin: kissing the tender folds of his neck, the curve of her back, and the inner surfaces of the knee, the foot, and the hand. When you have spent hours embracing each other in this manner, you will understand why the kiss is considered the most sacred form of love (and the only act of touch a prostitute will refuse).

Game #14
The Trust Walk

This game focuses on the theme of *bodily* trust as you guide your partner (whose eyes are closed) on a walk through nature. In order to appreciate the experience, participants must surrender their dependence upon the eyes and learn to trust that their partners will protect and safely guide them as they walk.

Begin by selecting a place in nature that you love—a park or a garden, or even your backyard—but make sure that it has easy places and paths on which to step. Stand in a clear, open place, holding your partner's hand. Ask your partner to close her eyes and walk, assuring her that you will guide every step she takes, warning her of obstacles or steps. At first, your partner will walk cautiously as she learns how to trust your guidance and support. Use words to reassure her: "It's clear and flat in front of you . . . there are three steps coming up . . . lift your foot . . . etc."

As she surrenders herself to the experience, she will begin to notice various sounds and smells. Start a conversation, asking her to describe what she senses and feels and thinks, and as you walk, introduce various objects that you find. Lead her to a tree, tell her when to stop, then take her hand and place it on the trunk or leaves. Ask her to explore the tree with both hands. She will probably take a great deal of time, because she will notice many qualities that are visually overlooked. When she has completed her tactile examination, find another object for her to explore. Take some dry leaves, crumple them near her ear, and then place them in her hand. Encourage her to appreciate how they feel and smell.

Try brushing various leaves across her face so that she can feel the different forms of touch. Have her lie down on the grass or lean against a very thick shrub, allowing her to experience nature with different parts of her body. Even if the place is intimately familiar, it will seem like a mysterious and foreign world.

You will find that she becomes very excited and pleased as she samples the different textures of rocks, smells the various aromas of plants, and feels the different kinds of surfaces beneath her feet. As her trust in your guidance increases, you can take her up a steeper path and even have her experiment with climbing on a rock.

After about twenty minutes, switch places so that she has the pleasure of guiding and surprising you. Notice how easy or difficult it is to surrender your control to your partner, and after the game is complete, talk about the issues of trust that the exercise brought up.

Game #15
The Sensual Bath

The perfect way to complete an afternoon's trust walk or hike is to give your partner a sensual bath. Begin by filling a large pot or bucket with hot water, to which you can add some fragrant oils. Place several soft washcloths in the water and bring it, with several towels, to your partner's side. Your partner, who is probably fully clothed, will be quite surprised, so tell him or her that you have prepared a special treat. Take one hot cloth, wring it out, and gently pat your partner's forehead and face. When the cloth gets cool, put it back into the water and remove another one.

Sponge all the parts of your partner's body that are not covered with clothes: the neck, arms, hands, etc. Then remove your spouse's shoes and socks: nothing feels better than a warm caress of the feet. You might also rub some of your partner's favorite lotion into his skin.

Game #16
The Sensual Afternoon

On the weekend, set aside a few hours and treat your spouse to a sensual afternoon, combining a number of the games from this chapter. To do so is a generous act of giving, and it makes a wonderful birthday gift. Better yet, initiate this game on an ordinary day: simply send a card to your partner announcing the date and time. Why an afternoon? Because it is the time when sensuality is least expected or given.

Begin the day by giving your partner (for this example, we'll assume it's a man) a long and sensual hug, following the directions that were given in the Melting Hug, the first game in this chapter. Look deeply into his eyes, gazing and smiling with love, then take a deep breath and share a kind word or two. Cover your partner's eyes with a bandana or a cloth (this is a particular turn-on for men, but not necessarily for women), then lead him to the dining-room table where a previously prepared meal or snack will be served. Feed your partner slowly, as described in Tangerine Love (game 5), and when you are finished, massage his shoulders and neck.

Next, drive your mate to a local playground or park. Lead him on a trust walk, as described in game 14. A playground, by the way, is an interesting place to be led through blindfolded, for it can stimulate long-forgotten memories from childhood.

After you have spent an hour on the trust walk, take off your partner's blindfold and give him another melting hug (add a little tickling—game 4—for fun). Bring him back home and prepare a sumptuous bath—bubbles, champagne, the works. Tell your partner that he is to do noth-

---

Tips for Giving a Sensual Massage

Giving a great massage is easy, for all you need to do is trust your intuition as you explore your partner's body. You do not need to use oil, nor even have your partner disrobe. To begin, gently rest your hands on your partner's shoulders, head, hands, or feet, for these are the safest and most comforting places to touch. When you first make contact, take a few breaths and let your own body and mind relax. Feel the weight of the person's body against your hands, and let your fingers press naturally against the surface of the skin. Feel the warmth in your hands, and then give a gentle squeeze, imagining that your partner's body is made of clay. Take your time, exploring the texture of the skin, the fleshiness of the muscles, and the contours of the body and bones. Lose yourself into your own sensuality, and do what feels good to you: sliding your hands slowly down the arms, legs, or back, rocking the head from side to side, gently lifting various parts of the body, etc. Experiment with different kinds of touch—from tickling to squeezing to stroking and shaking—and ask your partner to give you feedback as you proceed. For a special touch, try stroking your mate with a feather, paintbrush, tissue, or cloth, and if you want to go further, get George Downing's The Massage Book, *a classic text that will teach you how to give a luxuriously sensual massage.*

---

ing at all, for you will apply the lotions and soaps yourself. Begin with a luxurious shampoo, letting him smell its fragrance and then spending a full five minutes massaging his scalp. Then lather a washcloth with soap and let him enjoy the textures of the cloth as you rub his back, arms, hands, legs, and feet. Then ask your mate to step out so that you can dry him off with a towel. *Do not let him help!*

Ask your partner to lie down on the bed, or on a blanket that has been spread on the floor, and cover him with a sheet so that he will stay warm. If possible, turn on some gentle music and guide him through a relaxation exercise using one of the techniques from chapter 2—for example, The Relaxing Journey (game 5).

Place your hands on the sheet that covers your partner's body and begin to slowly stroke, being gentle but firm. Place your hands slightly underneath his body and slide them from head to toe. Lift the arms and legs, swinging them gently from side to side. Then place your hand on your partner's head and rock it slowly from side to side.

Continue the massage in the manner that feels right—trusting your intuition—and then explore his entire body with the tips of your fingers, giving special attention to those parts that are rarely touched by you (the secret strokes in game 6).

For a more intense experience, cover his body with kisses, and when you have completed the massage, lie down next to your mate and think about the loving experiences you have shared with each other that day.

Game #17
The Contemplative Love of Alan Watts

All the games in this chapter have focused on sensuality, but not specifically on the sexual act itself, for it is my belief that sexual games, in and of themselves, promote a mechanistic form of love. Sex is perhaps the most intimate communication, and thus it must make use of the best of your communication skills.

To have a truly satisfying sexual relationship, you will need to know as much about your partner's sexual history, desires, and fears as you possibly can, issues that can be explored using many of the discovery games in chapter 4, especially games 3, 6, 9, and 10.

Many of the previous games of sensuality can also be used to initiate

a sexual embrace, but the most important tool for obtaining sexual satisfaction is relaxation. If you cannot fully relax and surrender yourself to the myriad sensations, your pleasure will not reach the subtle erotic highs your body is capable of experiencing. And the easiest way to proceed is to focus on your breathing throughout the sexual embrace. Go slowly, shifting your attention back and forth between your partner's body, your own sensations, and your breathing. As you focus on your breath, surrender (at least for the moment) all your expectations and goals. By applying the principles of meditation, you can even suspend the incessant noises of the mind and experience the exquisite intensity of being in the present moment, free of all the ingrained notions of love that have accumulated within. This is the art of contemplative love, where body, mind, and spirit converge.

Contemplative love is a spontaneous form of sex: you don't try to make anything happen, nor do you strive for an orgasm or climax. You simply let things flow. Here's how Alan Watts describes this mystical embrace:

> Contemplative love—like contemplative meditation—is only quite secondarily a matter of technique. For it has no specific aim; there is nothing particular that has to be made to happen. It is simply that a man and a woman are together exploring their spontaneous feeling—without any preconceived idea of what it ought to be, since the sphere of contemplation is not what should be but what is. . . . One finds out what it can mean simply to look at the other person, to touch hands, or to listen to the voice. . . . The intimacy of a kiss or even lips in near proximity regains the "electric" quality which it had at the first meeting. In other words, they find out what the kiss really involves, just as profound love reveals what other people really are: beings in relation, not in isolation. . . .
>
> If no attempt is made to induce the orgasm by bodily motion, the interpenetration of the sexual centers becomes a channel of the most vivid psychic interchange. . . . The sense of identity with the other becomes peculiarly intense, though it is rather as if a new identity were formed between them with a life of its own. This life—one might say this Tao—lifts them

out of themselves so that they feel carried together upon a stream of vitality which can only be called cosmic, because it is no longer what "you" and "I" are doing. . . .

What lovers feel for each other in this moment is no other than adoration in its full religious sense, and its climax is almost literally the pouring of their lives into each other. . . . In that moment love takes away illusion and shows the beloved for what he or she in truth is—not the socially pretended person but the naturally divine.[25]

Contemplative love embraces the fundamental principles of conscious intimacy that underscore this book: it brings you into the present moment, it frees you from habituated patterns of the past, and it gives you access to the creative forces that lie dormant within. Contemplative love is a model for living the passionate life, a template for self-reflection, and a doorway to opening deeper layers of intimacy with your partner and within yourself.

CHAPTER 6

Fire-Fighting Games: Transforming Anger into Love

Anger is one of the most difficult and destructive emotions to work with in relationships, and so I have devoted an entire chapter to taming this fiery beast. Read through this section with your partner and experiment with as many exercises as you can to find out which games are the most useful for addressing the problems at hand. Then, when an emotional episode does occur, help each other to incorporate the lessons you have learned.

BENEATH OUR SOMETIMES confident and powerful exteriors, there lives a sensitive and fragile beast. But we, like other creatures of this earth, cover up our vulnerabilities with a variety of intimidating masks. The rattlesnake shakes its tail, the rabbit thumps, and we—sophisticated beings that we are—shake our fists, stomp our feet, and frown whenever we're threatened or hurt. With anger, we frighten off our opponents, disguising who we really are inside.

Anger is a defense that we are born with, but it is an enemy to intimacy, dialogue, and love. It interferes with empathy and trust, and until it subsides, we cannot negotiate or communicate our needs or resolve a conflict with ease. In relationships, anger seems to pose a double bind: if we express it openly, we push our loved ones away, but if we hold it in, it can easily turn into resentment, hostility, or self-hate. The only way out of this dilemma, the experts say, is to explore this destructive emotion and its many hidden forms (jealousy, hatred, prejudice, cynicism, sarcasm, criticism, selfishness, etc.) with thoroughness and care: to watch it and study it and search for the feelings it may hide. As Steven Levine suggests,

Rather than pushing [such feelings] down or spitting them out, we can let them come gently into awareness. We can start to give them space, to get a sense of their texture, of their voice, of their inclination. We begin to investigate the nature of *the* anger instead of getting lost in *my* anger.[26]

Processing Anger in Relationships

There are two parts in any conflict. The first is the problem itself: the situation, behavior, or activity that precipitated the relational rift. The second concerns all the reactions, emotions, and defenses that the conflict stirs up. These issues must be dealt with first before a problem itself can be addressed.

Sadly, many couples do not know how to effectively work through their anger, and most will usually distance themselves until the internal feelings die down. They sweep their feelings under the rug. Others may simply blurt out their feelings, but such expressions are almost always destructive. Anger hurts, putting us on the defensive and pushing us to withdraw or to provocatively lash back. To bear the brunt of a powerful display of anger is a traumatic event, but to bottle up one's anger is even worse, for such suppression can lead to a festering hostility, building up—sometimes for years—until it eventually explodes.

What, then, are we to do when we feel the furies boiling within? And how do we express ourselves safely without hurting those we love? The first step is to understand the nature of anger: to study it, to think about it, and to trace its family history and roots. The next step is to share this understanding with your partner and friends, exploring how anger works with them. Ask them how they perceive your anger, and what they think it is about, for our lovers and friends can see dimensions to which we are often blind. Finally, sit down with your partner and work out a plan for how to deal with future angry moods.

Eventually, anger will arise, and when it does, take some time to think about it *before* you talk to your mate. Follow it inwardly for an hour or a day. Meditate on it. Write about it in your journal, or discuss it with a therapist or friend. Or scream into a pillow if you need to let off some steam. With time and a little self-reflection, your anger will dissipate, leaving more room to approach your partner with gentleness and ease.

Some people believe that expressing anger is the most effective way . . . to influence another person. They may not realize, however, that the expression of anger can cause substantially negative results. Further, it does not generally change the other person's attitudes and may suppress only temporarily an unwanted behavior—which resurfaces when the threat of punishment has been removed. . . .

In general, couples do best if they try to keep their outbursts to a minimum. Since hostility is frequently based on misunderstandings or at least exaggerations, it is likely to aggravate rather than solve problems.

AARON T. BECK
Love Is Never Enough

Anger is a complex emotion, one that is embedded in our primitive mechanisms of defense, and thus it may take months—even years—to establish and refine your fire-fighting skills in creative and compassionate ways. Anger is a fact of life, but it is a feeling that always interrupts the intimate flow of dialogue, cooperation, and love. The key to working with anger is in the awareness we bring to each emotional situation as it erupts.

On the following pages, you will find many approaches for working with anger in constructive and imaginative ways. The first few exercises show you what you can do before you get angry: ways of understanding anger, techniques for dialoguing with your mate, and methods for charting anger's history and roots. The remaining exercises will show you how you can process anger internally, using meditation, visualization, and dramatic play. These games have the power to dissipate anger quickly, paving the way for effective dialogue between you and your partner.

As you read through this chapter, put a check mark by those games that you feel are important to explore with your partner. Then circle those games that would make you feel uncomfortable to play. These are the most important ones to discuss with your mate because they often hold the keys to unconscious anxieties and fears. With every game you play, you will gain greater self-control for those inevitable times when conflict does emerge.

Do You Get Angry. . . ?

When traffic or the car in front of you is going too slow?

When someone cancels an appointment with you at the last moment?

If the person in front of you at the checkout stand takes extra time?

When the elevator doesn't come as quickly as you wish?

When someone criticizes you?

When you fail to accomplish everything you had hoped to do in the day?

When you make a mistake and someone yells at you for it?

If somebody teases you?

If someone isn't paying full attention to you when you're talking?

When an item you recently bought doesn't work?

If someone blames you for something you didn't do?

Numerous studies suggest that if you get moderately angry at three or more of the above situations, you have a higher level of hidden anger than the average individual—anger that may spill over into your personal relationships at home and at work.

Game #1
Exploring the Meaning of Anger

Our first fire-fighting game begins with a dialogical exercise. When couples get angry, they often talk *from* their feelings—raising voices, shaking fists, threatening, etc.—but they often do not talk *about* them. But it is essential to talk about the underlying feelings, reactions, and concerns. In such discussions, we often learn important things about our partner's anxieties and fears—information that is essential to manage anger effectively. For example, does she feel frightened and overwhelmed when someone expresses anger? Does he feel humiliated or ashamed when he loses his temper? What happens inside when the feelings of rage take

over? Greater intimacy is established with our partners when we explore such questions in depth.

Invite your partner to have an intimate dialogue using the following questions as a guide. Each question, however, may lead to other questions and issues, and thus it may take several hour-long dialogues to address the items on this list. Listen carefully to what your partner says, without judgment or criticism, and try to respond with sensitivity and care.

1. What is anger?

2. Is it okay to feel angry?

3. Do you believe that it is "good" or "bad" to express anger toward others?

4. How does it feel when you get angry?

5. How does it feel to you when your partner gets angry, and how do you react?

6. What happens after you get angry?

7. What is the best way to respond to your own anger?

8. What is the best way to respond to your partner's anger?

9. How do you let your partner know that you are angry?

10. How long does your anger usually last?

According to Gerald R. Weeks and Larry Hof, professors of psychology and pastoral counseling at the University of Pennsylvania, exploring such questions can help couples diminish feelings of anger, especially if they expose the feelings that are hidden beneath the surface: "Anger is just the tip of many underlying and associated feelings . . . [like] hurt, fear, rejection, depression, guilt, insecurity, and shame. . . . These feelings need to be discussed just as much as, if not more than, the anger itself."[27]

Game #2
The Anger List

In this exercise, you and your partner will explore each other's emotional histories by sharing stories about the things that have made you angry in the past. As we come to understand the roots of our anger, we can redirect those childhood patterns and behaviors that interfere with adult responsibilities and concerns.

Step 1: Take two sheets of paper, fold them in half, and give one to your mate. In the first column, make a list of all the situations—big or small—that have made you angry as an adult. Examples might include: a rude salesman, a defective appliance, an income tax penalty, a careless driver, the glass your child broke, your husband's behavior, a forgotten anniversary, too much work, not enough money, a stain on your shirt, a congressman's attitude, disturbing news, ants in the kitchen, etc. In the second column, list all the things that made you angry when you were a kid (the bully at school, homework, not getting your way when . . . , breaking a toy, a parental punishment, eating lima beans, etc.). Make sure you have at least twenty items on each list to work with. As you compare your two lists, what patterns do you see? Do the same things make you angry now that enraged you as a child? Are you more or less angry than before, and has your anger changed or evolved? Such questions will deepen your awareness of your emotional patterns and beliefs. Read your list to your partner and talk about the feelings that the discussion brings up.

Step 2: Now exchange your list with your partner and add to it all the things you feel that your partner may have ignored or forgotten to include. This is an important step, because we are sometimes blind to our own emotional states. Be tactful in your wording, for this step may cause anxiety for your partner or even provoke anger! Read your additions to each other and ask your partner if he or she agrees with the observations you've made. Remember, though, that the purpose is to listen and to accept, not to argue or judge. You may find, as you dialogue, that there are many differences in what you and your partner perceive as anger, which can often explain why certain misunderstandings occur.

Step 3: For this next step, it is helpful to begin with a relaxation exercise, using the dialogical meditation techniques as described in chapter 3. Begin by facing your partner and, when you feel ready, describe one of the three angriest times in your life. Try to include as much of a *feeling sense* as you can, talking *from* the anxieties and fears. Share how you reacted to what you did, and how that event makes you feel now. Then let your partner ask questions until she or he fully grasps the impact of the memory you are describing. When you are done, switch roles and listen to your partner's story with your fullest attention, encouraging her or him to let the emotional expressions unfold. When your partner has finished, switch again and share another angry event from the past.

Step 4: When the two of you have finished sharing your stories, dialogue informally with each other. What patterns do you see in your partner, and how do they differ from yours? Tell each other how you felt as you listened to each story, exploring the questions it raised and the insights that it brought.

Step 5: As a final step, ask each other what you can do to reduce the situations that provoke anger. Brainstorm with your partner and write down as many solutions you can think of to defuse potential bombs. For example, if you tend to get angry at people who do irresponsible work, ask yourself how you would want to be confronted if someone felt the same about you. Could you then approach an irresponsible person in a similar way?

Game #3
Family Feuds

In this exercise, you will create a special type of chart—a genogram—to help you recognize the patterns of anger in your family histories and how it influences your behavior today.[28] How often did your parents get mad, and how did you react to their anger? What were the emotional styles of your family, and how did they influence your own? As we explore such questions with our partners, we can often unmask habituated patterns that interfere with our conflict-resolution skills, for once we understand our family's emotional histories, we can more easily recognize and interrupt these disruptive behaviors in ourselves.

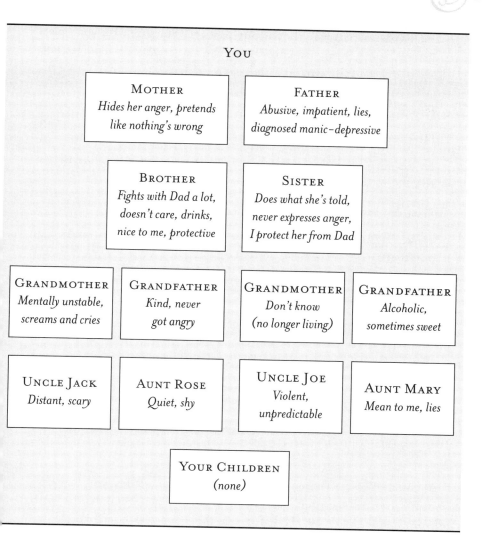

On a sheet of paper, make a family tree of all the relatives you have interacted with or know about through family stories and tales. Make a box for each relative, and write down a few key words describing each personality and the way he or she expressed anger. When you are finished, your chart should look something like the drawing above (the example shown was made by an adolescent girl who grew up in a house where everyone fought and yelled).

Talk about your drawing with your partner. Starting with your parents, describe everything you know about the way they handled anger and conflict, using the following questions as a guide:

1. How did your parents express anger?

2. How often did they express anger? Was anyone ever hurt?

3. How would fights start? Who would start them? Who got angry first?

3. How did your parents resolve their conflicts?

4. How did their expression of anger, or lack of expression, make you feel?

5. What did you do when they got angry? How did it affect you, and what did you learn?

6. How did other family members respond to your parents' anger?

7. When you got angry, how were you treated by your parents? Did you feel listened to?

8. Do you currently deal with anger in similar ways?

9. If you have children, do you treat them as your parents treated you?

As you and your partner explore each other's histories, you may discover why your own communication styles break down when dealing with emotional issues at home. Hal, for example, was very comfortable expressing his anger with others. When he was growing up, his parents had argued a lot, but they always seemed to work it out. Hal's wife, Suzy, however, grew up in a family where anger was never expressed. Even the slightest tone of irritation would cause her to withdraw. Needless to say, when conflicts arose in their current relationship with each other, they were both deeply frustrated and hurt. But when they shared their family feud charts, the family differences came to light. Hal and his wife could better understand why each one reacted so differently and had such opposing feelings about anger, and thus were able to be more sensitive and tolerant when a family conflict occurred. Hal became more careful about express-ing his anger, and when he occasionally failed, Suzy was more forgiving. By learning how to accept each other's differences, relationship expert Lib-erty Kovacs confirms, couples stop blaming and attacking each other and focus instead on developing constructive solutions for their problems.[29]

Game #4
Charting Your Anger Away

How often do you get angry or irritated? Once a month? Once a week? Several times a day? Sometimes it is the little things—the tiny hurts and subtle frustrations—that build up over time and turn into anger. By chart-ing your day-to-day mood shifts, this simple two-step process can help you uncover the seeds from which anger grows.

For the next few weeks, keep a daily chart of every irritable moment you experience, no matter how minor it may seem. Use the example on the following page (created by Joe, a manager at a high-tech company).

In the first three columns, record the day and time when each irritable moment occurs, describe the event, and then write down the correspond-ing angry thoughts that the event pro-voked. In the final column, give each emotional event an intensity rating: 1 for mild, 2 for moderate, and 3 for strong.

Rating the intensity of the mood allows you to observe how your moods fluctu-ate. Rating your moods also helps alert you to which situations or thoughts are associated with changes in moods. Fi-nally, you can use changes in emotional intensity to evaluate the effectiveness of strategies you are learning.

DENNIS GREENBERGER,
PH.D.

CHRISTINE A. PADESKY,
PH.D.
Mind over Mood

Just the simple act of keeping such a chart for several weeks can help one reduce the frequency and intensity of anger. Through his chart, Joe discovered many irritating events during his day that he had never noticed before. "I never realized how many things upset me, but when I started paying attention, I could stop myself and relax. Now, when I go home, I have the energy to enjoy my wife and kids. I never knew that the little stuff could make such a difference in my life."

JOE'S CHART

Day/Time	Event	Associated Thoughts and Feelings	Rating
Thursday, 10 A.M.	Computer problems at work, and I'm late turning in a report.	1. Pissed off at computer; the company won't upgrade old system—they're idiots, afraid of trying new things.	2
		2. My boss always pressures me; he never understands.	1
Friday, 9:30 A.M.	Slow traffic going to work; idiot driver cut me off.	3. Get out of my way, nobody knows how to drive, they're all idiots. I didn't need this today.	3
Friday, 2:30 P.M.	My son was called into the principal's office again.	4. He's doing it to spite me; he's lazy.	3
		5. I feel like screaming at him or grounding him.	2
Friday, 4:30 P.M.	Boss wants me to work overtime tonight.	6. He never takes my feelings or needs into consideration.	1
Saturday, 10 A.M.	The lawn mower breaks down, and I can't find my keys to the car.	7. Crummy piece of junk; ruins the plans I had today.	3
		8. There's just one crisis after another.	3
		Total Points for the Week:	18

Keeping a daily chart of your anger brings attention to the subtle events that contribute to an irritable mood. When you have it down on paper, you can more easily predict potential hot spots and redirect your energies before your anger kicks in. The act of writing itself helps transform the habituated ways in which one responds to emotional events, for the logic and organization that are required for keeping a chart interrupt the irrational chaos of the angry state. Chart keeping can even uncover other hidden problems: for example, a pattern of *seasonal* or *cyclic* depression, a hormonal or metabolic imbalance, or other conditions that may require psychological or medical care.

Emotionally charged thoughts are usually irrational, filled with exaggerations and distortions, and thus it is important to identify the distortions and reframe them in more constructive and realistic ways. Simply ask yourself the following questions about each emotionally charged and angry thought:

1. Is my impression of the situation really accurate?

2. Have I exaggerated any of my feelings and reactions?

3. Have I overgeneralized?

4. Am I using all-or-nothing thinking ("I never . . . ," "It always . . .")?

5. Have I jumped to conclusions?

6. Am I being judgmental ("I should have . . . ," "You ought to . . . ," "You're wrong")?

7. Am I using blame, making the problem solely about someone else?

When you review these questions, restate the upsetting event and your reaction to it in a more accurate, honest, and truthful way. Then write it down on your chart.

Let's take a look at one of Joe's emotional thoughts regarding his boss: *"My boss always pressures me; he never understands; he never takes my feelings or needs into consideration."* In this example, Joe uses all-or-nothing thinking, which distorts the reality of the situation and puts the bulk of the blame on his boss. He reframed his statement as follows: "My boss is under a lot of pressure, too. He's not the most sensitive person I've met, but he's treated me fairly in the past. He values me and he really needs my help. Besides, I've been under so much pressure myself that I'm sure I contribute to his stress." Two books that can help you to further develop these cognitive therapy skills are *Feeling Good,* by David Burns, and *Mind over Mood,* by Dennis Greenberger and Christine Padesky.

Game #5

The Hostility Checklist

In creating the Hostility Checklist, Aaron T. Beck, who pioneered the development of cognitive therapy, asks us to carefully consider the following question: When you are angry with your spouse, is it really worth it to openly express your feelings? Venting may let off steam, but it also strains the fabric of love and can knock a relationship off balance for weeks. Beck suggests that you wait until your anger dies down, which will allow you to see the problem with greater clarity.

Before venting your anger at your spouse, ask yourself these questions:

1. What do I expect to *gain* by reproaching, punishing, or criticizing my spouse?

2. What do I *lose* by using these tactics? Even if there are good short-term results, are the long-term results likely to be bad? For example, even if my spouse gives in or capitulates right now, is there a likelihood that this is only going to make the relationship more disagreeable or emotionally distant in the future?

3. What is the point that I want to get across to my mate? What is the best way to make this point? Am I likely to do this by reproaching or blaming my spouse?

4. Are there better ways than punishment to influence my spouse—for example, by having a serious discussion about his or her actions, or by offering a "reward" (a smile or compliment) when he or she does what I like?

To help you assess the costs and benefits of expressing anger, I have prepared a checklist which you can use to estimate whether the gains from the anger will exceed the losses. The best way to determine the overall value of expressing anger is to evaluate your past experiences. Use this checklist to assess the gains and losses from episodes of fighting, continue to consult it, and update your answers after future fights.

Checklist for Value of Expression of Hostility

Think back to your most recent expression of anger and try to determine its positive and negative effects. You may have to check with your spouse to determine how to answer many of these questions, since part of each answer depends upon your spouse's reaction. Check those that are true:

Positive Effects of My Expression of Anger

———— 1. My partner behaved better after the episode.
———— 2. I felt better.
———— 3. My partner felt better.
———— 4. Fighting back protected me when my partner became abusive.
———— 5. I could tell that my partner really heard me, which doesn't happen when I just talk in a normal fashion.
———— 6. I experienced a relief of anger and a release of tension.
———— 7. It cleared the air, and we were able to turn our attention to other things.
———— 8. We loved each other more after having "a good fight."
———— 9. We settled our argument.

Negative Effects of My Expression of Anger

———— 1. I was less effective, more clumsy, or even incoherent in presenting my argument or complaint.
———— 2. I said or did things that I regretted afterward.
———— 3. My partner discounted or discredited the validity of what I said, dismissing my ideas as based on emotionality or irrationality.
———— 4. My partner did not even hear my message—because it was buried in a cloud of hostility.

_____ 5. My partner responded only to my hostility, and retaliated.

_____ 6. My partner was wounded by my attack.

_____ 7. We got involved in a vicious cycle of attack and counterattack.

If you do decide to express your anger, you have a choice of tactics, some of which are more effective than others in simultaneously reducing your anger and getting your message across. For example, saying "I'm angry at you" may have a more constructive effect than attacking your partner's personality or giving him or her the silent treatment.

SEVENTEEN TIPS FOR BECOMING LESS HOSTILE

"Bottled up anger has long been suspect as a cause for illness," says Bradford Williams, M.D., director of the Behavioral Medicine Research Center at Duke University Medical Center. "It may increase the levels of stress hormones circulating in the blood, which can have a number of long-term effects on the cardiovascular system." If you or your spouse have difficulty with hostility, anger, or rage, review and practice these helpful hints and tips from Dr. Williams:

1. Admit to a friend that your hostility level is too high, and let her or him know you are trying to reduce it.

2. When cynical thoughts come into your head, yell "Stop!" (silently, if you are in public).

3. Try to talk yourself out of being angry. Reason with yourself.

4. Distract yourself when you're getting angry. For example, pick up a magazine from the rack if you're kept waiting in a supermarket checkout line.

5. Force yourself to be quiet and listen when other people are talking.

6. Learn how to meditate, and use this skill whenever you become aware of cynical thoughts or angry feelings.

7. Try to become more empathetic to the plight of others.

8. When someone is truly mistreating you, learn how to be effectively assertive, rather than aggressively lashing out.

9. Take steps to increase your connectedness to others, thereby countering the tendency of hostile people to ward off social support.

10. When people do you wrong, forgive them.

11. Cultivate friends at work or in your religious group.

12. Volunteer to help others less fortunate than yourself.

13. Learn to laugh at your hostile tendencies.

14. Engage in regular exercise.

15. Get a pet. People who have pets seem to live longer and be healthier, perhaps because animals, especially dogs, are so affectionate and undemanding. Unlike many people, pets give much more than they get.

16. Learn more about the core teachings of your chosen religion: A central principle of the major world religions is to treat others as we would have them treat us.

17. Pretend that this day is your last. Your hostile tendencies will come into perspective.

Game #6
Sitting with the Demons

Meditation is one of the most powerful ways to work through anger. When we meditate upon the demons within, we become more observant and relaxed, and thus we can go deeper into our emotions without losing control. We can safely experience our anger more fully, see it with greater clarity, and express it in nondestructive ways. Finally, meditation gives us insight into the existential roots of this primal emotional core. The more we learn about anger, the easier it becomes to redirect its energies into constructive actions and thoughts. The only trick is to *remember* to medi-

tate when you are angry, and so I suggest that you practice this game several times with your partner *before* a conflict comes up. Then, the next time anger erupts, you will be prepared to follow it into its depths, using the following steps as a guide:

1. Find a quiet place to sit, facing your partner, where you will not be disturbed by others or by the phone. Take about five minutes to relax, breathing deeply and slowly.

2. Focus on the feelings of anger that are there, and follow your emotions in any direction they take (in your practice sessions, focus on a recent event that made you angry. When you meditate upon anger, it often changes and moves. It may become more intense, then fade away, and return again with force. Or it may suddenly shift to another feeling state—to sadness or distrust, or to anxiety, boredom, or doubt—for anger often masks other emotions and moods.

3. Observe these feelings and thoughts as if you were watching a movie or listening to a tape, and label each one with a simple word or phrase: "I feel angry and hurt," or simply "Anger . . . doubt . . . hurt," etc., saying the words out loud or quietly to yourself.

4. After noting each feeling or thought, take a deep breath and let it go, paying attention to the next feeling that emerges. The internal dialogue might sound something like this: "Anger—anger—sadness—pain—I feel like running away—running away—I'm afraid of expressing my anger—I'm afraid of my partner being angry at me—I feel like crying—blackness—anger—sad . . ." If your mind wanders to some other topic, simply take another deep breath and refocus on your anger.

5. Begin a dialogue with your partner, focusing on the qualities of the anger. How does it make you feel? Where, in your body, do you feel it? How long does the feeling last? What preceded your feelings of anger, and what does it make you want to do? Do you feel like avoiding the feelings, or letting them run their course?

By passively observing the shifting of your emotions, you train yourself to observe your anger from a calmer mental state. As you do so, you will find that your anger influences your thoughts and behavior less and less. Your demons will have lost their grasp.

Game #7
Visions of Madness

In this simple meditation—given by Tenzin Gyatso, the Fourteenth Dalai Lama and spiritual leader of Tibet—we learn how to use the powers of imagination to eliminate the anger within. This is the first of several exercises that use visualization as a creative way to extinguish the fires within.

Let us do a meditation with a little bit of visualization. Imagine a scenario where someone that you know very well, someone who is close or dear to you loses his or her temper, either in a very acrimonious relationship, or in a situation where something else is happening. This person shows all signs of being in an intense state of anger or hatred, loses all mental composure, creates very negative "vibes," even goes to the extent of harming himself or herself and breaking things. Then reflect upon the immediate effects of intense anger or hatred. The reason why I think we should visualize this happening to others is because it is easier to see the faults of others than to see our own faults. So visualize this, and even see a physical transformation happening to that person. This person whom you feel close to, whom you like, the very sight of whom gave you pleasure in the past, now turns into this ugly, ugly person, even physically speaking. This is a kind of analytic meditation, so do this meditation and visualization for a few minutes, in an analytical way, using your imaginative faculty. At the end of it, relate that to your own experience. Then resolve, "I shall never let myself fall under the sway of such intense anger and hatred. Because if I do that, I will also be in the same position and suffer all these consequences—lose my peace of mind, lose my composure, assume this ugly physical appearance, and so on." Make that decision, and then remain in an absorptive meditation on this conclusion.

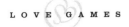

KILLING THE DEMONS WITH KINDNESS

Feeling irritable, anxious, a little depressed, or stuck? Is the freeway traffic driving you nuts? Do you find yourself snapping at others for no apparent reason, or mysteriously frustrated at yourself? There are times when we simply cannot recognize the conflict that lurks within. When meditation and self-reflection fail, try a compassionate diversion or two:

1. Treat yourself to a present or a special treat. Make your demons happy.

2. Take a walk in nature. Go to the beach and bury your demons in the sand.

3. Take a sauna, or a long, hot shower or bath. Melt those demons away.

4. Exercise. Run your demons to death.

5. Get a massage from someone you love and rub those demons away.

6. Make love. For demons, intimacy is like the plague.

Game #8
Revisioning the Angers of the Past

Roberto Assagioli, an early pioneer of psychoanalysis and the creator of Psychosynthesis (a psycho-spiritual therapy), found that people could form deeper, loving bonds if they first visualized and reexperienced the angers and hostilities from previous relationships, feelings that could unconsciously hinder one's ability to reach intimacy in one's present relationship.

The following visualization exercise is a modification of Assagioli's "imaginative evocation" technique.[30] When you recall a memory in the manner he suggests, the influence of that memory upon the present can be dissolved. I recommend that you use your partner or a friend to guide you through the following steps.

Sit or lie down in a comfortable place, close your eyes, breathe deeply, and relax as fully as you can. Remember an incident from a previous relationship where anger played a role. If nothing immediately comes to mind, take a few more deep breaths and let your imagination wander.

Eventually a memory will come to you. Describe it to your partner, with as much accuracy and detail as you can: what the person looked like, the place where the anger erupted, the shape of the room, the time of day, etc.

Take some more deep breaths, relax, and return to the scene that you just described. This time, replay it in your mind as if it were happening in the present. Feel the anger, the anxiety, and the tension in your body. If you deepen your breathing, the experience will become more intense, but do not spend more than five or ten minutes immersed in the emotional state, for longer periods may leave you feeling disturbed. If you feel yourself beginning to shake or involuntarily tense up, slow down your breathing and open your eyes—sitting up, if need be—until you feel more calm. And if you still feel overwhelmed, discontinue the exercise and return to it another day. When dealing with traumatic memories, you may need to repeat this step several more times until the intensity subsides.

Now bring yourself back to a state of relaxation by imagining a beautiful, serene place like a waterfall, forest, or beach. Assagioli recommends that the previous steps be repeated several times over the next few days until no emotional residue remains. But I have found that many people greatly benefit by immediately going through the following step: Take yourself back into the memory, but this time envision the scene unfolding in the way you would *ideally* want it to go. Try to come up with several creative scenarios, and share them with your partner.

Here's what happened with Paul when he revisioned the hurts and angers from his traumatic first love. His girlfriend dumped him without saying a word, and this sent Paul into a three-month depression. In revisioning this early memory, Paul realized that every time a fight ensued in his present relationship, he would immediately get depressed. Each time he replayed his first love scene, the emotional feelings lessened, but when he fantasied his ideal ending (in which his girlfriend sat down and gently told him that she wanted to end the relationship), he felt as if a great burden had been released. Now, whenever a relational conflict emerges, Paul does not get depressed, for he knows that his current partner would not just get up and walk out as his first love had done. By visualizing alternative solutions, we can actually reprogram our unconscious reactions to future conflicts and demands.

Game #9
Have Tomorrow's Fight Today

This technique uses creative visualization to help you to think through potential problem areas and to design effective solutions *before* a conflict occurs. By incorporating visualizations, problems and solutions can be grasped on a deeper level where intuitive insights emerge.

First, put yourself into a relaxed and meditative state, and then ask yourself this question: "In regard to my partner, what kinds of situations are most likely to make me angry?" Pick a situation that holds a strong emotional charge and allow your imagination to create a scenario around a make-believe fight. Visualize you and your partner having a fight, and watch it like a movie. How do you react to the fight? What does your partner do?

Imagine that a terrible fight takes place. Perhaps you'll smash a glass, or hit your spouse, or burn the entire house down. Exaggerate the outcome as much as you possibly can and watch the feelings that emerge. If this feels scary to you, remember that it's only a fantasy.

Once more, go back to the beginning of the scene. Ask your unconscious self—your intuition, your inner teacher—to provide you with a creative solution, and then see what your imagination provides.

Share your experience with your partner, and when a future conflict arises, quickly (in your imagination) run through the worst- and best-possible scenario you can think of. The solutions that you dream up are almost always more effective than those that have occurred to you in the past.

Game #10
Blurting (the Three-Minute Solution)

I don't know about you, but sometimes when I am engulfed in anger, the last thing I feel like doing is playing a structured game. I don't want to act rational or sensitive or kind. I'd rather complain and yell, for I know that if I take a few minutes to "get it off my chest," I'll feel better, calmer, and more capable of going on. But I also know that if I do this in front of my mate, I'll make a bad situation worse.

If you find yourself in a similar mood, then try this three-minute exercise the next time anger intrudes, completing the following sentences as fast as you can. Don't pause or think or censor anything—just blurt out whatever comes to mind. If you get stuck, make something up, *anything*, but keep on going. As you go along, make up other sentence stems to take you further into your feelings and thoughts, and if you are with another person, ask him or her to read the sentences to you, making up others that seem appropriate to your mood. Are you ready? On your mark, get set, BLURT:

1. I'm so angry that I could _____ .

2. And I feel like I _____ .

3. I even think that I could _____ .

4. The thing that bothers me the most is _____ .

5. And the basic problem is this: _____ .

6. If I could make things go the way I wanted them to go, _____ .

7. But in order to make that happen, I'd have to _____ .

8. Now, if I really wanted to get past my anger, I would need to _____ .

9. A simple solution could be _____ .

10. Another solution would be _____ .

Now see how you feel. Has your anger shifted? Has a more effective solution been found? Blurting promotes intuitive and creative responses, even when you are being gripped by rage. But sometimes it doesn't work, for a person can be so caught up in feelings of rage that he or she cannot get past the destructive impulses inside. When this occurs, ask a friend to guide you through the exercise again, write down your thoughts on paper, or try out game 17, Killing the Couch, to help blow off the steam.

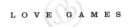

Game #11
Scripting Your Anger (the Ten-Minute Solution)

Your client's check just bounced, your partner embarrassed you in public, and your kid spilled soda on your suit. You are, shall we say, enraged,
and a confrontation is assured. But it helps to be prepared. Before you
engage in battle, take a few minutes to try a scripting technique—an imaginary rehearsal of how you will confront your partner—that University of
California, Irvine, psychologists Dennis Greenberger and Christine
Padesky use to help couples achieve the outcomes they want when they
must confront a problem with their mates.[31]

The next time a conflict erupts, take a piece of paper and write down
as briefly as possible the problem that occurred and explain why it made you
upset. Then briefly state your suggestions for a solution. Then mentally
rehearse what you plan to say (your "script") to your partner. Think about
your opening remarks—the most important part of the script—and how
you would like your partner to respond. What is the best way to get this
person to listen without creating a defensive reaction or response?

Practice reading your script out loud, in front of a mirror, or with a
tape recorder, for it will help to polish your approach. You can also rehearse it with a friend who can provide further clarity and advice. When
you feel ready, approach your partner and carry out your script.

Game #12
The Seven-Day Cure

"The only factor that can give refuge or protection from the destructive
effects of anger and hatred is the practice of tolerance and patience," the
Dalai Lama once said.[32] But the practice is not as simple as it sounds. It
may be easy to feel loving for brief periods of time, especially when you are
happy and surrounded by compassionate people, but it is very difficult to
practice compassion around the clock, especially toward those who have
little ability for showing you respect.

Here's a suggestion: For one week, generate kind thoughts and actions
toward everyone you meet—on the freeway, in line at the grocery store,
when your kid breaks your favorite dish, toward the gardener with the

thousand-decibel leaf blower, and even toward yourself. For seven days, hold compassion for every moment of the day, interrupting any hint of anger or irritability that you feel. But do not suppress feelings of sadness or fear, for these are often the genuine emotions behind the angry mood.

I decided to try this exercise at the end of a particularly frustrating week, one in which everything seemed to go wrong. Everyone seemed like a royal pain, and I hated the state I was in. I had meditated on it, played it out in my imagination, screamed, and kicked the couch. Nothing seemed to work, so I forced myself to send compassionate thoughts to every irritating soul in my life—to the grumpy neighbor, the hostile homeowner's association, and to the maniac on the road.

> ## THE TWO-WORD SOLUTION
>
> *In big bold letters, write "THANK YOU!" across the top of every check you sign: to the phone company, the IRS, even to the municipal clerk for that ticket you got last week. It may brighten someone's day.*
>
> SUSAN VAN VONDEREN

The first day was the most difficult, for I really wanted to let my anger out, but I placated myself with the thought that it would only be a week. By the fifth day, however, I was feeling so much better that I extended my experiment for another week. And then I continued it for a month. Now I do it without thinking, and it seems to have made a significant difference in my life. Little things that used to annoy me—the construction noise next door, the endless traffic jams—I barely notice at all. I'm relaxed and happy a majority of the time. Sometimes I fall off track, but only for a day or two.

I'm not sure why it took me so long to try this simple approach, but I do know this: when I ask my clients and friends to try this exercise, they, too, have reported great success. Even Cindy, a self-proclaimed road warrior, had her armor pierced. "No way," she said, when I suggested this game. "I'm not giving in to those other jerks on the road." But several weeks later, she brought the subject up. "I didn't really believe it would do any good, and besides, I really like my anger. It gives me strength and I don't feel pushed around. But I tried it anyway, and maybe it's my imagination, but I couldn't find any jerks on the road. It really seems to work!"

Game #13
Tapeworms

When you are angry, are you aware of the changes in your facial expressions, in the cadence and tone of your voice? If you are like most people, the answer is probably no.

Anger has a curious way of blinding us. It distorts the way we think and feel and even hear. But if we could glimpse our anger through the eyes of someone else, a behavioral transformation might occur. All we need is a little piece of tape, in the form of a cassette or video recorder.

Make an agreement with your spouse to record the next fight you have. Just knowing that a tape recorder is running will keep your anger in check, but if you can, try to allow a typical fight to unfold. Then play it back and analyze what you see. For most couples, a single tape recording will promote dramatic changes in their confrontational styles and the ways they handle disputes.

You might also try the following experiment. Using a video or tape recorder, stage a playfully dramatic fight, using your partner, friends, or members of your family. This is actually quite fun to do, often promoting intimate dialogues about feelings and communication skills. Such an exercise brings tremendous consciousness to the experience of anger, for it lets us see how we are perceived by others when our emotions carry us away.

Game #14
The Empty Chair

In this game, popularized by the gestalt therapist Fritz Perls,[33] you conduct an imaginary conversation with a person you are angry with, but instead of just playing yourself, you act out both roles. This exercise works best when a support person (someone other than the one you are angry with) is present to act as your "director," keeping you on track as you work toward solving the problem at hand. This game can bring you in touch with different aspects of yourself that have been suppressed or projected onto others, and it will help you to understand more clearly how other people think and feel and react.

Set up two chairs facing each other. Begin by sitting in one chair and imagining that the person you are angry with is sitting in the other. Start the conversation by playing yourself and saying whatever you feel like, and then sit in the other chair and respond *as if you were the other person.* Your support person can assist by telling you when the conversation seems unreal and may intervene if the dialogue gets stuck. You may also want to experiment by asking your friend to play the role of the other person or to take the position of a devil's advocate. You may even end up laughing as the emotional layers unfold.

When you have finished, discuss the experience with your friend, and then share your insights with the person with whom you were angry. You will find that you can now engage this person with optimism, care, and strength.

Game #15
Hollywood

This is a variation of the Empty Chair game, to be played when you do not have a support person to work with. With paper and pen, write down a dialogue on paper between you and the person you are angry with. As with the previous exercise, this game will help to illuminate many hidden dimensions of your anger, helping you to reach clarity and insight about yourself, the other person, and the problems you may face.

As you write, allow your imagination to roam. You can add other "characters" to your play—a support person, a devil's advocate, a therapist, your kid, even an angel—to help explore different facets of your personality. As you allow these imaginary characters to interact creatively with your real emotions and thoughts, some surprising scenarios may emerge. When you have finished, and your anger has subsided, share your screenplay (if appropriate) with your mate.

Game #16
The Artist's Revenge

This game was inspired by Al Bauman, a Reichian therapist, who told me the following story: One day, many years ago, someone came knocking at his door. There stood an old friend, an artist by trade, with an expression

> *Symbolic imagery techniques often allow patients to release pent-up feelings like anger and resentment, without further harming the relationship with the partner. For example, such a patient may experience himself gradually smashing a huge boulder in the mountains while simultaneously venting his angry feelings. Other patients may imagine breaking through a barrier, discarding old parental messages that evoke negative emotions, or placing feelings of guilt in the gondola of a hot air balloon and watching it float away.*
>
> D. CORYDON HAMMOND
> *Handbook of Hypnotic Suggestions and Metaphors*

of rage on his face. "I'm so angry and frustrated about my marriage that I haven't been able to paint for weeks," the young man raged. Al listened patiently and then he told his friend to go home, to get some crayons and a pad of paper, and cover it with angry little marks. "But," Al said, "you are not to stop until you have covered every single spot on the page." It took hours to complete, but when the artist stepped back, he saw that he had created a potent but beautiful sketch. It was alive, vibrant, and disturbing, but, most important, he was free to paint again. And his anger was under control.

I do not know whether the artist's marriage succeeded or not, but his story has impressed me for years, for it exemplifies one of the few instances when anger can be expressed in a constructive and creative way. The next time you feel angry, try directing that emotion into a work of art. The easiest approach is to pour your feelings onto a piece of paper. It's quick and cheap and ultimately fun. Felt pens, pencils, crayons, and chalk work best because you can grab them in your fist and shove them across the page. Just let yourself go, scribbling and poking and jabbing until the entire page is full. But don't try to make a design—just let the feelings come out through the tips of your fingers and hand—and keep going until your emotions subside.

Bauman's innovative work with anger grew out of his conversations with a man named Wilhelm Reich, a controversial psychoanalyst who was known for encouraging people to express their anger through pillow pounding and screams. But Reich also believed that anger could be processed through art. A frustrated musician could put his feelings into sounds, and a dancer could gambol her rage away. Behind the anger, said Reich, were the deeper feelings of sexual intimacy and love. One simply had to break through the anger to be free.

The next time you have some anger to spare, try turning it into art. If all else fails, then try taking it out on your couch—the more typical Reichian approach, as the following game describes.

Game #17
Killing the Couch

Sometimes internal feelings of anger are so strong, or so locked up inside, that a self-ventilation session may help. In the following exercises—to be done when you are alone—you can safely release your anger through yelling, hitting, or kicking something soft. This technique can be very helpful for those who are shy or withdrawn, for it allows a person to get in touch with feelings that may have been buried for years.

The rationale to this approach comes from the Reichian notion that feelings can be stored in the body as well as the mind. Anger, in particular, can cause a person to tense the muscles of the jaw, neck, back, and arms. This is the physiology of rage, which can be released through vigorous movements and sounds.

As you read through the following techniques, try to visualize yourself enraged, throwing an all-out temper tantrum—like a two-year-old. Then, when you feel consumed by anger, try out a tantrum for real:

1. Scream as loud as you can into a pillow for at least a minute, which will seem and feel like a very long time to yell. The first few screams won't do the trick, but after about a dozen or so, you should feel an underlying rage break through. Breathing is essential, for the deeper you breathe, the easier it will be to scream. You can also yell out any expression or expletive that comes to mind, such as "I HATE YOU, I HATE YOU, I HATE YOU, I WISH YOU'D DROP DEAD AND ROT . . ." Once your underlying anger fully surfaces, continue screaming until it subsides, and if sadness or grief comes up, allow those feelings to unfold. Then breathe slowly until you are fully relaxed, meditating on the experience and the meanings that it may hold.

2. Lie on your bed, and with your arms and legs, hit and kick as fast and as hard as you can—for five minutes, if you can—making as

much noise as you can. When you are done, roll yourself back and forth in a sensual way for several minutes more. Quietly reflect upon the feelings and thoughts that emerge.

3. Sit in front of a couch or a bed. Take a deep breath and raise your arms above your head, and as you exhale, bring your fists down as hard as you can into the pillows. As you hit the pillows, yell as loud a sound as you can (if that feels too uncomfortable, then a closed-lipped *"umph"* will do). Continue until your anger subsides, and observe how your feelings and thoughts now flow.

As an alternative to yelling and hitting, you can also direct your anger into a vigorous activity. You can run as hard as you can or hit a punching bag with all your might. You can even dig a hole in the backyard or tear an old shirt to shreds. In these ways, you can set free the anger from your body as well as from your mind.

Game #18
The Wise Old Man

Of all the imagination games that work with anger, this is one of my favorites. It is a variation of Assagioli's inner teacher work, a creative fantasy that shares elements from psychodrama, gestalt, and Jungian imaginative techniques. You can play it when you are angry or calm, and each time you do so, you will discover something new: a simple insight, a new idea, or a solution you haven't tried.

The best way to play this game is with your partner or a friend, where one of you reads the instructions and the story and the other fills in the missing parts of the dialogue. When you get the hang of it, the reader can begin to improvise, playing the part of the wise old man. To begin, ask your partner to lie down and relax as you read the following text:

You are about to take a journey to a special place within, where you will meet an unusually wise but ornery old man. He is, according to the rumors, the Master of Rage, knowing everything there is to know about those nasty demons within.

Feel yourself entering into a state of relaxation, breathing deeply and relaxing every part of your body. With each exhalation, feel yourself falling deeper into peace. Your arms and legs and body are getting heavy and warm, melting into the surface that supports your weight. You feel yourself sinking even further, through the floor and into the soft dark earth below.

You are drifting down a tunnel deep inside the earth, darker and darker, deeper and deeper, until you suddenly see a light. You find yourself in a cave, and in the center there is a fire burning. Feel its warmth as you come closer to the flames.

There, on the other side of fire, an old man sits, shrouded in a cloak of rags. "Sit down," he curtly says.

You feel a little irritated, but you do as he commands. You are tired from your journey, very tired and worn. You say hello, but the old man doesn't reply. You try again, but you still don't get a response. You feel your anger grow and are about to get up and leave when suddenly he speaks.

"Open the box at your feet. It's a present from me to you." *Arrogant little man,* you think, but you take the box in your hands. You open it carefully and read the note you find inside. You cannot help but follow the instructions it gives:

Breathe deeply into the place inside where your anger quietly resides, allowing all your thoughts and feelings to unfold. With each deep breath you feel your anger growing, flowing through your head, your body, and your blood. The anger almost makes you tingle and shake, and you can feel it in your veins. But still you keep on breathing. Think angry thoughts. Visualize angry people. Recall an angry event. Who made you angry in the past, and who makes you angry now? Feel the anger flowing through your veins.

A fire is burning inside, like the fire in the cave, and every time you add a log, it burns brighter with light and heat. You perspire and start to sweat. "Why have you done this to me?" you ask the raggedy man. But he does not utter a word.

"Why won't you answer me, old man?" you say with irritation. Inside, the anger continues to grow. You feel it in your hands, you taste it in your mouth. You are angry and tense, and

every muscle aches. Your irritation grows and grows and grows, but the little old man does nothing but laugh.

That's it! You won't take any more. You're mad as hell and about to explode. You're just about to do something terrible, when suddenly the old man speaks.

"Okay, I'll talk with you if you want," he says. "But I doubt if you will listen."

And so a dialogue begins, but you must use your imagination and speak for the wise old man. He begins by saying something rude: "_____."

You say something angry in return: "_____."

And he responds: "_____"

You argue with him, and he responds: "_____" (let your fantasy run free).

You threaten and insult him, and he responds: "_____" (anything goes).

You plead with him, and he responds: "_____" (don't censor anything).

You even arm-wrestle with him, but all he does is _____ (have fun with it; it doesn't matter what you say).

Finally you give up and ask him for advice. A warm smile inches across his face, and a twinkle is discerned in his eye. He sits down in front of the fire and begins to tell you all he has learned about anger.

He tells you why your ancestors were angry: "_____" (let your intuition unfold). And your anger begins to dissolve.

He tells you why society is mad: "_____." And your anger dissolves some more.

He tells you about the nature of anger, and the secrets that it holds: "_____." Your anger falls away.

And then he tells you about you, about your anger and what it is about: "_____." You feel warm and relaxed and at peace.

Finally, he tells you something interesting and wise, but it wasn't what you expected: "_____."

"Now you may ask me one question before I disappear," the old man says, and so you ask the following: "_____."

He replies: "_____."

You look up and he vanishes into the dark. You're feeling very, very relaxed and calm, and you thank the man in the darkness for his help. The fire starts to dim, and you feel yourself being pulled back to the surface of the world, up through the tunnel and back into your room. You take ten slow, deep breaths and sink into a peaceful, relaxed state, awake and rested and wise.

When the exercise has been completed, reverse positions with your mate and let yourself be led into the center of your soul, where both anger and wisdom reside.

Anger and Forgiveness: Concluding Remarks

In this chapter, we have dealt with anger in many ways: thinking about it, charting it, talking it through, defusing it, reframing it, visualizing it, listening to it, and blurting it out to a chair. We have even tried to kill it with kindness and run it into the ground. By now, your anger should be history.

But even in history, anger can stay alive as disappointment, bitterness, distrust, and fear, cutting us off

THE OLD, WISE SELF

Think about yourself as an older, wiser person of about eighty or so years of age. What would the older, wiser you say to you and your partner that might help in getting you to feel close and loving; what advice, suggestions, or support could the older, wiser self give to help during these times?

GEORGE J. STEINFELD
Journal of Couples Therapy

It is necessary to practice, practice, and practice alternative responses to anger. Your characteristic way of responding to anger did not develop overnight, and new patterns will also not develop overnight. . . . Begin practicing alternative ways of thinking (e.g., replacing "hot thoughts" that generate anger with "cool thoughts" that promote conversation and problem solving); quieting physiological arousal with relaxation techniques; and avoiding critical remarks that make others defensive.

CLIFFORD NOTARIUS,
SAMUEL LASHLEY, AND
DEBRA J. SULLIVAN
Satisfaction in Close Relationships

from ourselves and each other. One final step is needed to dissolve the grudges that remain: a forgiveness step that has its roots in the spiritual traditions of the both the East and the West.

Forgiveness means to release and let go, to pardon and exonerate, to embrace the future by freeing one's self from the past. The next time anger intrudes, be it justified or displaced, work it through the best you can, without self-criticism or blame, giving it your fullest understanding and care. And when the anger has passed, give a gentle prayer of thanks, and hug your partner well. With forgiveness, we open the doors to compassion and to the deeper layers of love.

Once the storm has past and the furies have been laid to rest, we can turn our attention to the problem itself—to the issues behind the anger—and to the development of effective problem-solving skills, illuminated by the games in the following chapter of this book.

CHAPTER 7

Problem-Solving Games: Refining Your Relationship Skills

In this chapter, you will find tools to help you work through conflicts, dis-agreements, and other problems that frequently occur in relationships. You will learn about the art of confrontation, rules for fighting fairly, and strategies for defusing emotional bombs before they explode. The advice in this chapter comes from many expert sources, including Aaron T. Beck, Harville Hendrix, and Thich Nhat Hanh.

THERE IS A WELL-KNOWN STORY about a couple who were in the midst of a terrible fight. They could not come to an agreement, and so they decided to consult a local rabbi for advice.

The rabbi listened carefully to the husband and replied, "Your arguments are sensible and wise, and I fully agree with what you say."

But when the woman spoke, the rabbi was impressed. "You are quite right," he said. "Your opinion is sound, and I must fully agree with what you say."

Another person, listening in the back of the room, suddenly sat up and exclaimed, "Rabbi, you have just agreed with each one. Certainly they can't both possibly be right."

To which the rabbi responded, "Yes, I most certainly agree. You, dear friend, are absolutely right!"

No matter what the conflict is, both parties often hold valid points of view. Even in the best of relationships, conflicts—large or small—are bound to occur. Poor communication, small misunderstandings, unconscious motivations, value discrepancies, illnesses, fears, and even personal growth can challenge stability and love. But conflicts can also arise

163

when two people simply see things from differing points of view. In such cases, as the story above depicts, neither person is necessarily wrong. One man thinks that his wife spends too much money, but she just thinks he's tight. She wants to wallpaper the bathroom, but he wants to paint it white. He feels sexually deprived, but she feels romantically starved. Whether it's about money or sex or religion or friends, we all have different beliefs and concerns.

What, then, are we to do when we find ourselves at odds with each other, and what is the best way to proceed? Do we give in to our mate, insist upon our way, or do we ignore the problem and hope that it quietly disappears?

> *Couples can overcome their difficulties if they recognize first that much of their disappointment, frustration, and anger stems not from a basic incompatibility but from unfortunate misunderstandings that result from faulty communications and biased interpretations of each other's behavior.*
>
> AARON T. BECK
> *Love Is Never Enough*

Problem solving begins with a mutual willingness to sit down and talk the issue through. This may seem obvious, but many couples overlook this simple step. One person simply imposes his or her solution on the other, not out of hostility, but because we unconsciously assume that *our* solution is right. After all, it makes perfect sense to us. But our partners have different, yet equally valid, views.

Effective problem solving depends upon sensitive negotiation and dialogue, and it requires that each person listen carefully to the other's perspective. It takes time to find a mutually satisfying solution, and many alternatives may have to be explored, as Bill and Sharon discovered when they tried to plan for their annual summer trip. Bill wanted to lie on the beach, as they had done in previous years, but his wife wanted to do something new. Sharon suggested a cruise, but Bill was reticent to commit.

In many relationships, the stronger personality often prevails, but this often provokes resentment in the other partner, which may linger in the background for years. Other couples might compromise, going to the beach one summer and then taking a cruise the next. But Sharon and Bill decided to take a more creative approach. They spent a few hours brainstorming (which we will explore in game 5 of this chapter) and came up with an exciting idea: a wilderness trek in the mountains. They both enjoyed hiking, and Bill loved the mountains as much as the beach. Through supportive listening and touch of imagination, they resolved their vacation plans in a way that included each other.

Serious conflicts, however, may require a more sophisticated strategy. Strong emotions may first need to subside before you can approach your mate. An appropriate time and place must be found to discuss the problem, and an agreed-upon set of "rules" must be used to guide your conversation smoothly through the complexity of thoughts and feelings that every conflict contains. The next few pages will outline twenty-four basic strategies, which have been summarized from hundreds of expert sources,[34] for solving problems effectively. Study them carefully with your partner before you try out the games that will follow.

Problem-Solving Strategies: Twenty-Four Rules for Keeping the Peace

There are two nonnegotiable rules in resolving emotional issues and fights. The first is that **all confrontations are *by appointment only,*** for you will both need time to prepare. This, however, is not so easily done, for when we are upset, there is a tendency to blurt out our feelings or ignore the issue in its entirety. When you find yourself upset, describe your problem *briefly* to your partner and then make an appointment to sit down and talk. Wait for at least an hour to allow your partner to become emotionally prepared, and if either of you feels it necessary, take a few days to prepare (game 4, The Friday-Night Solution, is a very effective strategy to use).

The second nonnegotiable rule is that **either person may call for a time-out at any time he or she**

Making an appointment shows respect and consideration for our partner, and it prevents spontaneous combustion. Making an appointment gives the person who's angry or frustrated a cooldown period to cool his or her thoughts. The person on the receiving end has a chance to prepare for the onslaught and doesn't feel invaded.

—HARVILLE HENDRIX AND
HELEN HUNT
The Couples Companion

chooses. A time-out may last for only five minutes or may take several hours or days, but it is the responsibility of the person who calls for the break to immediately suggest a specific time to reconvene. This rule, too, is difficult to follow because it interrupts the conversational flow, but not to take a break when one person feels overwhelmed can ruin the chances of resolving a major conflict adequately. The result is a problem that can undermine the stability of a relationship for months.

I also suggest that you try to incorporate the dialogical meditation technique described in chapter 3, game 1, because it will help you to process any conflict with greater ease. In fact, dialogical meditation will make every game in this chapter more effective when you play.

Three Strategies for Beginning a Constructive Dialogue

1. Pick the Right Time.

Briefly describe the problem you wish to address with your partner and set up a mutually agreed-upon time to discuss it. But before you engage in dialogue, ask yourself the following question: "Can my partner really hear me and respond to me at this time?" If not, consider waiting for a better time. Avoid discussing difficult issues prior to going to work or sleep, and give yourself at least two hours to talk and then unwind afterward.

2. Find the Best Location.

Select a place where the two of you won't be disturbed. Avoid confrontations in the bedroom; studies show that people unconsciously associate fights with where they occur, and the bedroom should be used primarily for lovemaking and rest. Consider having your discussion outdoors while taking a walk, which will help to ground you in your body (see chapter 3, game 8). You might also meet in a restaurant or other public place, which will help you to stay calm, or talk on the phone if a face-to-face meeting feels too threatening.

3. Open Your Dialogue with Kindness.

Begin a confrontation with an expression of love by giving a compliment, a small gift, or a tender embrace. This lets your partner know that you are entering the dispute with a willingness to protect the underlying love that you share.

Six Strategies for Containing Disruptive Emotions

1. Avoid Provocative Language.

No insults. No accusations. No denunciations. No condemnations. No blaming. No character assassinations. No sarcasm. No swearing. No threats. No yelling. Ask your partner to inform you if your communication feels like an attack: even if you think you are calm, your partner may require greater sensitivity and care.

2. Soften the Tone of Your Voice.

Pay close attention to your voice as you speak: hostility can be communicated through tone as well as words. Your communication will be more effective if you speak slowly, with warmth. Soothing, gentle speech goes a long way in getting your message across.

3. Be Aware of Nonverbal Communication.

Feelings and emotions can be communicated nonverbally through facial expressions and body movements. Looking away, frowning, giving an exaggerated smile, or rolling your eyes can be easily interpreted as anger, hostility, sarcasm, or disbelief. These cues can stimulate an unwanted reaction from your partner, so ask him or her for feedback about any nonverbal message you may send.

4. Monitor Your Anger.

If you find yourself getting more upset as you talk or listen, take a few minutes to calm down. Close your eyes, take deep breaths, and stretch your arms and legs. Ask your mate for help: the contact of your partner's hand can have a soothing effect. Monitor your pulse rate; if it rises, take a twenty-minute break.[35] Consider playing one of the anger-reducing games in chapter 6.

5. Recognize the Danger Zone.

Shakiness, increased perspiration, clamminess of the skin, muscle tension, a tight jaw, chest pressure, clenched arms or fists, exaggerated facial expressions, and other intimidating body motions are signs that you may soon lose emotional control. Ask your partner to point out any warning signs that you may fail to notice, and then take a break.

6. Call for a Time-Out.

If you feel stuck or overwhelmed, call for a five- to thirty-minute break—but don't just walk away or suddenly hang up the phone. An abrupt interruption can really upset your partner because you have not given her

or him enough time to prepare for a time-out. Take a minute to explain why you need to take a break, and then set a time to resume. During the time-out, practice the relaxation exercises from chapter 2. If communication breaks down again, consider rescheduling for the next day.

Eight Strategies to Improve Communication Between You and Your Partner

1. Talk about Yourself.

Begin sentences with "I feel . . ." rather than "You are . . ." Talk about what is going on inside of you, but be specific: avoid overgeneralities and vague descriptions. For example, instead of saying *"I feel hurt when I'm criticized,"* identify the specific event and the feelings it brought up for you at the moment: *"Whenever I'm criticized, I feel like a little boy and I think that I'm going to be rejected. I know I tend to overreact, but I feel as if I'm being punished for something that I didn't do."* Because it is very difficult to talk about a relational conflict without using the word *you,* try having several practice dialogues with your partner about a prior conflict or fight.

2. Avoid Mind Reading.

Don't assume that you know what your partner thinks or feels; ask questions instead. Instead of saying *"You always get defensive when we have company over,"* which is an example of mind reading, turn it into a question: *"When we have company over, do you get defensive?"* Your partner may say no, and even though you may think that he or she does get defensive, your viewpoint is still an opinion, and to say so may cause your partner to withdraw. Your partner will often see things in a different light.

3. Show Respect for Your Partner's Point of View.

It is important to acknowledge your partner's perspectives and criticisms, even if you don't agree, for no two people see a problem in exactly the same way. Let your partner know that you appreciate hearing what he or she thinks: *"I really want to know what you think and how you feel about this problem,"* or *"It really helps me to understand you better when you explain your perspective to me."*

4. Take Equal Responsibility.

Learn to think about conflicts as a conjoint problem. Rarely is the problem simply "yours" or "mine."

5. Take Turns.

Talk for five minutes without interruption. Then let your partner talk for five minutes without interruption. If you need more time to talk, ask your partner if he or she would be willing to listen for an extended period.

6. Be Specific.

Focus on one problem at a time. If you're talking about a hurtful statement that your partner recently made, for example, don't bring up other events from the past. Stay focused on the specific event that occurred. Provide concrete details and complete explanations of the problem and ways in which it can be resolved.

7. Provide Empathic Feedback.

Let your partner know that you are listening carefully. Use a gentle tone of voice and smile to show that you are interested in what your partner says. Mirror back what you have heard and what you think the other person is trying to communicate. "Mirroring is a deceptively simple exercise," says marital therapist Harville Hendrix. "When one of you has something to communicate, whether it's a thought or a feeling, you simply state it in a short, declarative sentence. . . . Your partner then paraphrases your remark and asks for confirmation."[36]

8. Ask for Clarification.

If you are unclear about what your partner is saying, ask him or her to restate the issue: *"I'm not sure if I really understand; can you tell me again, or in a different way?"* Ask for details to help your partner illuminate subtle but important points.

Seven Strategies for Resolving Problems and Finding Solutions

1. Search for Constructive Ideas.

Offer specific suggestions and ask your partner for alternative ideas. *Write all of them down on a separate sheet of paper* and talk about them in depth. Search for solutions that are mutually satisfying as you look for ways to include the other person's ideas in your plan.

2. Review the Past.

Many problems stem from the past and are rooted in family history. When you talk about these past connections, many problems will be reframed, allowing you to find new solutions to the current issues at hand.

3. Try Brainstorming.

Turn on your creativity. Be silly, and use your imagination, writing down every notion that pops up. After about ten minutes, you will often find a useful solution or two.

4. Sit with Your Problem for a Week.

If an effective solution is not found, sit with the problem for a week. Don't try to solve it; just be aware of it and watch the feelings and thoughts that occur. Often, by week's end, a practical solution will appear. Ask your friends for additional ideas and then discuss them with your mate.

5. Implement Your Plan.

Using your imagination, play with different solutions ("If we did A, then B could happen, possibly leading us to C . . ."). When you "test-drive" your plans in this way, you can often identify and resolve unrecognized difficulties before they occur. Work out a step-by-step solution to your problem—who will do what, when, where, and how—and write it down.

6. Close with Kindness.

Give supportive remarks ("I really appreciate your willingness to go through this process—I know how hard it is") and give each other a hug, doing everything possible to generate kindness before your conversation ends.

7. Get a Progress Report.

Keep checking in with your partner over the next few days and weeks, requesting feedback ("How do you feel about our plan?" or "Do you think we are making progress?") and evaluating your problem-solving skills ("What did you like the most about the process, and what did you like the least?" or "What would you do differently the next time a problem occurs?").

Twenty-four rules—from making an appointment to following up with progress reports—are a lot to remember when you are in conflict with your mate. Therefore, I suggest that you make a photocopy of these rules. Place them in a conspicuous location and review them once a month. Leave the rules posted for an entire year, and then evaluate the progress of your problem-solving skills with your partner.

The following games will help you to develop these skills by focusing on specific ways to identify problems and find creative solutions to common relational ills. These tried-and-true techniques have been used to bring conscious intimacy into thousands of relationships throughout the world.

Game #1
Hot Spots: Identifying Potential Problems

The most important time to explore relationship problems is *before* they get stirred up, for it is easier to maintain a loving attitude toward your mate as you explore possible solutions. But many people tend to avoid such discussions until a crisis erupts, when conflict is far more difficult to work through. This game has been adapted from a study that identified ten specific hot spots commonly found in marriages. The study found that couples who complete the following survey report substantial improvements in their relationship.[37]

For each of the following issues, decide to what degree a problem may exist in your current or most recent relationship. Rate how serious you believe the problem may be, circling a number between ① (for mild or nonexistent) and ⑩ (for severe). Write down when you think the problem began—for example: in a previous relationship, when you got married, when financial problems occurred, etc.—and then mark how often the problem occurs: never, rarely, sometimes, or often.

After you have recorded your answers, ask your partner to evaluate each issue, and record his or her answers with a different-colored pen. Then compare your responses, paying particular attention to the differences that emerge. If you come across an issue that seems to be a problem for one of you but not the other, discuss how you might work together to improve the issue at hand. Write down possible solutions and then work with them over the next few months. Then review this survey again to see how your ratings have changed.

1. Do You Have a Problem with Communication?

mild problem ⤙ 0 1 2 3 4 5 6 7 8 9 10 ⤚ *serious problem*

This problem began _____

How often does this problem arise? *never rarely sometimes often*

We could improve the situation by: _____

2. Do You Have a Problem with Money?

mild ≺ 0   1   2   3   4   5   6   7   8   9   10 ≻ *serious*

This problem began _____

How often does this problem arise?   *never*   *rarely*   *sometimes*   *often*

We could improve the situation by: _____

3. Do You Have a Problem with Sex?

mild ≺ 0   1   2   3   4   5   6   7   8   9   10 ≻ *serious*

This problem began _____

How often does this problem arise?   *never*   *rarely*   *sometimes*   *often*

We could improve the situation by: _____

4. Do You Have a Problem with Jealousy?

mild ≺ 0   1   2   3   4   5   6   7   8   9   10 ≻ *serious*

This problem began _____

How often does this problem arise?   *never*   *rarely*   *sometimes*   *often*

We could improve the situation by: _____

5. Do You Have a Problem with Religion or Spirituality?

mild ≺ 0   1   2   3   4   5   6   7   8   9   10 ≻ *serious*

This problem began _____

How often does this problem arise?   *never*   *rarely*   *sometimes*   *often*

We could improve the situation by: _____

6. Do You Have a Problem Dealing with or Having Children?

mild ≺ 0   1   2   3   4   5   6   7   8   9   10 ≻ *serious*

This problem began _____

How often does this problem arise?   *never*   *rarely*   *sometimes*   *often*

We could improve the situation by: _____

7. Do You Have a Problem with In-Laws?

mild ≺ 0   1   2   3   4   5   6   7   8   9   10 ≻ *serious*

This problem began _____

How often does this problem arise?   *never*   *rarely*   *sometimes*   *often*

We could improve the situation by: _____

8. Do You Have a Problem with Your or Your Partner's Friends?

mild ≺ 0   1   2   3   4   5   6   7   8   9   10 ≻ *serious*

This problem began _____

How often does this problem arise?   *never*   *rarely*   *sometimes*   *often*
We could improve the situation by: _____

9. Do You Have a Problem with Recreation, Relaxation, or Play?
   mild ≺ 0 1 2 3 4 5 6 7 8 9 10 ≻ *serious*
   This problem began _____
   How often does this problem arise?   *never*   *rarely*   *sometimes*   *often*
   We could improve the situation by: _____

10. Do You Have a Problem with Alcohol, Food, or Drugs?
    mild ≺ 0 1 2 3 4 5 6 7 8 9 10 ≻ *serious*
    This problem began _____
    How often does this problem arise?   *never*   *rarely*   *sometimes*   *often*
    We could improve the situation by: _____

Game #2
Tuning Up

Sometimes it is a seemingly insignificant problem that disrupts the flow of intimacy and love. Minor problems often go unaddressed, but the feelings behind them can build up over time and suddenly erupt when you or your partner least expects it. On the surface, it may look as though the person is overreacting, but these little problems often contain clues to major issues and concerns. This exercise, and the one that follows, will help you to identify those hidden trouble spots that could later turn into a fight.

Take out a piece of paper and write down minor issues that have bothered you about your partner but that you may not have talked about in depth. Ask your partner to do the same. For example, perhaps you are bothered by the way your spouse drives, organizes the bills, helps out around the house, cooks, etc. List five minor irritants (no more, or you'll have to respond to your partner's complaint that you criticize too much!) and then talk to each other about your lists. By working on minor problems, we intuitively learn how best to approach more serious problems and fights.

Game #3
Checking In

By checking in with our partners every week, we not only nurture our love and communication skills, we can also identify and resolve the little irritations that may have quietly built up during the week. Perhaps your partner left a mess in the kitchen on Monday, forgot to hug you before leaving for work on Wednesday, and ate the last piece of dessert without offering you a bite. Trivial things, but by the end of the week you may feel disappointed, irritable, or hurt, and if these little problems do not get addressed in a compassionate way, the foundation for a more serious altercation may be laid. So take ten minutes—Friday night or Saturday morning is ideal—to consciously assess the quality of your relationship for that week. In my opinion, this is one of the most important exercises you can perform, so make an agreement with your partner to try this game for a month.

At the beginning of each weekend, sit down with your partner and talk about the things you said or did during the previous week that caused each other pleasure and pain. Begin with the positive deeds, listing all the little acts that made you feel cared for and loved. For example: "I just wanted to let you know how much I love it when you kiss me before going to work. And I really enjoyed the walk we took in the park and the breakfast you prepared the other day." Even the tiniest things can warm your lover's heart when you acknowledge the pleasure he or she has brought, and it also makes it easier to talk about the minor disappointments of the week.

After your partner has absorbed your compliments, talk about the things that made you feel irritated or hurt. Be gentle and specific as you describe how you would like to be treated in the future: "When I get upset, please don't give me advice or try to fix the problem, as you did last night. Just hold me and listen and let me talk it out." If you practice this game for just a few weeks, you will see how much more loving your relationship becomes.

As a variation, ask your partner the following two questions at the end of each week: "What did I do to please you this past week?" and "What would you like me to do or improve upon during the following week?"

This approach is particularly effective when one person has difficulty acknowledging kindness or asking for something in return.

Game #4
Thich Nhat Hanh's "Friday-Night Solution"

Sometimes, when a problem occurs, it can be more effective to wait a few days to talk about it rather than bringing it immediately to your partner's attention. It gives you time to think about the problem, to calm down if you feel angry or upset, and to contemplate various ways to address and resolve the problem you are struggling with. The best time to do this, says Buddhist teacher Thich Nhat Hanh, is Friday night:

> Suppose your partner says something unkind to you, and you feel hurt. If you reply right away, you risk making the situation worse. The best practice is to breathe in and out to calm yourself, and when you are calm enough, say, "Darling, what you just said hurt me. I would like to look deeply into it, and I would like you to look deeply into it, also." Then you can make an appointment for Friday evening to look at it together. One person looking at the roots of your suffering is good, two people looking at it is better, and two people looking together is best.
>
> I propose Friday evening for two reasons. First, you are still hurt, and if you begin discussing it now, it may be too risky. You might say things that will make the situation worse. From now until Friday evening, you can practice looking deeply into the nature of your suffering, and the other person can also. While driving the car, he might ask himself, "What is so serious? Why did she get so upset? There must be a reason." While driving, you will also have a chance to look deeply into it. Before Friday night, one or both of you may see the root of the problem and be able to tell the other and apologize. Then on Friday night, you can have a cup of tea together and enjoy each other. If you make an appointment, you will both have time to calm down and look deeply. This is the practice of meditation. Meditation is to calm ourselves and to look deeply into the nature of our suffering.

When Friday night comes, if the suffering has not been transformed, you will be able to practice the art of Avalokiteshvara—one person expressing herself, while the other person listens deeply. When you speak, you tell the deepest kind of truth, using loving speech, the kind of speech the other person can understand and accept. While listening, you know that your listening must be of a good quality to relieve the other person of his suffering. A second reason for waiting until Friday is that when you neutralize that feeling on Friday evening, you have Saturday and Sunday to enjoy being together.

Game #5

Brainstorming

A problem has arisen, and the two of you have talked about it for hours on end. You've analyzed it, meditated upon it, reframed it, ignored it, traced its history into the past, and looked at it through each other's eyes. But you still can't find a satisfactory solution. The problem remains, pulling like an untrained dog upon its leash. Now is the time to brainstorm, to pull out all the rational plugs and let your imagination soar. This game was devised by Tina Tessina and Riley Smith, two well-known therapists and authors of the popular book *True Partners.*

If you're having difficulty developing an option that will solve the problem so that both of you are satisfied, you can stir your creative imagination by learning to *brainstorm.* Brainstorming is a technique developed by high-powered "think tank" scientists to put their creativity to work to invent new solutions for previously unsolvable problems in aerospace, engineering, and chemistry. The object is to develop a list of ideas, many of which may be useless, but enough of which are fresh and feasible to choose from. Brainstorming was created to overcome limitations on creativity, and it will help you and your partner free up your thinking and explore options. It will also help you decide if you need further information and, when it is necessary, to set up a research project.

Learning to brainstorm shows you how to overcome criticism and its blockage of your creative ideas by getting playful and energetic, and allowing even silly or impossible ideas to be part of the process. By not considering the reasonableness of options until after brainstorming, you give your creativity free reign. To brainstorm, you think of and make a list of all kinds of ideas for solving the problem, as many as you possibly can, as quickly as you can. It is important to write down every idea, *whether or not it seems to make sense, be possible, or be reasonable.* If you eliminate ideas because they are not reasonable, practical, sensible, or acceptable at this point, you will block the flow of new ideas and stifle your creativity. Brainstorming breaks through old familiar concepts and stimulates new, more creative ideas by creating conditions (moving around physically, writing large, setting a time limit, being playful, and stating rapid-fire, excited suggestions) that encourage a noncritical, unrestricted, free flow of ideas.

In brainstorming, you and your partner learn to move around to loosen yourselves up, freely generate ideas you haven't thought of before, write them down, review them, evaluate them, and choose the best solution. The point of brainstorming is to break through the limits of your previous thinking, by getting outrageous, silly, creative, and inventive. Through this energetic, fun process, you will be able to find innovative solutions to seemingly unsolvable problems. If you allow ideas like "my fairy godmother will come and fix it," or "I'll win the lottery" to be OK, you will not stifle the new *sensible* idea that may just be perfect to solve your problem.

> *A far-out idea may seem nonsensical but it may provide, in seed form, the solution that is finally adopted. I am told that the managers of a major airport were brainstorming ways of removing snow from the runways. One of the participants suggested putting a giant frog on the control tower which could push the snow aside with its enormous tongue. In time that idea was reshaped to the solution they ultimately selected—a revolving cannon that shoots a jet airstream.*
>
> —ROBERT BOLTON, PH.D.
> *People Skills*

You will know that your thinking is not restricted when you have as many silly ideas as usable ones. When your thinking *is* restricted, the exercise will show you how to loosen it up. The intention of brainstorming is to generate new ideas and remove the limitations that normally would inhibit the flow.

Choose a place where you won't be interrupted, and allow twenty to forty-five minutes, depending on the difficulty of the problem. Have a large pad, piece of paper, chalkboard, or marking board and crayons, chalk, or markers for writing your ideas because physically moving around helps you to stay loose and energized.

1. *Write the problem down.* Write down the problem in terms of each of your basic wants so that it is in plain sight while you brainstorm. It's the reason you are trying to generate the options, and having it in front of you will be a constant reminder to help you stay on track.

2. *Write as many ideas as you can in ten minutes.* We recommend that you each write your ideas on the board or pad as you come up with them, to keep you moving, and raise the energy level. Set a timer for ten minutes. During that time, each of you should try to contribute as many ideas as you can, calling them out and writing them down. Saying your ideas out loud as well as writing them creates a playful atmosphere, reminiscent of a game of charades or a TV game show. Be silly, be boisterous, shout ideas out, don't worry about being sensible or reasonable, get as excited as a game-show contestant does. Remember, the first ideas may be hesitant, but as you get into the "game" and begin to toss ideas back and forth, your energy will rise. The more your energy flows, the more your ideas will flow. Don't criticize or comment on the ideas. You can evaluate each other's ideas later.

Game #6
The Referee in a Box

Here is a powerful tool that you can use to help subdue a potentially volatile dispute. It is particularly effective for couples who lose control of their emotions when they fight or have difficulty communicating with clarity and sensitivity. Simply turn on a tape recorder as the two of you talk the problem through. When you play back the recording, you will clearly hear what does and doesn't work in your communication styles and problem-solving strategies. You will be able to hear who interrupts whom, who strays from the central issue, and who offers the most rational solution. Couples will be able to point out overly emotional displays and can often see where one person overreacted or misinterpreted what the other person had said.

Even if you do not turn it on, the presence of this little box can help to bring more focus to the negotiating bench. Even if you are skilled at conflict resolution, record one of your conversations with your partner and play it back. You will often discover many areas of communication on which to improve, and if you use a video recorder, you can observe how your facial expressions and body movements affect how your partner responds.

When a conversation is being taped, both people will be more conscious of what is said, and thus the tape recorder assumes the role of an observing referee.

Game #7

Rating Your Partner and the "Post-it" Solution

When we are angry or upset, we often fail to see the acts of kindness our partners give to us. Psychologist Mark Goldstein uses two creative approaches for helping couples become more conscious of actions that bring pleasure into their relational lives. These simple techniques, as described by Aaron T. Beck,[38] the father of cognitive therapy, can even cut through severe conflicts in just a few days:

> Mark Kane Goldstein, a psychologist at the University of Florida, has used a simple method to help husbands and wives keep track of their partner's pleasant actions. Each spouse is given several sheets of graph paper on which to record whatever his or her partner does that is pleasing. The spouse rates these acts on a ten-point scale, indicating degree of satisfaction. Dr. Goldstein found that 70 percent of the couples who tried this simple method reported an improvement in their relationship.

Simply keeping track of the small pleasures of their married life makes a couple more aware of the actual degree of satisfaction. Prior to making these systematic observations, the couples had rated their marital satisfaction lower than they did after they kept a systematic score. All that had changed was their *awareness* of what was going on. Before keeping track, they had underestimated the pleasures of their marriage.

You can try Dr. Goldstein's method as a way to determine whether you may be underestimating the satisfaction in your marriage. You may discover, as did many of his clients, that you have more satisfying moments together than you had realized. And, as your relationship begins to change for the better, keeping track of pleasant experiences gives you a baseline for later comparisons.

Dr. Goldstein showed me another technique which I subsequently found very helpful for many couples. The technique aims to open up the blinders that prevent many angry partners from seeing, or at least appreciating, their spouse's pleasing acts. With this method, both husband and wife (or either one) are asked to place several sticky labels somewhere on the other mate's clothing, such as on the lapel of the jacket or on the collar. Each time the husband, for example, does something that pleases his wife, she removes one of the labels. The couples keep track of the number of labels removed each day. Usually, most or all of the labels have been removed by bedtime.

Although this technique may seem simplistic to some, it yields powerful results. In order to note pleasing actions, spouses begin to really *look at* each other. (When they were angry, they had tended to look away from each other.) This method forces spouses to break through the barriers that obstruct their vision of their partner's good deeds. The assignment prompts them to be on the lookout for their mate's pleasing actions, and then to do something that shows they have seen these acts. This, in turn, helps both to reinforce the acts, so they will be repeated, and to highlight them in their minds. Finally, the technique of applying and removing labels brings a distressed couple into closer physical contact.

After you have observed your spouse's spontaneous good behavior for a while, you should start to tell him or her what else you would find pleasing. This should be stated in a straightforward manner, without sarcasm, accusations, or innuendos. For example, avoid making conditional requests— veiled attacks, really—such as "I'd like you to help me with the dishes, but take that pained expression off your face" or "I'd like you to talk to me when you come home from the office instead of dashing in to watch the six o'clock news." The simple request is much more likely to get you what you want. . . .

But just asking is not enough. Whenever your spouse does something that pleases you, it should be followed up with a reward of some kind—an appreciative note, or a kiss, for example. Rewards are a far better way than punishment to change how your spouse acts.

Game #8
Caring Days

This is an exercise that therapists use to help couples establish nurturing dialogues and rapport.[39] Once each morning, you simply ask your partner what form of affection he or she would like to receive from you during the day. We all need positive reinforcement, for it helps to build trust and self-esteem, but we must be willing to tell our partners what we like. By clearly articulating these desires, you can transform even a troubled relationship into a respectful partnership. Here are several versions of this love-enhancing game:

1. Once each morning (or in the evening, if you prefer), name one or two specific acts of kindness that you would like your partner to perform during the following twenty-four hours. The request must be simple, specific, and small (hug me when you come home, wash the dishes, talk with me during dinner, take me out to lunch, tell me how much you love me, rub my feet), *and not be the subject of a current conflict.* For example, if you have been quarreling about money, do not ask your mate to buy you something, or if you have been arguing about a sexual issue, do not request an

erotic activity. If your partner does not feel comfortable granting your request, ask for something else (at a later time, you can talk about the reasons your request was denied). Then ask your partner what she or he would like from you in return.

2. Make a list of ten to twenty simple things that would bring you pleasure or joy (getting flowers or a special note, being read to, taking a walk on the beach), and ask your partner to do the same. Exchange lists and do at least three things per week that are on your partner's list. Try to add several items to your list each week.

3. Agree to surprise each other in some small, but pleasurable, way over the next few days. It's really exciting to know that you are going to be surprised. See how many surprises you can squeeze in during the week.

4. Indulge each other for an entire day. Tell your partner that, for a specified period of time (between three to eight hours, on a Saturday or Sunday), you will cater to his or her every whim. Make a list of all the things your partner would like you to do (that are acceptable and agreeable to you), and then indulge him or her to the hilt. Prepare breakfast in bed, complete with the peeling of grapes and followed by an exotic massage, trying to fulfill your partner's deepest fantasies and needs. Then set a time to switch roles, so that you can be catered to in style.

5. Make a list of all the romantic behaviors and activities you used to do when you were dating and highlight the ones that still turn you on. Ask your partner to do the same, and then spend the next week flirting with each other, applying as many of the enjoyable behaviors as you can. Take each other out on a "first" date, and see if you can recapture that original spark. By applying all your years of romantic experience, the two of you should have a wonderful time!

Game #9
Critical Mass

Critical thoughts and feelings—complaints, disappointments, feelings of anger or contempt—can easily undermine the foundations of communication. These thoughts can indicate that there are deeper issues that are being overlooked, and, if they go unaddressed, they may lead to more serious problems and fights. In fact, many studies have found that when critical thoughts outnumber positive feeling and thoughts, the marriage is headed for trouble.[40] This game will help you to identify and defuse surreptitious attitudes before they reach an explosive critical mass.

Make a list of all your partner's negative traits and every criticism and complaint that you can remember having about him or her. Then highlight the ones that you feel are current and valid: Are they really true? Have you exaggerated their importance? Are they projections of personal problems or old feelings carried over from the past? When you carefully analyze your list in this way, the number of criticisms should decrease. Next to each remaining criticism, write down one or two things that you and your partner could do to address the problem or trait.

Now make a second list of all of the things you praise about your mate (the traits you like, the qualities you admire, the little things that make you smile and feel happy). How does this list compare to the first? If there are fewer qualities on your positive list than on your critical list, try to add to it so that there are more.

Ask yourself this question: How often do you express your critical thoughts to your partner, and how often do you tell your partner the positive thoughts you have? Make a point to sit down with your partner and share all the positive thoughts on your list. Then ask your partner to share with you one critical thought he or she has had about you. Talk about various ways to address that criticism, and when you have completed that task, ask your partner if you can share one critical thought about him or her.

Game #10
I Should, You Should

Critical thoughts can be hazardous to your relational health, but there are other subtle beliefs that we often impose upon ourselves and others—beliefs that can hold us back from fully enjoying life. These are the shoulds and shouldn'ts that we have accumulated over the years—from our parents, our teachers, our playmates, and ourselves: "I should always smile. . . . I should never yell. . . . I should be more neat. . . . I shouldn't watch so

much TV. . . . I should exercise more. . . . I should make more money. . . .
I shouldn't eat so many sweets. . . . I should call my parents more often. . . .
I should, I shouldn't, I should!"

One day, many years ago, I decided to make a list of all my shoulds
and shouldn'ts. By the time I had finished, I had accumulated two hundred and seventy-five! No wonder I felt so anxious! With such a list, who
could possibly feel free to do what he or she really wanted to do?

"Shoulds" and "shouldn'ts" can also act as barriers to intimacy and
love. "Shoulds are dangerous to partnerships," say relationship experts
Harville Hendrix and Helen Hunt, for "they define an imaginary partner, blinding us to our real mate."[41] When we impose a should or
shouldn't upon our partners, we are telling them how to be, and we are
saying that they are not good enough as they are. It is, in essence, a form of
control.

Sit down with your partner and take turns completing the following
sentence stems, saying whatever comes to mind as fast as you can:

I should _____ but I shouldn't _____.

*And you should _____ but you shouldn't
_____.*

> *Make a list of at least three shoulds
> you've been laying on your partner. Then
> pick out the one most important to you
> and reframe it as a behavior-change re-
> quest for your partner tonight. In your
> mind, turn the rest of "shoulds" back into
> "hopes."*
>
> HARVILLE HENDRIX AND
> HELEN HUNT
> *The Couples Companion*

Don't pause, or think, or censor what
you say—just blurt it out and then let
your partner take a turn. Here's an example of how the game might unfold:

Kathy:

I should <u>always be polite,</u> and I shouldn't <u>interrupt.</u> And you should
<u>hug me every day</u> but you shouldn't <u>tell me what to do.</u>

Tom:

I should <u>work harder at my job,</u> but I shouldn't <u>be such a slob.</u> But you
should <u>be more assertive</u> and you shouldn't <u>cry so much.</u>

As the game continues, you will be guided into deeper areas of criticism and complaint, and you will become more aware of how pervasive and

influential those little shoulds can be. If you find yourself running out of things to say, you can use as a guide any of the following topics, which often conceal many expectations and rules (for example, *"Regarding sex, I should...."*):

sex	intimacy	anger
money	work	education
marriage	parenting	friendship
religion	honesty	health

When you have finished, talk about the most "influential" shoulds and shouldn'ts—the ones that hold you back and the ones that feel the most stifling to you and your partner. Try reframing them with positive suggestions in terms of your own desires and needs. For example, it may really bother you that your partner is habitually late. Instead of making a generalization like "People should be on time," you might say, "It would mean a great deal to me if we can be on time to events. What could I do to help you be on time? Perhaps I can remind you, or do the dishes while you dress." Then offer to meet one of your partner's requests.

Game #11
The Behavior Change Request

One of the most delicate dilemmas couples face is when one person asks the other to alter a personal behavior. The other person is likely to resist even the simplest request—even if it is clear that a change would improve the relationship—because it usually feels like an imposition (a "should") and because it requires effort to alter a habituated pattern of behavior. Because all relationships require adjusting one's behavior to meet essential needs, this exercise, created by Harville Hendrix, will show you how to compassionately request a behavioral change from your partner:

The purpose of this exercise is to educate you to your partner's deepest needs and to give you the opportunity to change your behavior so that you meet those needs. As you stretch against your resistance, your partner will be healed and you will become a more whole and loving individual.

This is a very important exercise. I recommend that you give it your highest priority.

Directions

1. The first step in this exercise is to identify the desires that lie behind your frustrations. On a separate sheet of paper, make a comprehensive list of all the things that bother you about your partner. When does your partner make you feel angry, annoyed, afraid, suspicious, resentful, hurt, or bitter? Here's a partial list:

Jenny's List

I don't like it when you . . .

drive too fast.

leave the house without telling me where you are going.

criticize me in front of the children.

undermine my authority with the children.

read the newspaper during dinner.

criticize me in a joking manner in front of friends.

don't pay attention to what I'm saying.

turn away from me when I'm upset or crying.

criticize me for being indecisive.

criticize me for being a poor housekeeper.

keep pointing out the fact that you earn more money than I do.

2. Now get out a second sheet of paper and write down the desire that lies hidden in each frustration. Skip several lines after each desire. Do not write down the frustration, only the desire. (This is necessary, because you will be showing this second sheet to your partner.)

Example:

Desire

(corresponds to the first frustration listed above): I would like to feel safe and relaxed when you are driving.

3. Underneath each desire, write a specific request that would help you satisfy that desire. It is important that your requests be positive and that they describe a specific behavior.
Examples:

Desire:

I would like to feel safe and relaxed when you are driving.

Request:

When you are driving, I would like you to obey the speed limit. If the road conditions are bad, I would like you to drive even more slowly.

Desire:

I would like you to comfort me when I'm upset.

Request:

When I tell you that I am upset, I would like you to put your arms around me and give me your full attention.

Notice that these requests are for specific, positive behaviors. The following request is a bad example because it is not specific.

Vague request:

I would like you to be more attentive.
It should be rewritten to make it more detailed:

Specific request:

I would like you to give me a warm hug as soon as you come home from work.

This next request is a bad example because it is negative:

Negative request:

I would like you to stop yelling at me when you're upset.

This should be rewritten so that it describes a positive behavior:

Positive request:

When you are mad at me, I would like you to use a normal tone of voice.

4. Share your second list (the one that lists desires and requests but not frustrations) with each other. Use your communication skills to clarify each desire and request so that it is clearly understood. Rewrite the request if necessary so that the partner knows exactly what kind of behavior you want.

5. Now take back your own list and rank each request on the left side of the page with a number from I to 5 indicating its relative importance to you, I indicating "very important," 5 "not very important."

6. Exchange lists once again so that you now have your partner's requests, and assign a number from I to 5 on the right side of the paper indicating how difficult it would be for you to grant each request, with I indicating "very difficult," 5 "not at all difficult."

7. Keep your partner's list. Starting today, you have the opportunity to grant your partner three or four of the easiest requests each week. Remember that these behaviors are gifts. Regardless of how you feel and regardless of how many changes your partner is making, keep to a reliable schedule of at least three or four behavior changes a week. (You are encouraged to add more requests to your lists as time goes on.)

FOUR CHARACTERISTICS OF GOOD FEEDBACK

1. **Feedback is descriptive rather than evaluative.** When behavior is described rather than judged, the individual can hear the feedback nondefensively and use it as he or she sees fit. . . .

2. **Feedback is specific rather than general.** To be told that one is "dominating" will probably not be as useful as to be told that "just now when we were deciding the issue, you talked more than anyone else."

3. **Feedback takes into account the needs of both the receiver and giver of feedback.** Feedback can be destructive when it serves only our own needs and fails to consider the needs of the person on the receiving end.

4. **Feedback is directed toward behavior that the receiver can do something about.** Frustration is only increased when people are reminded of shortcomings over which they have no control.

VONDA OLSON LONG
Communication Skills in Helping Relationships

Game #12

Making Wishes Come True

Problems in a relationship may often arise from a feeling that our needs are not being met. We all wish to be loved and recognized, and the stronger our needs, the more we may expect or demand of others. If our basic need for love is not acknowledged or responded to, we may slip into anger or withdraw into depression and fear. With this exercise, you will learn how to acknowledge your partner's needs.

First, play a free-associative game with your partner by completing the sentence *"I wish you would (or could) _____."* Jill and Jerry, for example, sparred back and forth, coming up with as many spontaneous wishes as they could: "I wish you would spend more romantic evenings with me," "I wish you could make a million dollars," "I wish you didn't worry so much about work," . . .

After you have done about twenty rounds, take out two sheets of paper—one for you and one for your mate—and write down three of the twenty wishes that you would like your partner to grant. These wishes could be about communication, or sex, or taking a vacation, or anything that you feel would be nurturing or healing to you. Exchange lists, and ask your partner if he or she could grant just one of your wishes. If not, explore the reasons why, and then write down three more wishes from which your partner can choose.

Not every desire can be met, but if we carefully reflect upon our needs and then ask our partners for a special request, we may be happily surprised by what we receive. In an intimate relationship, couples will attempt to meet, in some form, many of the items that are on each other's list.

Game #13
Writing Off Your Problems

Letter writing is an excellent way to clearly articulate a problem to your mate. In this exercise, you will experiment with three types of letter-writing techniques. The first step is to write a highly emotional letter, which will *not* be given to your mate. Pick up a pen, and for the next five minutes, write down as quickly as possible all the negative feelings you have concerning a problem you wish to address with your mate. Jot down your anger, fears, sadness, insecurities, and hurt. Keep writing until the emotions subside. Reread your letter and, if you still feel emotionally charged, write a little more. When you have finished, save this letter in your personal diary.

Your second letter will be written with the intention of delivering it to your mate, but you have the option to keep it, rewrite it, or throw it away. Use the following tips as you address your conflict and the solutions you propose:

1. Open the letter with a word of kindness, a compliment, or other expression of love.

2. State the problem as clearly and simply as you can.

3. Talk about your feelings (anger, fear, hope, etc.) in a calm and rational way.

4. Avoid provocative language: no insults, accusations, sarcasm, threats, or condemnations.

5. Talk about yourself, beginning sentences with "I" instead of "you": "I felt hurt. . . . I wanted to be listened to. . . . I needed time to relax. . . ."

6. Acknowledge your partner's point of view. Try to articulate the problem in writing from his or her perspective ("I imagine that you see the problem in the following way. . . .").

7. Offer constructive ideas and specific suggestions for solutions.

8. Request an appointment to discuss the problem, asking for your partner's suggestions and help.

9. Close your letter stating to your partner your commitment and love.

After you have written your letter, put it aside and read it the following day. Does the letter still make sense? Did it express what you wanted to say in a constructive and loving way? If not, take a few minutes to rewrite your letter. You may give the letter to your mate, or choose to read it to him or her at an appropriate time. Or, you can put your letter aside and save it as an entry in your personal diary or journal, to be shared at a later time.

Letters help you organize your thoughts, and when you give them to your partner, he or she can read them several times to absorb your message and prepare an appropriate response. When dealing with emotionally charged issues, letters can be very effective because they eliminate expressions of hostility that might can be communicated through tone of voice or bodily expressions.

Another effective technique is to

> *Writing love letters to yourself is one of the most powerful ways to heal your relationship with the most important person in your life—you. . . . [It] will help you to forgive yourself for your imperfections, motivate yourself out of self-recrimination and into action, and move you from depression and despair to hope and clarity.*
>
> BARBARA DE ANGELES
> *How to Make Love All the Time*

write a letter to yourself as if you were your partner responding to the letter you just wrote. In this letter, you write down the ideal response you would like to receive from your partner. It feels good to acknowledge and praise yourself, and if you choose to share it with your mate, you will be demonstrating how you want to be responded to and cared for. "Sometimes writing a response letter is even more powerful than writing a love letter," adds author John Gray. "Writing out what we actually want and need increases our openness to receiving the support we deserve. In addition, when we imagine our partners responding lovingly, we actually make it easier for them to do so."[42]

Game #14
Forgiving Difficult People

The exercises in this chapter are geared toward working through conflicts with someone you love. But what about others with whom problems arise? Day to day, we encounter difficult people—nosey neighbors, rude clerks, selfish colleagues, or demanding friends—who are angry, upset, or simply need more attention and love. How can we internally work with ourselves to relieve or resolve such tensions?

Sharon Salzberg, a highly respected meditation teacher, suggests that you can send loving thoughts to the difficult people in your life through an Eastern practice known as "metta," or lovingkindness, a challenging but highly rewarding meditation:

> The first time I was given the instruction to look for one good quality in a person I found difficult, I rebelled. I thought, "That's what superficial, gullible people do—they just look for the good in someone. I don't want to do that!" As I actually did the practice, however, I discovered that it had an important and powerful effect. In fact, it was doing just what it was supposed to do: looking for the good in someone did not cover up any of the genuine difficulties I found with that person, but allowed me to relate to them without my habituated defensiveness and withdrawal. . . .
>
> Perhaps you can most easily feel metta [lovingkindness] for a difficult person if you imagine them as a vulnerable infant, or on their deathbed (but not with eager anticipation—be care-

ful). You should allow yourself to be creative, daring, even humorous, in imagining situations where you can more readily feel kindness toward a difficult person. One student of mine chose as a difficult person someone who was loud, intrusive, and extremely talkative. She found she could only start sending this person metta if she imagined her sitting in a chair, bound and gagged. Another student was so afraid of his difficult person that he could only send him metta while imagining him well restrained in prison. As the strength of our metta grows, we can eventually reach a place where we sincerely extend wishes of well-being to the difficult people in our lives, even while we work to counter their actions and activities of which we disapprove.

Sit comfortably, and start with directing metta phrases toward yourself ["may I be happy; may I be peaceful"], enveloping yourself with your own loving care. After some time, direct the phrases toward a benefactor, then a friend. If you have found a neutral person, you can then include them. You should turn your attention to the difficult person only after spending some time sending metta toward yourself and to those you find it relatively easy to feel metta for. Imagine the difficult person in any situation you wish. Get a sense of them by visualizing them or saying their name. If you can, contemplate one good thing about them. If you can't, remember that this person, just like ourselves, wishes to be happy, and makes mistakes out of ignorance. Direct the metta phrases toward them, whichever phrases you have been using. If saying, "May *you* be free from danger, may *you* be happy," brings up too much fear or sense of isolation for you, you can include yourself in the recitation: "May *we* be free from danger. May *we* be happy."

> *Compassion makes life easier, but is in no way a retreat from life nor is it an easy road to take. In establishing an increasingly realistic frame of reference, compassion has the effect of thrusting us into the very middle of ourselves and into the middle of life generally.*
>
> THEODORE ISAAC RUBIN, M.D.
> *Compassion and Self-Hate*

Gently continue to direct metta toward the difficult person, and accept the different feelings that may come and go.
There may be sorrow, grief, anger—allow them to pass through
you. If they become overwhelming, go back to sending metta to
yourself or a good friend. You can also do some reflections to
help hold those feelings in a different perspective. A classical
one is to ask yourself, "Who is the one suffering from this
anger? The person who has harmed me has gone on to live
their life (or perhaps has died), while I am the one sitting here
feeling the persecution, burning, and constriction of anger.
Out of compassion for myself, to ease my own heart, may I
let go."

Another reflection is done by turning your mind to the suffering of the difficult person, rather than viewing their actions only as bad or wrong. Compassion is the refinement of
love that opens to suffering. When we feel anger, fear, or jealousy, if we feel open to the pain of these states rather than dis-
graced by their arising, then we will have compassion for
ourselves. When we see others lost in states of anger, fear, and
so on, and we remember how painful those states are, we can
have compassion for those people as well.

Game #15
Discovering the "Write" Solution

Using a journal or a diary is a powerful technique for solving relationship
problems. When a problem comes up, writing about it can help you sort
through and organize the opinions and feelings that are filtering through
your mind. When you later review your pages, you will often discover underlying issues that you did not notice before.

There are no hard-and-fast rules when working with a diary. The
object is to be spontaneous and record the flow of intuitive thoughts. You
can jot down the events of the day, record your dreams, draw a picture,
pour out your emotions, or construct a playful fantasy. The following
story will exemplify how one woman used journaling to work through her
relational pain.

June had been feeling terrible for months, but every time she engaged in a dialogue with her husband, Bill, both became emotionally upset. She knew that neither person was to blame, but there were just too many issues to sort through. Following her therapist's advice, June started a diary. The first few pages were filled with poisonous thoughts about Bill. At first, it felt frightening to commit such words to paper, but after writing for ten or twenty minutes she would feel much calmer and clearer. However, by the end of the day, the emotional turmoil would return. Once again, before going to sleep, she took out her pen and created an affirmation to focus upon for the following day.

> Writing gives the mind a disciplined means of expression. It allows one to record events and experiences so that they can be easily recalled, and relived in the future. It is a way to analyze and understand experiences, a self-communication that brings order to them.
>
> MIHALY CSIKSZENTMIHALYI
> *Flow: The Psychology of Optimal Experience*

June wrote daily for a month, and then she went back and reread her work. She was surprised at how emotional she had been, for she had not realized how often she swung between feelings of misery and joy. Now she could more easily identify the problems and clarify what her major issues were. She also saw how she could improve her communication with her husband, for her thoughts were no longer governed by her emotional ups and downs. The journaling process made her feel better, and she felt that her relationship with her husband had improved.

June shared parts of her journal with Bill, and they began to talk—seemingly for the first time in years—about their innermost feelings and concerns. Suddenly, what seemed to be an insurmountable impasse in communication became an easy and enjoyable exchange. And the diary? It was incorporated into a book and accepted for publication: her personal journey became, in essence, a gift to others throughout the world.

CHAPTER 8

Romantic Writing Games: Wooing Your Partner with Paper and Pen

In this chapter, you will learn how to deepen communication and intimacy by composing romantic letters and notes, playing reading games, keeping a couple's journal, and plagiarizing your favorite poet. With a little imagination and some paper, you can ink your way to love.

IF YOU HAVE ever given or received a love letter, you know how meaningful the experience can be. Yet in today's hectic world, we often forgo or forget about this special act of intimacy. To nurture the soul of relationship, says author and psychologist Thomas Moore, we must cultivate the art of conversation, through writing as well as speech. As Moore so eloquently writes:

> Something happens to our thoughts and emotions when we put them into a letter; they are then not the same as spoken words. They are placed in a different, special context, and they speak at a different level, serving the soul's organ of rumination rather than the mind's capacity for understanding. A woman who was in a touch-and-go struggle in her marriage, not sure if it was going to survive, told me that even after hours of conversation with her husband, she would sometimes write him a letter, feeling an added dimension of intimacy in that form. Another woman described how in moments of extreme

frustration she would stop talking to her husband and instead sit down and write him a letter, delivering it from the kitchen to the living room. Each of these women felt that a letter might somehow touch her mate's heart more deeply than the spoken word.[43]

A letter or a note of kindness is an important expression of love, for just a few words can open one's heart and heal relational wounds. But, for some individuals, writing may feel like a daunting task, bringing up fears of vulnerability and doubt, or concerns that you will be laughed at or judged. But with a little guidance from the following games, you will see how easy it can be to write an endearing but playful note and speak deeply from your heart and soul.

Game #1
The Note of Appreciation

Do you remember the scene from the movie *When Harry Met Sally* when Harry blurts out his reasons for wanting Sally in his life? It went some-thing like this: "I love the way you get cold when it's seventy-one degrees outside, the way it takes you an hour and a half to order a sandwich, and the way you crinkle your nose when you get mad," Harry began. "But the most important reason for wanting you in my life is that you are the first person I want to see in the morning and the last person I want to talk to before I go to bed." In these few sentences—by describing the little things he appreciated and loved—he regained his girlfriend's trust.

To keep love sacred and alive, we often need to hear such words, and a note of appreciation is an easy way to begin. On a card or a sheet of paper,

You want to get in the habit of having a lot of surprises in your relationship that can range anywhere from an affection-ate note slipped into a briefcase to an unexpected dinner. Again, keep in mind that the surprise has to be something that your partner wants. . . . You might be going through the mall, and you'll hear her say, "Those are nice earrings"; or "I want to get this book one day." Make a note of this, and go back and buy it for her as a surprise.

WADE LUQUET
Short-Term Couples Therapy

make a list of ten things—big and small, silly and sweet—that you really appreciate about your partner. Then leave it in her purse or his car, or someplace where it will be discovered during the day. That evening, when you reunite, you can savor the sparkle in your partner's eyes.

Game #2
The Envelope Trail

I came across this very sweet game in a book by Caryl Krueger,[44] to be used when you are away from your lover for an extended period of time. Before leaving, write a brief, loving message on a sheet of paper for each day that you will be gone. Be imaginative: one note can be a simple endearing comment, the next can be provocative or sexy, the third can include a humorous comment or poem.

Put each letter in a separate envelope and write the date on which it is to be opened—one for each day that you are gone. You can even include some flower petals or other romantic token. Tie your bundle of letters together and hand them to your lover just before you leave, with the instructions that only one can be opened each day. Your partner will love the excitement of having to wait twenty-four hours before the next letter can be read.

Game #3
Post Office

In this exercise, Susan Page offers suggestions and guidelines for writing a love letter to your mate, but what really makes it special is the romantic place from which the letter is mailed:

> Do whatever you need to get yourself in the mood to write a love letter. Pretend you and your partner have been separated for a month, and that you miss him or her terribly. Pretend it is your anniversary. Or pretend you are not yet married and you are trying to woo him or her.
>
> Put yourself in a romantic environment. Maybe take a bubble bath first, or light a candle and put fresh flowers on the table or desk where you will write. Play romantic music.

Then sit down and write a love letter.

It doesn't have to be mushy or corny. And it doesn't have to be long, although it certainly can be if you get into it. Maybe it will be funny. Write it in your own style. Be sincere. Be yourself. Write from your heart.

This is not the time to dredge up all the rough spots you have been through. This letter is not about *all* your feelings, only your love and appreciation.

If a "formula" would be helpful, use this one (borrowed from an old boyfriend of mine who actually did this for me): Write "I love you because you are _____." Keep writing the sentence over and over, filling in with all the different qualities you appreciate. If you like, write each line in a different color. (That's what my boyfriend did.)

Do you have a favorite poet who expresses your sentiments? Include a sonnet from Shakespeare or a poem by Browning or Gibran. Or use the words from a favorite romantic song.

Here's a little outline for a love letter. Use it if it helps:

Why I love you.

Things I love about you.

Why I love our relationship.

How you make me feel.

What I want for you.

What I want for us.

What I want to give you.

Now, mail your letter. Would it be more fun for your mate to receive it at home or at work? If you like, you can arrange to have your love letter mailed from a romantic-sounding city or town. Just put your stamped, addressed envelope inside a second envelope addressed to the Postmaster of the town you choose. Attach a note requesting that your letter be hand-stamped and mailed.

Loveland, Colorado 80537

Loving, New Mexico 88256

Romance, West Virginia 25175

Game #4
Treasure Hunt

Using index cards or stationery, create two or three romantic notes for your partner and leave them in unusual spots: way down under the sheets, under a jar of pickles, in a cereal box, or under a dinner plate. You can leave a coupon in the freezer treating your lover to an ice cream cone, or an invitation on the shower faucet for a stimulating massage. Or simply write "I Love You" with lipstick on the bathroom mirror. These little acts of kindness bring many happy returns.

As an alternative, make up a dozen cards and hide them around the house, and then tell your partner what you've done. You can check in every day to see which notes were found, giving little hints to tease your partner on. Sometimes, a few notes will be forgotten, only to be discovered months later and surprising you with a lovely note from *yourself!*

What makes these notes so endearing is that they are unexpected. They symbolize that you are doing something special for your lover, and they add a touch of playfulness to your life. They can even turn an ordinary day into a memorable and loving event.

Game #5

The "Anatomy" of Love

> *Knotted bodies*
> *are the book of the soul:*
> *with eyes closed,*
> *with my touch and my tongue, I*
> *write out on your body*
> *the scripture of the world. . . .*
>
> OCTAVIO PAZ

For this exercise, I will share with you a secret that many great writers have used to touch another's soul: They simply focus one part of their lover's body as they compose their poems and prose.

Take out a piece of paper and make love to your partner

with your words. Write a paragraph on the beauty and texture of his hair. Describe in detail her smile and the color of her lips, contrasting them with the shapes and forms in nature:

> *"Your crimson lips are like the fires that light the summer skies."*

Or write about the ways that you could stroke his hand:

> *"Slowly, with the tips of my fingers, I trace the curves within your palm, lingering for a moment at the wrist before retreating to the tips of your hand."*

You might, for example, compare her eyes to a famous work of art:

> *"If your eyes could talk, they would betray the secrets of your youth, bringing forth the envy of Raphael."*

By noticing the smallest details, we let our partners know how much we care about every aspect of their being. It's really quite easy, for all you have to do is to trust the imaginative flow within. But if this seems difficult, try the following technique: Take a piece of paper and pick one part of your partner's body, writing down the first three impressions that come to mind. Tom, for example, when he reflected on his partner's hair, came up with this:

> *Wild and curly*
> *I just want to run my fingers through those curls*
> *I love it when you rest your head upon my chest*

By making simple additions and revisions, you will have written a beautiful letter of love. *"Dear Corrine,"* Tom wrote. *"Your hair is wild and curly, and all I want to do is run my fingers through those auburn curls. I love it when you rest your head upon my chest, especially when we are asleep. With all my love, Tom."* With brevity and simplicity, a tender moment can be created and shared.

Game #6
The Poet's Touch

! hope
faith !
! life
love ! . . .

e. e. cummings

It is easier to write a poem than to compose a letter of love, for all you need are a few choice words and a free-associative phrase. Here's how to write a knockout poem that will melt your partner's heart. On a fancy piece of stationery, write down three words that come to mind when you think lovingly of your partner: For example, you might come up with "smile," "softness," and "grace." Then, compose a simple sentence that expresses one aspect of your love, and write it down below the other words. When you are done, your poem will be similar in form to this:

Smile
Softness
Grace . . .
My love grows fonder daily.

ESCAPE me?
Never—
Beloved ! . . .

ROBERT BROWNING

Write your poem on a piece of good-quality stationery. Sign it, and then burn one edge of the paper for an aesthetic touch. Roll it up, tie it with a ribbon or string, and leave it somewhere special for your partner to find. These little touches—the paper you choose, the ink you use, and the way you fold or roll up the note—symbolize the unique love you hold for your mate. Then place your poem next to your partner's pillow before he or she wakes up, as the ancient lovers in Japan would do a thousand years ago!

Game #7
The Poet Thief

When we cannot find the words to express our deepest thoughts, another's voice will do just fine: you can "borrow" someone else's writing and share it with your lover. Choose a poem that expresses, in some small way, the feelings of your heart. Even when the words aren't yours, you are communicating something that everyday language can't reach.

The idea for this game came from a lovely movie called *Il Postino,* in which an ignorant fisherman tries to woo the most beautiful woman in town. Barely literate, he is tongue-tied in her presence and can only utter a clumsy word or two. But he has a plan: he will ask a visiting poet, the famous Pablo Neruda, for help. Neruda encourages the fisherman to trust his inner muse. But the fisherman's pen refuses to write, and so he copies one of Neruda's poems and passes it off as his own. The woman is bewitched—indeed, the entire town is stirred; it was quite an erotic piece—but Neruda does not betray his student, and the fisherman wins the woman's heart.

The first step is to find a poet whose style you really like. Look through your partner's books for clues about his or her taste, and visit a bookstore or library to see what captures your eye: a dark and moody verse, a Shakespearean vignette, a spiritual melody from the East. My own favorites include:

100 Love Sonnets, by Pablo Neruda

Selected Poems of Rainer Maria Rilke, translated by Robert Bly

The Love Poems of Elizabeth and Robert Browning

No Nature, by Gary Snyder

A Tree Within, by Octavio Paz

Rumi: In the Arms of the Beloved, translated by Jonathan Star

Call Me by My True Names, by Thich Nhat Hanh

Once you have selected a poem, call your lover on the phone and read it aloud. Or copy it onto a card, adding a personal note to the end

("I just wanted to share this poem with you . . ."). Give the book itself as a present, reading selections to your lover at a strategically romantic time. Try lighting candles and playing background music as you read.

You can also rewrite parts of the poem, and thus turn it into your own, a technique that many teachers use to help others develop their writing skills. Here is an example of how you might personalize a passage from the German poet Rilke. The original poem went like this:

> *I love the dark hours of my being*
> *in which my senses drop into the deep.*
> *I have found in them, as in old letters,*
> *my private life, that is already lived through,*
> *and become wide and powerful now, like legends.*
> *Then I know that there is room in me*
> *for a second huge and timeless life. . . .*[45]

Here is how I revised it for a person I held dear to my soul:

> *I love the fullness of your being*
> *in which my senses fall.*
> *I have found in my love for you*
> *my fullest self,*
> *wide and powerful, as with legends of the old.*
> *And I know that there is room in me*
> *to hold you in this huge and timeless life.*

You can even create a marvelous piece by taking single lines from different poems, weaving them together, and giving them to your mate. It is a gift that will be cherished for years.

Game #8
Musical Chairs

Music, they say, is the language of the heart, so why not borrow a few lines from your favorite songs and put them into a letter of love? But be careful what you choose, for I once rearranged a Stevie Wonder tune with unexpected results. *"My dearest Jackie,"* it began:

Your body moves with grace and song
like symphonies by Bach or Brahms.
A female Shakespeare of your time
With looks to blow Picasso's mind—
You are the best!

I signed it *"With all my love, from Stevie and me,"* thinking it was pretty sexy, but the woman I was dating couldn't get over the image of Picasso's work with all those eyes and breasts and noses sticking out all over the place. I must have hit a nerve, for that night, I slept alone.

Think about the songs that have moved your heart and write down the lyrics as you remember them. It doesn't matter if they are exact or not. You can also sort through your partner's albums and, assuming the lyrics are printed, write them down on a piece of stationery or a card. The more poetic and metaphoric the verse is, the more romantic it will feel. The songs of Joni Mitchell, Enya, Paul Simon, and Gordon Lightfoot are excellent examples of lyrical prose.

Game #9
Zen Telegrams

This game was inspired by Mary Clancy and Roger Lauer, who created it as a therapeutic technique to help people reduce their inhibitions when sharing intimate thoughts.[46] It encourages spontaneous dialogue by engaging in symbolic play.

The dining-room table is the perfect surface to use, but first cover it with several layers of newspaper for protection. Place a stack of plain white paper on which to draw. You can use felt pens, crayons, chalk, or pencils, but the ideal media to work with are watercolor, inks, and brushes.

With your partner, put a sheet of paper in front of each of you, saturate your brushes with paint (or hold a pen in your hand), and then close your eyes. Place your brush or pen on the paper, and rapidly move your arm and hand to create a spontaneous design. Open your eyes, and without judging your work, take another sheet of paper and make another design, experimenting with different movements of your arm. Try drawing from a feeling—anger, sadness, joy, etc.—and see how that affects the

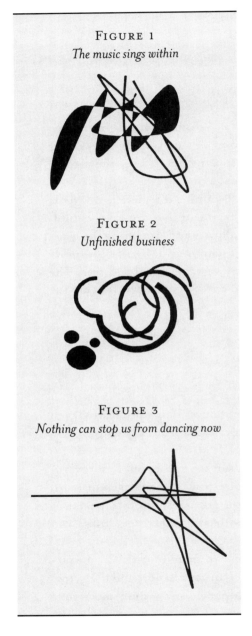

FIGURE 1

The music sings within

FIGURE 2

Unfinished business

FIGURE 3

Nothing can stop us from dancing now

image that you make. Continue to do this until you have made about twenty designs.

Exchange your drawings with your partner, and quickly write down whatever thoughts or expressions come to mind as you look at the designs. Here (at left) are several examples of one couple's work (they were experimenting with computer-generated forms), and the captions they came up with for each design.

You may be met with laughter and delight, discover a glimmer of personal truth, or recall a fond memory or fear. But by the time you have finished, you will feel more confident and relaxed. Have a conversation about your drawings. Do they really capture how you feel? Do they symbolize an unspoken fantasy or wish? In essence, you are using your designs in a fashion similar to the inkblot test that psychiatrists use to bring out hidden feelings and thoughts.

Game #10
Poetry for Two

In this exercise, you will create a poem with your partner, taking turns writing one line at a time. Spontaneous poems have a way of bringing up hidden feelings and moods, but when they are embedded in a playful form of writing, they rarely stir up the concerns and anxieties that couples often have when they consciously express their inner private thoughts.

Like the Zen telegrams in the previous game, spontaneous poems help to bring unconscious desires to the surface, allowing you and your partner to talk about them in a playfully creative way.

Take a sheet of paper and select a title on a topic that you would like to explore. Write it at the top of the page (for example: *Growing Old, Friendship, Secret Love, The Money Mess, Eros, Family Fun,* etc.). Then quickly compose the first line of a poem, saying anything that comes to mind. Write it down and read it to your partner, who will then spontaneously compose the next line, be it serious, silly, or sweet. Continue taking turns writing lines, and keep going until you have about twenty lines of free-associative verse. Then read the entire poem aloud. Often, you will find deeply meaningful expressions of love intermixed with vulnerability and wit.

When you have completed one poem, ask your partner to pick a new title and to compose the first line of a new piece, going through the process again. If you find yourself getting stuck, say something absurd and write it down, and let your partner figure out how to respond. Keep it playful, and when you have finished, talk about your experience, which may stimulate important discussions concerning intimacy and love.

Game #11
The Couple's Journal

A "couple's journal" is a combination diary, letter, and experimental play—a powerful tool for deepening conscious intimacy and love. I recommend that you make this game a high priority. Try it for several months to see how it affects your communication with your partner.

Purchase a spiral notebook, and on the first page write a brief note to your partner, inviting him or her to create a diary with you. Ask for a simple commitment: to read what you write each day and to respond by jotting down any feeling or thought that comes to mind, filling up as much of the page as he or she can. On the following day, read what your partner has written, and then add another page of your own writing to the journal.

After a month has gone by, read the journal out loud together and talk about the experience it provoked. A couple's journal can bring to light many new perspectives about your personal and relational lives that may not have been reached through verbal dialogue.

Feel free to write whatever you want. You may want to respond to your partner's entry (following Jennifer Louden's guidelines, below) or simply share something personal or sweet. Topics may include:

- a nurturing thought

- a vulnerable feeling

- a question that you would like to ask of your partner

- a personal problem you are struggling with

- last night's dream

- a spontaneous poem

- a memory from the past

- something silly or humorous

- a fantasy or a wish

If you don't feel like writing, you can draw a picture, or make a design, or glue in a clipping from a magazine. It only takes a few minutes each day to open new doors of communication and listening.

Before you begin your journey, share with your mate the following comments by Jennifer Louden, author of *The Couple's Comfort Book,* as she guides you through the basic rules of the game:

> Keeping a couple's journal is an act of courageous communication. A balance is needed between the free-flowing-I-can-write-anything of personal journal writing and the need to respect your partner's feelings. This balance can be achieved with a few guidelines.
>
> 1. Never make fun of what your mate has written. Don't bring up material from the journal during a fight. Don't share what is written in the journal with another person.
>
> 2. Remember that this is *raw* material. Written words on a page can take on a powerful, permanent quality. Try to

remember the words are coming straight from the heart, unedited. Keep your sense of humor and remember, nothing is written in stone.

3. If you are in doubt about whether to write something, consider this question: What is my hoped-for result? If it is to manipulate, injure, or impress, reconsider.

4. Above all, aspire to be honest and caring in what you write.

Decide *together* how often and approximately how long or how much you will write in your journal. Once a day for three months? Twice a week for a month? Once a week for six months? Make a defined commitment to each other and write this in the front of your journal to avoid confusion.

One way journal keeping could work: You come home from work and spend fifteen minutes relaxing before making dinner. This is the time you like to write in the journal. Your partner prefers to write just before bed. You pick a topic and write it across the top of the page, then write as long as you feel like it (although you have agreed to always try to write at least a paragraph). You put the book back in its special place by your bed. That night, your partner reads what you wrote, then writes. The next time you write, you read what she or he wrote and either respond or add to it, or you pick a new topic and start a new entry. And so your journal grows.

Decide ahead of time how you will discuss what you've been writing. Will you have a weekly check-in or will you bring up insights or questions based on journal entries anytime? Be clear. Some couples feel that writing their innermost thoughts is okay, but discussing them face-to-face is too touchy. If this is the case, it helps to make a small ritual out of talking about journal material. Other couples like to weave the journal stuff right into their lives. Decide *before* you start writing.

Keeping a journal together does require commitment and effort. The first or second week, one of you will most likely hit some resistance. Use this resistance. Write about why you don't want to write. Stream-of-consciousness writing works well for exploring resistance, as does timed writing. *Immediately* after making an entry, reward yourself with something that makes you feel good—a baseball game with your son, frozen yogurt, or a favorite old movie.

Game #12
Bedtime Stories

In the evening, when my son climbs into bed, I love to read him stories. It is an intimate time for both of us as we relax into a world of fantasy, imagination, and myth. But reading aloud can be equally valuable for adults, as a way to explore new relational themes. Reading can be an ideal way to introduce new ideas in a nonthreatening way, especially for couples who have difficulty expressing themselves to each other.

Reading games can be used to repair relationships in which communication has broken down.[47] In these situations, couples can pick out books on relationships and read them together. By discussing the authors' ideas from an "outsider's" perspective, couples can often address their personal difficulties with less defensiveness. The ideas and concepts described in books have been carefully organized and thus can offer the couple a clear and more comprehensive understanding of the problems each may face.

Take turns reading to your partner at least once each month. You can experiment with fiction and poetry as well as psychology. Read to each other in bed, at the beach, or over breakfast or lunch. Read slowly, with passion and warmth, and when you are being read to, listen as carefully as you can. The following suggestions will help you to create a reading plan that can bring you both insight and pleasure for many years to come:

Favorites: Pick a book that you have already read, a favorite one, and select a passage to read aloud. But first tell your partner why this book was meaningful to you. After you have finished, ask your partner to respond to the passage you selected, but do not criticize or judge what is said. Just listen with an open heart. Then ask your partner to share a passage from one of his or her favorite books.

Currents: When you get a new book, tell your partner about it and read a brief passage from the cover or the introduction, to give your partner a sense of the author's voice. As you read through your book, mark various passages that you think your partner may like to hear, and share them before going to bed.

Swapping: Pick one of your favorite books that you would like your partner to read, and have your partner pick one for you. You can read the entire book, or you can simply find a passage that was meaningful to you and read it to your mate.

Browsing: Take your partner to the library or bookstore and browse through the aisles together, pointing out the books that catch your eye and explaining to your partner why. Then switch roles. Before you leave, find a book that you both are interested in and take turns reading chapters to each other.

Issues: When a specific problem emerges between you and your partner, find a book on relationship dynamics that talks about that issue. Read a pertinent passage and see how you can apply the author's wisdom to your problem.

One final suggestion: Spend a few hours browsing through your partner's books and the libraries of your friends. For it is there, among those worn pages, that you will find the seeds that fostered their values and beliefs.

"All through life we may read books for enjoyment and for the information we gain, arousing and at the same time satisfying our curiosity," wrote the renowned psychoanalyst Bruno Bettelheim. "But only at certain periods in our lives will we read books in the hope that they will influence it, give it direction, solve pressing problems. This is especially true when we find ourselves in a crisis of life or when we are undergoing obscure inner developments. Then a book can influence our whole being."[48] In our relationships, when we choose a path of conscious intimacy, we are shaking up the patterns of the past to give us a moment to embrace our partners anew. In such moments of transition, there are many opportunities to gain insight and love, be it through a book, a game, or an intimate dialogue with our mates.

CHAPTER 9

Playful Games: Surprising Your Partner and Having Fun

Take a break from the serious work of intimacy and literally engage your partner in play. Play catch with an invisible ball, have a conversation between thumbs, make a portrait of your partner à la Picasso, and then end your day by switching roles—and clothes—with your partner. In the process, you will laughingly fall into love.

RELATIONSHIPS are serious work. But there is also a time to play, bringing a touch of spontaneity and joy into the intimate corners of our lives. In our final chapter, we will explore some playful ways to make your partner smile and laugh.

> *Do something today to make your partner's jaw drop: start a tickling match while they're still in the shower, scatter Hershey's kisses in their underwear drawer, drive them blindfolded to a new restaurant for dinner.*
>
> HARVILLE HENDRIX
> AND HELEN HUNT
> *The Couples Companion*

Playfulness can take the edge off a stressful day and lift our partner's spirits when she or he is feeling down. Couples who have fun have an easier time dealing with difficult issues. They see their partners as a source of pleasure which deepens their emotional bond.[49] When integrated into serious discussions, playfulness can melt away defenses that keep us from opening up during a vulnerable moment of intimacy.

There are many ways to bring

playfulness into our relationships. We can surprise our partners with an unusual gift, or by sending a Valentine's Day card in June. We can laugh and act silly, or reenact a childhood pleasure from our past. Jennifer Louden, author of *The Couple's Comfort Book,* suggests that partners nurture each other's merriment by sharing a joke a week, tickling each other, playing hide-and-seek without the kids, collecting and sharing humorous cartoons, sending absurd postcards to each other, creating funny videos or audiotapes, giving each other preposterous gifts, or watching comedy films together. To take the edge off conflicts, she encourages couples to use squirt guns or do something silly like wearing Groucho glasses.[50] Such mischievous acts not only bring people together by breaking monotonous patterns of behavior; they can even be employed to heal illness and disease, as Patch Williams, the well-loved doctor of medicine, demonstrated when he would dress up as a clown to relieve his patients' worries and fears.

In this chapter, you will be shown how to rediscover the playful pleasures of childhood, bringing them into your dialogues with your partner, family, and friends. In these moments of creative fun, we can even illuminate forgotten qualities that add richness to our distinctive personalities and traits, qualities that may have been suppressed by parents and teachers who did not appreciate the art of play.

Game #1
The Pleasure List

This game was created by Jean Houston, who has taken note of how often we ignore the little pleasures in our lives. This exercise will help you recall the pleasurable moments you have had so that you can consciously reintegrate them into your life. After you complete the game, share with your partner and ask him or her to talk about the little pleasures of life. Houston writes:

> *Don't get too old and forget that inside each of us there is still a child that wants to come out and play with their best friend.*
>
> HARVILLE HENDRIX AND HELEN HUNT
> *The Couples Companion*

One day, as an experiment, I asked a group of friends who were in the house to jot down a

list of their most pleasurable experiences and associations. After some initial laughter and skepticism, they came up with the following list, their enthusiasm growing noticeably as they continued with this project. The sampling that follows is a regular Noah's ark of pleasure, an adventure into lands forgotten but now found again, a banquet to regale the body and captivate the soul:

Lying on the beach listening to the waves, with my toes wriggling in the hot sand.

Climbing between freshly ironed sheets that have been dried in the sun.

Nursing my baby in the middle of the night, curled up in a big chair.

Roller-skating at breakneck speed down a steep hill.

Picking! My own navel, my own scalp, ears, nose.

Cuddling, singing to, and rocking my children, and scratching their backs—which I did every night until they were at least eleven. It was like the evening blessing for me.

Walking in the quiet of New York City after a heavy snowfall.

Listening to a Beethoven symphony and imagining that I'm the conductor.

The electricity in the air after a thunderstorm has blown away.

The sensation of a purring, enraptured cat as she kneads my body with her paws.

Saturday afternoon at the movies with a giant Mr. Goodbar.

Dancing with my huge dog.

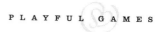

Hearing a choir rehearsing as I walk down the street.

Sitting by a fireplace and watching the images come and go in the crackling flames.

Blowing the paper wrapper off the straw into the fans at Robinson's Drug Store before guzzling my strawberry ice cream soda.

Reading a great novel in a hot bath on a cold night.

Diving naked into a cool lake.

Telling ghost stories while the wind demons howl outside the house.

Cool green grapes in July.

Watching the cork disappear beneath the water and feeling the sudden tug of a big fish on the line.

How often do we make such lists? Most lists are lists of things to be done, reminders of duties unattended and obligations reluctantly remembered. For our doctors we list our symptoms, for our therapists our problems. A catalogue of woes is much more frequent in our society than a catalogue of pleasures. . . .

Make a list of your own pleasures and delights. If you are anything like my friends, once you start, the remembered pleasures will trigger more memories to relish and you will not want to stop. These memories prime your sensorium, and you may find, after making and recalling this list, that your awareness will have a keener edge, your capacity for pleasure will deepen, and your body will feel lighter. More important, the recovery of more skeins in the tapestry of pleasure will give you a larger room upon which to weave delight.

Having listed your pleasures, choose one that is particularly vivid for you right now and feel it intensely. Visualize the experience as strongly as possible, hear it, taste it, smell it, let it fill your entire body. Experience it down your spine, breathe

into it, laugh into it, smile into it. Reach out and hug it. Hold it to you and then let it go. Begin now to move with this knowing flooding your body.

Sing or draw or paint or write or cook or garden with this knowing flooding your being—and note the difference. What has happened? And now remember some "problem" or something that may have been bothering you when you began this exercise. How does it look now?

After doing this exercise one person commented, "What problems? They're gone!" For others, their problems look smaller and more manageable. Another person in the philosophy department of a large university said later that she had tried this before going to a particularly difficult meeting with her department chairman, who had previously terrified her. She found herself smiling as she went in, barely able to contain her mirth. (She had been remembering the time she won the children's pie-eating contest at the county fair.) Her good will toward the world in general encompassed the chairman as well, and the meeting resulted in a new spirit of cooperation and the beginning of a lasting and productive working relationship.

I have found this to be true over and over again in my work. Those people who are in touch with their pleasures inevitably share this pleasure with those around them.

Game #2
Child's Play

In this game, you will have a chance to relive some of the playful moments of childhood. Doing so can help you discover forgotten parts of your personality that can bring you deeper joy with your mate.

Take two sheets of paper and give one to your partner. Write down twenty childhood activities that you each recall as being fun: pillow fights, playing Monopoly, roller skating, eating whipped cream for breakfast, etc. When you are done, put your paper next to your partner's list, and cross out any activity that either of you would not enjoy doing. Then pick two activities—one from your list and one from your partner's—that you can immediately put into action. Have a tickle fight, go to an amusement park, or run through the neighborhood playing tag. Every few days, pick another item from your lists, continuing until all the activities have been tried.

Game #3
Wrappers

This game involves experimenting with the *way* in which a gift is given. If we take the time to wrap a present differently, or deliver it in an unusual way, we add a special touch to the gift-giving process.

Once, for my son's seventh birthday, I handed him the end of a ribbon and told him to follow it wherever it led. The ribbon went under furniture, through cupboards, and meandered through every room in the house. Along the way, I left small presents, which he opened with glee. The trail eventually led to the garage, where the ribbon was tied to a blanket that was draped over a large, lumpy mass.

Before I would let him unwrap the mystery gift, he had to try to guess what it was. A playful tension built as I gave him some hints: perhaps it was a dinosaur bone, or a petrified monster, or some other yucky mess that little boys love. Finally, when he could stand it no more, I let him uncover the gift. It turned out to be a ten-speed bike, and he was thrilled. But it was really the way in which the bike was given that made the gift especially memorable to him.

The next time you give a gift of love, surprise your partner by wrapping or giving it in an unusual way. Here are some ideas to try that have been tested by my colleagues and friends:

- Hide the present, leaving written clues to where it can be found.

- Tape a small gift to your body and invite your lover to find it.

- Put a tiny gift in a giant box filled with newspaper.

- Blindfold your partner, who must unwrap the gift and guess what it is.

- Put five layers of wrapping around your present, with a card attached to each layer.

- Wrap your gift with colorful cloth, aluminum foil, or the Sunday comics.

- Use acrylic paint or watercolors to decorate the box that the gift is in.

- Glue flowers, leaves, confetti, or balloons onto the box or wrapping paper.

- Give a gift to your lover in an unexpected place, like a restaurant or a park.

- Hang the gift from the ceiling, or place it in the branch of a tree.

- Have a stranger deliver an anonymous gift from you; reveal your identity later.

Game #4
Lighten Up!

Instead of just wrapping a present, why not surprise your spouse by wrapping the house? Take some Christmas lights and pin them to the underside of your bed or dresser and around the frame of the bedroom door. Then fill the room with candles, turn on the music, and watch the look on your partner's face when she or he walks in. By changing the environment of your space, you can add a touch of enchantment to your romance.

You can also turn your abode into an exotic, romantic space by placing two or three small, portable lights in the corners of the room, behind a plant, or underneath the bed. If you put colored bulbs in your fixtures, you can create different tones and moods. Purchase a paper lampshade and decorate it with paint, or drape colored fabrics around your existing shade for a playfully romantic look.

Game #5
The Alphabet Game

This sweet game was inspired by Jennifer Louden, author of *The Couple's Comfort Book*. Tell your partner that, for each of the following twenty-six days, you are going do something special that is connected to a letter of the alphabet. On the first day, for example, you might bake him an *a*pple pie, *a*pply some lotion to her feet, or take her to an *A*rmenian restaurant to celebrate the day. On the second day, dream up a surprise beginning with the letter *B* (giving her *b*acon and eggs in *b*ed). Continue through the alphabet for each succeeding day. By the twenty-sixth day, you should find yourself sleeping with your partner intimately embraced in your arms, sharing those *ZZZZZ*s of love. Have a contest: play the game together and surprise each other with letters of fun each day.

Game #6
The Surprise Outing

"Try to surprise at least one person every day," advises Mihaly Csikszent-mihalyi,[51] an expert on bringing creativity and flow into relationships. "Instead of being your predictable self, say something unexpected, express an opinion that you have not dared to reveal, ask a question you wouldn't ordinarily ask. Or break the routine of your activities."

Csikszentmihalyi suggests that we occasionally arrange special trips for our partners when they least expect it—in the middle of the week, for example—taking them out to breakfast, to a museum, a poetry reading, a movie, or to a picnic in the park. Call up the boss and see if you can arrange for your mate to leave early from the office, or if your partner is self-employed, ask him or her to set aside one half of the day for a very special surprise. Playful outings like these provide a sense of romance that will be remembered for years to come.

> *Make a commitment to surprise each other once a month. Just the anticipation of the surprise can keep you on a happy edge.*
>
> WADE LUQUET
> *Short-Term Couples Therapy*

Game #7
The Surprise Party

Instead of waiting for someone else to treat you in a special way, take control and do it yourself by creating the kind of event that would bring you the greatest pleasure and joy. To bring your fantasies to life, Dallas radio personality Suzie Humphreys suggests that you give yourself a surprise party, orchestrated exactly as you would like:

I was married to one of those husbands who wasn't going to give me a surprise birthday party. And I'd always wanted a surprise birthday party. Women want that! We give 'em to you guys!— You neeever do it back! You think a single rose from the grocery store is gonna cut it.

So I decided to plan my own surprise birthday party. We were at a dinner party one night and I said, "Mark down the twenty-fourth on your calendar. I'm givin' myself a surprise birthday party." Everybody laughed—just like you are—until the invitation arrived in the mail. It invited them to the First Annual Suzie Humphreys Surprise Birthday Party. It had the time and place, and it had a little map to show you where to park your car so I wouldn't get suspicious. Then it charged 'em twenty bucks a couple.—Well why should I pay for the food, I was cookin' it!—And then it said, "Don't waste your money on a silly gag gift; put it all together and buy me something real nice. I'd like a silver chafing dish!"

Come the night of the party, I blew up 350 helium balloons, painted signs that said "We love you, Suzie! You're the greatest!" I assigned my two best friends to take me out to get a drink so everybody'd have time to get in there and hide. Seven o'clock, I walked into a pitch black room and twenty-four people yelled, "Surprise!"—And I cried!

The point is, who can plan your surprise birthday party better than you can! And if we do it for ourselves, we are not waiting for someone else to make our lives exciting. We can live together in marriage or friendship and know we have all within us to do what we need to do.

Game #8
Two Thumbs Up

In this game, created by therapist John Rowan,[52] you will create a dialogue between you and your partner's thumb. Yes, thumb! Not only will this exercise leave you rolling on the floor with laughter; it will also help you and your partner identify patterns of behavior that can interfere with communication and other acts of intimacy. For added excitement, incorporate this game into your next party or social activity.

Begin by sitting in a chair, facing your partner. Stretch your right hand out in front of you—with your thumb sticking up in the air—and bend your fingers into your palm. Have your partner do the same. Now clasp each other's fingertips (the same position you used for the childhood game of thumb wrestling). Both of your thumbs should be pointing up and facing each other.

Give your thumb a personality and a name, as if it were a puppet. Your thumb, for example, can take on the persona of a famous actor or actress, a gangster, a shy little girl—any personality that strikes your fancy at that moment. Tell your partner who your thumb is, and together decide upon a scenario to play. Examples might include going out on a date, kissing and making love, having a political debate, engaging in a heroic fight, pretending to be emperor of the world. Then start to dialogue with your partner, thumb to thumb. You add the words, and your thumbs act out the part. Be as imaginative as you can and play out the scenario for approximately two minutes. Then switch to your left hands and thumbs and play out another two-minute scenario.

After you have completed the second round, talk about your experience with your partner. Did one person take an active, aggressive role while the other assumed a passive role (a very common occurrence that often reflects one's underlying personality weakness or strength)? If you played a sensual role, did you perceive your partner as romantic, or did the scene appear to be a little hostile or sexist (this can uncover unexpressed fears)? As you talk, see if deeper issues have been touched, for this game often exposes aspects of one's personality that may have been hidden for years.

Game #9
The Invisible Ball

This game and the one that follows have been adapted from the work of theatrical trainer Viola Spolin, who uses such games to help people develop their imagination, intuition, and communication skills.[53] When played at home (with your partner or with a group of friends), these games become a wonderful tool for enhancing intimacy by tapping into inner feelings that can only emerge through nonverbal play.

Drama games also help couples recapture a sense of spontaneity and play that is essential for keeping love and romance alive. They illustrate the importance of using body language in our dialogues with each other, and they help us to express our feelings with greater clarity and ease.

> *Drama games teach people to communicate more fully and accurately by expanding their repertoire of ideas. It helps them put thought into action through a conscious process that is within their control.*
>
> TIAN DAYTON
> *Drama Games*

To begin, face your partner, standing about four feet apart. Extend your arms, palms up, and trace the shape of an invisible ball. Move your palms all over the ball, visualizing how it looks and feels and moves. Without using words, find a way to show your partner how heavy the ball is, and then hand it over. Slowly pass the ball back and forth between the two of you, pushing, pulling, lifting, and dropping. Play with the ball, using your whole body. Roll it, throw it, and bounce it off your head. When you toss it into the air, follow it with your eyes.

Once you have a good feel for this technique, imagine that your ball has just turned into flubber, an elastic blob that can be pulled into strange and unusual shapes. Stretch it apart in your hands and drape it over your partner's arms. Your partner then shapes it into something else and hands it back to you. Try wrapping it around your body or pouring it over your head. Step over it, into it, under it, and through it. Demonstrate how sticky it is.

Now create a fantasy dialogue with your partner about this object, exaggerating the tone of your voice: "Susan, help! It's stuck to my hair and I can't get it out!" "Look out, Tim, it's coming alive and crawling up the wall!" When you have completed this exercise, talk about the feelings it brought up and what it shows you about your styles of communication. For example, did you or your partner find it embarrassing to play? Was it difficult or uncomfortable to use your body language to express a concept or idea? Did one of you have an easier time "communicating" to the other and, if so, why? Over the next few weeks, pay closer attention to your and your partner's body language and try to bring more expressiveness into your daily activities and talks.

Game #10

Tug-of-War

Games like tug-of-war encourage children to be more expressive and to redirect their aggressive energies into cooperative activities with others. By playing an imaginary game of tug-of-war with your partner, you can also refine your adult skills of cooperative exchange.

Begin by imagining that you and your partner are holding an invisible rope. As you initiate a game of tug-of-war, use your facial expressions and body positions to describe how hard you are pulling. Keep visual contact with your partner, responding as best you can to his or her movements. If your partner pulls really hard, for example, you will have to respond by being knocked off balance. As you "struggle" with your partner, you must demonstrate which one of you has the greater strength, and then you must figure out, without using words, who will win. This game can help partners become more sensitive to the nonverbal power struggles that are hidden in many relationships.

> *Imaginative play is so very important because it provides the primary means for integrating inner and outer worlds.*
>
> BRUNO BETTELHEIM
> *A Good Enough Parent*

Continue to play tug-of-war for about five minutes, then talk about the attitudes that were symbolized by your styles of interaction. For example, did one of you give in easily or become excessively manipulative, reflecting a pattern that occurs in other interpersonal exchanges? If you

are a person who gets easily intimidated when problems and conflicts occur, this game can help you be more assertive, bringing greater equality to your interactions with your spouse.

Game #11
Body Language

This game, inspired by theater professor Nancy King, teaches couples how to bring more bodily expression into their conversations.[54] This game is effective for helping shy individuals open up and become more comfortable with their bodies when they interact with others.

In this game, you are going to ask your partner out for a date—describing in detail what you are going to do (dinner, theater, a movie, lover's lane), but you cannot use any words. Instead, you have to "communicate" using only your elbows, knees, feet, or hands. Your partner, in turn, must guess what you are trying to say. As the conversation unfolds, your partner controls which part of your body you must use to communicate with.

When Julie and Joel played this game, Joel began by making a fist and knocking on an invisible door. Julie had no problem guessing what Joel was "saying" with his hands. She invited him in, and he then used his hands to describe an old-fashioned movie camera, cranking the invisible shaft with one hand and looking through the circle he shaped with his other fingers and palm. Julie readily picked up his charadelike clue that he wanted to take her to a movie, but she decided to play hard to get: "I'd love to go to a movie with you, but tell me what it's about." Mischievously, she told him that he had to use his feet.

"How am I ever going to suggest a romantic movie with my *feet*?" Joel thought. He picked up his foot and pretended to stroke her body. Julie

> *Stand facing each other with your eyes closed, fingertips touching. The partner leading uses his or her hands to express an emotion: nurturance, love, freedom, passion, desire, or whatever feels right. Do two or three different emotions while your partner tries to guess the feelings. Repeat with the other person leading. You can also use your entire body or just your feet (touching big toes, for instance).*
>
> JENNIFER LOUDEN
> *The Couple's Comfort Book*

could hardly stop laughing. "Okay, okay," she finally said, "I'll go to the movies with you. But I need to know one thing more. How are you going to say good night? Tell me using your knees!"

After you have played one round, switch roles and go out for a second date. A great way to end this game is to actually invite your partner out for an evening of romance.

<h2 align="center">Game #12</h2>
<h3 align="center">It's Alive!</h3>

In this game, imagine that you come into contact with an animal—it could be a cat, an insect, a bear, etc.—and let it interact with you. Act it out in the style of a charade, and see if your partner can guess what kind of creature it is. Switch roles, and see if you can guess the imaginary animal your partner has chosen to meet.

Next, become an animal that expresses a side of yourself that your partner rarely sees, act it out, and see if your partner can identify the side of your personality you are portraying. When your partner correctly guesses the trait, switch roles and try to guess what animal personality your partner has picked. Tom, who had a strong and outgoing persona, decided to act as a squirrel to highlight the way he worries about money and obsessively "squirrels" his savings away. By expressing a hidden side of yourself through the symbol of an animal, you may find it easier to talk about it with your mate and include it in your life.

Now pick an animal that describes a positive quality that you feel is missing from your life. Act it out and let your partner identify the trait. Lara, a shy midwestern girl, chose to be a ferocious tiger because she wanted to feel more assertive at work. Playing such a role with her husband gave her the confidence she needed to handle the aggressive job she was in.

Finally, pick a quality of your partner's personality that you think he or she keeps hidden or masked. Portray it as an animal and let your partner guess what aspect you are trying to depict. Switch roles, and then talk with each other about the feelings and thoughts that these exercises brought up.

Game #13
"Lights, Camera . . . Action!"

For this game, you need a prop: a video camera, which can be real or make-believe (a cereal box with a bottle cap on the end will do nicely). Tell your partner that you're making a documentary film and that he or she must answer all the questions you wish to ask. Your partner can answer these questions in any way he or she sees fit: with humor, truthfulness, or deceit (just as in the movies!). In your interview, begin with a few warm-up questions ("Where did you grow up? What are your favorite hobbies? . . .") and then ask more provocative questions ("What is one of your biggest secrets . . . your greatest fear? . . .").

When you have finished your interview, talk with your partner about the experience. If you used a real camera, play back your tape, and then share with your partner how it felt to be actually recorded. Did you worry about what you might say? Did you wonder how others would react if they actually saw the interview? How do you think you'd respond to an interview that would actually be shown on TV?

This game helps people to reflect more deeply upon themselves because a camera makes one exceptionally self-conscious. It also encourages a person to communicate with greater clarity and conciseness. And for couples who have difficulty talking about themselves, this technique can help to break the ice.

Game #14
Picasso

In this game, you will learn how to creatively work with your partner in a more cooperative and coordinated way. You and your partner will draw a picture together that represents some aspect of your relationship, but you must work on the picture at the same time, without talking, *using only one pen!*

For your drawing, pick an activity that you enjoy doing with your partner. For example, you might choose to draw a picture of the two of you kissing, going for a walk, or sitting down for a romantic dinner. When you have agreed upon the subject, take a sheet of paper and sit next to each other. First, you must figure out the best way for both of you to hold one pen in your hands (putting your arm around your partner, crossing arms, etc.). Then begin drawing, but you cannot communicate with words. You may, however, use body language and sounds.

Your drawing is to have structure and form, but don't worry about how it actually turns out—it will look more like a painting by Picasso than one by Da Vinci or Rembrandt! When you have finished, talk about the feelings that came up as you worked to coordinate your efforts with each other. For example, did you find yourself fighting with your partner for control over the pen, or did you just give in and follow his or her lead? Did you enjoy the experience of drawing together? Did you actually feel that you captured a semblance of the activity you attempted to draw, or were you disappointed if you failed (it's almost impossible to make a realistic drawing when two people hold one pen)? Did you find a way to communicate easily without the use of words? Couples who have completed this exercise often comment that they work better together on real-life projects at home.

> *Finger paint together, blindfolded. Put down plastic or do it outside. Or do it blindfolded, outside, and naked! Watercolor together on the same piece of paper. Mold Play-Doh or clay together. Feel your fingers slipping over one another, your creative minds working together, without purpose, delighting in the sensations.*
>
> JENNIFER LOUDEN
> *The Couple's Comfort Book*

Game #15
On Your Mark, Get Set, Draw!

This two-part drawing game can help you get in touch with unspoken feelings that many people have about self-image and the way they are seen by others. Find a table where you and your partner can sit down facing each other, and place a dozen sheets of paper and several pencils in front of you. The object is to draw each other's face and body *in ten seconds or less.* To do this, you must reduce the elements of the human figure to impressionistic squiggles and marks: a few curvy lines will give a semblance of hair and the outline of the body and face, and a couple of dashes can complete the mouth and eyes.

When your time has elapsed (you can use a timer or just guess), grab a second sheet of paper and make another sketch, experimenting with different styles and techniques. Compose a picture entirely out of dashes and dots, draw with your eyes closed, or hold the pencil in your other hand, repeating the process until you have completed seven or eight designs. Allow your feelings to guide you, as opposed to following your ideas about how you should draw.

When you have completed your drawings, share them with your partner—along with your feelings, reactions, and thoughts. Did you feel nervous about drawing your mate, or having your mate sketch you? Did a self-critical voice kick in that criticized your drawing skills, or were you able to surrender yourself to the joy of spontaneous play? Each time you give yourself over to nonjudgmental creativity, the emotional distance between you and your partner will decrease.

Now, take two more sheets of paper, and draw each other with as much detail as possible. The catch is *you cannot use your hands!* You can hold the pencil in the fold of your elbow, with your toes or teeth, or with any other body part that you want. You may laugh to the point of tears, but you will find that a greater intimacy has emerged, for on an unconscious level, this game reduces many of the judgmental feelings we hold about our self-image: how we think we should look to ourselves and to others. Ask your partner if this game had any effect upon his or her ideas about beauty, attractiveness, or self-image.

Game #16
Role-Playing Each Other

In this final game, you will have a chance to experience in a playful but dramatic manner the way in which you are seen by your partner. Role-playing—moving, talking, and behaving as if you were someone else—is a psychodrama technique that can help couples establish greater empathy and understanding for each other.[55] Variations of role-playing have been used throughout this book: to help you see a problem through your partner's eyes, through imaginary conversations with your mate, etc. Role-playing helps you to see the world through another's eyes and makes you more sensitive to your partner's needs. It can show your partner how a certain behavior appears and can serve to change ineffective patterns of communication.

This unique version of the role-reversal technique was developed by Margo Anand, author of *The Art of Sexual Ecstasy*. In this game, you will "be" your partner in every way imaginable, imitating attitudes, gestures, tone of voice, wearing the other's clothes, and even putting on makeup and cologne to accentuate the role. In essence, you will create a living mirror of each other as you take on the persona of your mate. This game will help you discover what it means to be male and female and how these roles are played out in your intimate relations with others. Anand explains:

> This is one of the most delightful games I have ever played. It involves role-playing your partner and then having your part- ner role-play you. You exchange names, clothes, makeup, per- sonality, gait, everything. For a while you become the other person, adopting as best you can every aspect of his or her be- havior, from speech patterns to stance to quirky gestures.
>
> Ordinarily you do not see yourself through the eyes of someone else. This game gives you the chance to experience how you come across to your partner. You hear how you talk— both your distinctive speaking style, and what you tend to talk about. You see how you walk, gesture, listen, kiss, and hug, and in return you show how your partner comes across to you. The game can be incredibly funny, and it's surprising how many deep revelations can emerge in this atmosphere of mer- riment and parody.
>
> Both men and women can get in touch with their own mas- culine and feminine sides by role-playing their partners. This will create more flexibility and freedom from gender stereo- types. You can reveal to your partner—and vice versa—in a play- ful, nonthreatening way, those things that make it difficult for you to relate and that stand in the way of harmony. You can disclose those character traits that your partner is not aware of because they are so ingrained and habitual. In this mutual ex- change of roles, you also reveal to each other the fixed attitudes you both have about what it means to be a man or a woman, and how these assumptions affect and determine your relationship.
>
> In role-playing each other, you can illustrate patterns of jealousy, clinging, inattention, controlling, and interrupting.

It takes courage to expose your partner's foibles, and it can be unnerving to have your own blind spots revealed. But the atmosphere of the game should render this healing communication innocent and even erotic.

Allow at least an hour or two for this practice. Be clear about the time frame, and stick to it. It is important for this practice to have a definite beginning and ending so that you can establish boundaries to the dramatic comedy you will be enacting.

It's more effective if you start in separate rooms, dressing up in each other's clothes. Try to find clothes that more or less fit you—a few temporary alterations should do the trick.

See if you can arrange your hair like that of your partner—a wig may help, if you can find one. If not, a hat is a useful way of hiding your own hair, or perhaps you can find a substitute for a wig—colored paper, perhaps, or a piece of cloth.

Remember your partner's face, and try to reproduce it on your own—putting on makeup, penciling in or pasting on a mustache or a beard. Fill in the accessories that distinguish your partner: jewelry, shoes, scarves, vests, ties. . . .

Suggestions for Women

Your challenge is to submerge yourself in your male partner's personality. Become him. Feel how he carries himself. Are his shoulders sloped, hunched, or level? Is his torso drooping forward, leaning back, erect? Does his manner of walking flow sensually from the hips, or is the movement confined to his knees and lower legs? Try walking as he does. Is it fast or slow? How do his feet meet the floor? Does he stand on the balls of his feet or on his heels? Do his toes point in or out? How does he hold his neck, rigidly or loosely? How about his head—does it remain fixed, bent forward, jerk around, have a habitual twitch? How do his eyes and mouth move? Keep adding the characteristic features, gradually becoming more and more like him, externally and internally.

Remember how your male partner speaks, and try talking that way. Is it more from the belly or from the throat? Is his voice high-pitched or deep? How does he gesture when he speaks? What does he talk about? Rehearse some lines, capturing his speech patterns. And be sure to exaggerate so that you can let him know what it's like to hear some of his common refrains.

Depending on how you plan to spend the next hours, you can also recall how he eats, how he drives, and so on. Get ready to be him in every possible way.

Suggestions for Men

You are becoming like your female partner. You are imagining and feeling how she moves her body, how it feels to have her hips, how it feels to have her breasts, her skin. Imitate how she carries herself, how she stands, walks, carries her head, and moves her arms. Feel the pleasures, the sensations, the surprises of being in a woman's body. Is she fluid, sensual, and overtly sexy, or stiff, withdrawn, and uptight? Imagine that you're a great actor, and immerse yourself in the role of your female partner.

Then, when you feel that you have successfully impersonated your partner, let him or her know that you are ready, and stay in your new role.

When you meet, the first thing you are both likely to do is burst out laughing. It takes a little discipline to maintain your new roles, but remember this is the vital ingredient that makes the game work. So be dedicated actors, even if you're playing comedy.

These first moments offer a precious opportunity to meet again, as if for the very first time. So before throwing yourself into the more familiar task of playing each other in the context of your current relationship, imagine that you have never seen each other before this moment.

Introduce yourselves. If it feels right, the man can be shy in playing the woman, and the woman can feel what it is like to be the man in this situation—the initiator, the one is who supposed to make all the right moves. Think for a moment—how

did you feel when you met? What was the attraction? You may wish to enact a whole evening in which you come to know each other for the first time—not necessarily repeating the exact situation in which you met, but staying firmly in character. This could include flirting and seduction, but don't be in a hurry to jump into bed. Take your time, and feel the person you are playing as deeply as possible.

Once you have played these opening scenes, you can proceed to the current situation, reenacting some daily activities, such as cooking a meal, talking about your plans and your concerns, dancing together, seducing each other. As you make the transition from newly introduced strangers to familiar partners, notice whether anything has been lost through this increasing familiarity. Are you taking each other for granted? Are you less open, more demanding? Do not hesitate to enact those behavior patterns in your partner that you feel have made it difficult for you to be heard, seen, and understood.

When watching your partner impersonating you, try not to get upset by what you are seeing. Rather, learn about yourself through this opportunity. This can be a moment of great insight in which you clearly see the patterns that have prevented a deeper intimacy in your relationship. Most people find they can laugh at themselves, because the whole exercise is well-intentioned. If feelings of anger or embarrassment arise, do not try to hide them, but open yourself to the truth of the portrait you are seeing.

Make sure you end the game at the appointed time.

Sit facing each other. Close your eyes and be silent, taking a few deep breaths and integrating all that has happened.

End with a Melting Hug [chapter 5, game 1].

For the next half hour do not speak about the game you have just played. Then give each other feedback, recollecting the most difficult, revealing, and humorous moments. Tell your partner what you learned that can improve your relationship.

Pointers

At first you may wish to role-play for an hour or so. Then, as you get better at the game, see if you want to play for a whole evening, acting each other around the house and possibly even in bed.

Even if you feel that your acting is amateurish, that you can't mimic the details of your partner's looks and habits, do your best to stay with the basic feeling of being him or her. After a while you may discover a natural ability to play this character. You'll soon see that your observations of your partner are keener than you realized.

In my seminars people often play this game over an extended lunch, with the whole group participating. It's also a hilarious and healing game to play at parties, once you get a little experience of doing it and reaping its benefits.

A word of caution: The aim here is to use role-playing to create more understanding and harmony with a loving and humorous attitude, not to humiliate. So if the temptation to be hurtful comes up, resist it and carefully toe the delicate line that divides revelation from revenge.

You may stumble into awkward moments when the easiest thing would be to say, "Let's stop being silly. I'm me, you're you. Let's drop this charade." But be courageous and stay in the roles. Your play-acting will deepen in these moments if, instead of quitting, you sincerely share your feelings while staying in character.

Vera, a young singer from San Francisco, had this to say after playing the game with Don, her husband: "Don acted 'me' to perfection. I saw myself as never before. It's true I am spoiled, always demanding, impossible. I see it now. And I am much more aware of what I say, how I say it, what I do, and the consequences of my acts. As a result, I feel more at ease with myself and with Don. I am able to see that he and I are two different, autonomous beings. Now I can listen to him and really *hear* him. Before I couldn't. I was always reacting to him without thinking. Now I observe myself while I act. It feels so good to be able to take some distance."

Endgame

Inventing Your Own Game

I suggest that you play one last game, a game that is personally tailored for your partner because it is created by *you!* You can do this alone, but the easiest way to invent a game is by sitting down with your partner and brainstorming to see what comes to mind. Take out a sheet of paper and let your imagination roam, writing down everything silly and serious that comes to your and your partner's mind. You can also jot down an idea for each of the categories I used in this book: a discovery game, a sensual game, a problem-solving game, a romantic writing game, a playful game, or even a game for processing emotional turmoil. Turn to the listing of games in the table of contents and see if one of the game titles gives you an idea.

Put down at least a dozen ideas on your paper, and then pick one that seems most promising to you. The game can be simple, or a variation of one of the games in this book. If nothing comes to mind, tape your sheet of paper to the refrigerator as a reminder and ruminate on it over the next few days. Sometimes a great idea will come to you seemingly from out of the blue. Indirectly, of course, you will be contemplating the dynamics of your relationship as you think about ways to playfully increase intimacy and love.

The next step is to clarify the purpose of your game. On a separate sheet of paper, compose a few sentences to describe the purpose of the game and what you hope will be gained by playing it with your mate. Then describe, step-by-step, how the game is to be played. When you have completed this step, give your game an intriguing title. Then try it out with your partner. If you created the game alone, introduce it to your mate, play it, and see what happens. Whether it is successful or not, write down what you learned.

The benefits of inventing a love game are many: it stimulates cooperative creativity between you and your mate; it challenges you to think about areas that may need to be addressed in your relationship; and it encourages you to interact with your partner in new and imaginative ways. These are some of the keys for deepening intimacy and keeping romance alive. Even if you do not actually come up with a game and simply think about a possible approach, you will find that you become more conscious of the complex layers of love in which you are immersed.

Publishing Your Game

I would like to offer you one further enticement to create a game of your own: I will consider its inclusion in a second volume of games that I am currently putting together. Type up your game (no more than a thousand words) and mail it to *21241 Ventura Boulevard, Suite 269, Woodland Hills, CA 91364* (e-mail: *markwaldman@hotmail.com*). Your story should describe what happened—including any funny, unusual, or disastrous results—and a brief description of how it helped your relationship. If your game is used, you will receive credit and a copy of the book in which it appears. But you must include your name, address, a brief one-paragraph biographical statement about yourself, and a letter giving me permission to include your game in a book.

The Therapy Game

No matter how skilled we are at the game of love, there are times when communication breaks down and intimacy falters. Our personal attempts at reconciliation seemed blocked at every turn. At such vulnerable times, a therapist may be able to assist you in rebuilding an intimate bridge.

In counseling, individuals and couples learn how to see themselves and their partners in different ways. Often they are given tailor-made tools (i.e., love games) to show them how to communicate more effectively. In therapy, people who are struggling with issues of intimacy become more conscious, more open, and more in touch with their feelings. And when working with volatile emotions, the therapist's office may be the safest place to express such feelings and thoughts.

Finding an adequate therapist is not difficult, for the qualities one looks for are similar to what we expect in a personal relationship: compassion, understanding, interest, empathy, and an ability to respond with care. Ideally, our spouses and friends should fill this vital role, but there may be times when outside help must be sought. "A therapist," Harville Hendrix adds, "can help you maneuver around your blind spots and assimilate material from your unconscious that might take you months or years to assimilate on your own."[56]

When working with a therapist, pay close attention to how you feel during and after the therapeutic exchange. Did you feel listened to and understood? Were the insights meaningful and the suggestions helpful? Did you feel respected as a person, and was it easy for you to open up?

But opening up to a therapist can be as difficult as opening up to one's mate. Feelings of vulnerability, fear,

> A therapist's ability bears very little relationship to any credentials he or she might have. Love and courage and wisdom cannot be certified by academic degrees.
>
> M. SCOTT PECK
> The Road Less Traveled

and shame can erupt, and there is always the risk of being rejected or misunderstood. Yet one must take such risks—in therapy, with friends, and with life.

To enrich the therapeutic experience, I recommend that you review the dialogical meditation technique described in chapter 3. This game incorporates the essential principles of psychoanalytic free-association and will rapidly take you into the core issues of your problem. Dialogical meditation is the game I teach my clients, the game I play with my most intimate friends, and the game that initiated the writing of this book.

If you would like help in finding a therapist in your area, or would like to arrange for a counseling session with me—in person, or by telephone—you may contact my office in Woodland Hills, California: (818) 888-6690—or e-mail me at *markwaldman@hotmail.com.*

A Note of Appreciation

*We live our lives
in growing orbits of awareness—
a delicate balance
between reality and myth.*

M.R.W.
February 14, 1999

It is Valentine's Day—a day to reflect upon love—and I am filled with appreciation and awe. I have traveled the path of conscious intimacy for many years, yet I feel that I have only scratched the surface of what it means to be compassionate toward those I have honored and loved. There is so much more to learn, and there are so many people to thank.

Like love, writing a book can be filled with excitement and fear: a combination of imagination, fortitude, and luck. Fundamentally, writing is a dialogue among many parts of one's self. First there is the idea, then the inspiration to write, followed by the constant turmoil to express one's feelings and thoughts. Inner voices nag as you try to please the imaginary critics of the mind. Finally, with trepidation and hope, you share your ink-stained pages with someone in the flesh. Feedback comes—encouragement, confusion, debate—and you return to your desk to clarify and revise. Agents, publishers, and editors intervene, but somehow you persevere. From romance to conflict, from conflict to resolution, from resolution to joy—you finish your book, you consummate the marriage, and a personal vision is transformed.

In the creation *of Love Games,* there are many people who have earned my appreciation and respect: To Irene Prokob, who had the vision to see the potential of this project when it was little more than a whim. To Jeremy Tarcher, who provided ceaseless inspiration through many times of doubt. To Wendy Hubbert, who guided me through the most difficult parts of organization and brought clarity to every page of this book. To David Groff, Kristen Giorgio, Lily Chin, and the dedicated Tarcher staff who exemplify excellence in the publishing world. Thank you, one and all. But, most of all, I want to express my love to Susan, my wife who supported me through endless hours with patience, spiritual joy, and faith.

There are many paths to conscious intimacy: through gentleness and self-reflection, through open dialogue and self-disclosure, through listening and creative play, through kindness and compassion, and through a careful vigilance toward destructive feelings and moods. Throughout this book—through the metaphor of a game—I have tried to offer a glimpse of some of the paths we can take.

References and Notes

1. Mihaly Csikszentmihalyi, in *Flow: The Psychology of Optimal Experience* (New York: Harper Collins, 1990) and Bruno Bettelheim, in *A Good Enough Parent* (Knopf, 1987) provide excellent perspectives on the importance of games and play in the development of child and adult skills.

2. B. Bettelheim, *A Good Enough Parent* (New York: Vintage, 1987).

3. M. Csikszentmihalyi, *Flow: The Psychology of Optimal Experience* (New York: HarperCollins, 1990).

4. V. Long, *Communication Skills in Helping Relationships* (Pacific Grove, Calif.: Brooks/Cole, 1996).

5. N. Branden, *The Art of Living Consciously* (New York: Simon and Schuster, 1997).

6. E. Berne, *Games People Play* (New York: Grove Press, 1964).

7. D. Goleman, ed., *Mind/Body Medicine* (Yonkers, NY: Consumer Reports Books, 1993).

8. M. Murphy, *The Future of the Body* (Los Angeles: Tarcher, 1992).

9. T. Hanh, *Present Moment, Wonderful Moment* (Berkeley, Calif.: Parallax, 1990).

10. J. Kornfield, *A Path with Heart* (New York: Bantam, 1993).

11. J. Hadley and C. Staudacher, *Hypnosis for Change* (Oakland, Calif.: New Harbinger, 1989).

12. H. Benson, "The Relaxation Response," in *Mind/Body Medicine,* ed. D. Goleman (Yonkers, N.Y.: Consumer Reports Books, 1993).

13. Ibid.

14. R. Assagioli, *Psychosynthesis* (New York: Penguin, 1965).

15. Swami Vivekananda, ed., *The Complete Works of Vivekananda* (Almora: Mayavatl Memorial Edition, 1915).

16. M. S. Peck, *The Road Less Traveled* (New York: Simon and Schuster, 1978).

17. T. Reik, *Listening with the Third Ear* (New York: Pyramid, 1948).

18. This version of Adam and Eve is adapted from Steven Mitchell's *Genesis: A New Translation of the Classic Biblical Stories* (New York: HarperCollins, 1996).

19. M. Anand, *The Art of Sexual Ecstasy* (Los Angeles: Tarcher, 1989).

20. Sentence-completion games have been used since the beginning of this century in many therapeutic contexts: for exploring family histories and personal values, for identifying conflicts and resistance, and for promoting deeper consciousness and intimacy. They have even been used to overcome sexual difficulties and fears. Distinguished psychologist Nathaniel Branden uses this technique as a central part of his work with couples. I have used his model for the structuring of this game.

21. L. Gordon, *Passage to Intimacy* (New York: Fireside, 1993).

22. T. Hanh, *Teachings on Love* (Berkeley: Parallax Press, 1997).

23. M. Shaw, *Passionate Enlightenment: Women in Tantric Buddhism* (Princeton: Princeton University Press, 1994). A comprehensive, delightful, and scholarly overview of this often misunderstood practice.

24. A. Phillips, *On Kissing, Tickling, and Being Bored* (Cambridge: Harvard University Press, 1993).

25. A. Watts, *Nature, Man and Woman* (New York: Pantheon, 1958).

26. S. Levine, *Healing into Life and Death* (New York: Doubleday, 1987).

27. G. Weeks and L. Hof, *Integrative Solutions: Treating Common Problems in Couples Therapy* (New York: Brunner/Mazel, 1995).

28. M. Bowen, *Family Therapy in Clinical Practice* (New York: Jason Aronson, 1978).

29. L. Kovacs, "The Power Struggle Stage: From Polarization to Empathy," *Journal of Couples Therapy* 7(1), 27–37.

30. Assagioli, *Psychosynthesis.*

31. D. Greenberger and C. Padesky, *Mind over Mood: A Cognitive Therapy Treatment Manual for Clients* (New York: Guilford Press, 1995).

32. Dalai Lama, *Healing Anger* (Ithaca, N.Y.: Snow Lion, 1997).

33. F. Perls, R. Hefferline, and P. Goodman, *Gestalt Therapy* (New York: Julian, 1951).

34. The following books are excellent sources for helping couples improve their conflict-resolution skills: Aaron T. Beck, *Love Is Never Enough* (New York: Harper and Row, 1988), Weeks and Hof, *Integrative Solutions,* Mark Robert Waldman, ed., *The Art of Staying Together* (New York: Tarcher, 1998), and Robert Bolton, *People Skills* (New York: Simon and Schuster, 1979).

35. D. Goleman, *Emotional Intelligence* (New York: Bantam, 1995).

36. H. Hendrix, *Getting the Love You Want* (New York: Henry Holt, 1988).

37. J. Gottman, C. Notarius, J. Gonso, and H. Markman, *A Couples Guide to Communication* (Champaign, Ill.: Research Press, 1976).

38. A. Beck, *Love Is Never Enough* (New York: Harper and Row, 1988).

39. R. Sherman and N. Fredman, *Handbook of Structured Techniques in Marriage and Family Therapy* (New York: Brunner/Mazel, 1986).

40. M. Whisman, *Satisfaction in Close Relationships* (New York: Guilford, 1997).

41. H. Hendrix and H. Hunt, *The Couples Companion* (New York: Pocket Books, 1994).

42. J. Gray, *Men Are from Mars, Women Are from Venus* (New York: HarperCollins, 1992).

43. T. Moore, *Soul Mates* (New York: HarperCollins, 1994).

44. C. Krueger, *222 Terrific Tips for Two* (Nashville: Abingdon Press, 1995).

45. R. Bly, trans., *Selected Poems of Rainer Maria Rilke* (New York: Harper and Row, 1981).

46. M. Clancy and R. Lauer, "Zen Telegrams: A Warm-up Technique for Poetry Therapy Groups," in *Poetry in the Therapeutic Experience,* ed. A. Lerner (New York: Pergamon Press, 1978).

47. S. R. Hamburg, "Reading Aloud As an Initial Assignment in Marital Therapy," *Jour-*

nal of Marital and Family Therapy 9, no. 1 (1983): 81–87. (Also described in R. Sherman and N. Fredman, *Handbook of Structured Techniques in Marriage and Family Therapy* (New York: Brunner/Mazel, 1986).

48. B. Bettelheim, *Freud's Vienna and Other Essays* (New York: Knopf, 1989).
49. Hendrix, *Getting the Love You Want*.
50. J. Louden, *The Couple's Comfort Book* (San Francisco: HarperSanFrancisco, 1994).
51. M. Csikszentmihalyi, *Creativity* (New York: HarperCollins, 1996).
52. J. Rowan, *Healing the Male Psyche* (New York: Routledge, 1998).
53. V. Spolin, *Theater Games for the Classroom* (Evanston, Ill.: Northwestern University Press, 1986).
54. N. King, *Giving Form to Feeling* (New York: Drama Book Specialists, 1975).
55. Sherman and Fredman, *Handbook of Structured Techniques*.
56. Hendrix, *Getting the Love You Want*.

Permissions

Contributors

Margo Anand teaches and lectures on tantric love and spirituality. She is the author of *The Art of Sexual Ecstasy* and *The Art of Sexual Magic*.

Aaron T. Beck, M.D., is Professor of Psychiatry at the University of Pennsylvania. He is recognized as the father of cognitive therapy and is the author of many articles and books, including *Love Is Never Enough*.

Herbert Benson, M.D., is the Mind/Body Medical Institute Associate Professor of Medicine at Harvard Medical School and author of numerous scientific publications and popular books, including *The Relaxation Response*.

Nathaniel Branden, Ph.D., is a California psychotherapist and author of numerous books on love and self-esteem, including *The Psychology of Romantic Love* and *The Art of Living Consciously*.

Judith and Erich Coché are professors at the University of Pennsylvania and authors of *Couple's Group Psychotherapy: A Clinical Practice Model*.

Jenny Davidow, M.A., is a Doctor of Clinical Hypnotherapy, a dream therapist, and and a creativity coach in Santa Cruz, California. She is the author of *Embracing Your Subconscious* (Tidal Wave Press, P.O. Box 2392, Aptos, CA 95001).

Tenzin Gyatso is the fourteenth Dalai Lama and spiritual leader of Tibet. Winner of the 1989 Nobel Peace Prize, he has authored many books, including *Healing Anger*.

Josie Hadley and Carol Staudacher are the authors of *Hypnosis for Change*. Ms. Hadley is a certified hypnotherapist, and Ms. Staudacher is a widely published author and poet.

Thich Nhat Hanh is a Buddhist teacher nominated by Dr. Martin Luther King, Jr., for the Nobel Peace Prize and author of seventy-five books, including *Teachings on Love* and *Being Peace*.

Harville Hendrix, Ph.D., is a therapist, pastoral counselor, former professor, and author of many books on relationships, including *Getting the Love You Want*.

Jean Houston, Ph.D., is past president of the Association for Humanistic Psychology and author of many books, including *The Possible Human* and *A Mythic Life*.

Suzie Humphreys is a noted keynote speaker for conventions, associations, and conferences. She can be reached at (830) 997-9721.

Jack Kornfield, Ph.D., is a psychotherapist, founding teacher of the Insight Meditation Society and Spirit Rock Center, and author of numerous books on meditation and spirituality, including *A Path with Heart*.

Jennifer Louden is a workshop leader and author of *The Couple's Comfort Book*.

Susan Page is a Protestant minister, former Director of Women's Programs at the University of California, Berkeley, and author of several books, including *How One of You Can Bring the Two of You Together*.

Sharon Salzberg is a founder of the Insight Meditation Society in Barre, Massachusetts, and author of *Loving-Kindness*.

Charles T. Tart, Ph.D., is a professor at the University of California, Davis, and the Institute of Integral Studies. He has authored many books, including *Living the Mindful Life*.

Tina B. Tessina, Ph.D., and Riley K. Smith, M.A., are authors of *True Partners,* lecture widely, and counsel couples and individuals in Southern California.

Redford B. Williams, M.D., is a professor, director of the Behavioral Medicine Research Center, and head of the Division of Behavioral Medicine at Duke University Medical Center.

About the Author

MARK ROBERT WALDMAN is a therapist in Woodland Hills, California. He is the author of *The Art of Staying Together,* an anthology of writings on the essence of love, intimacy, and communication, and coauthor of *Dreamscaping: New and Creative Ways to Work with Your Dreams.* He was the founding editor of the *Transpersonal Review,* chairperson for the Los Angeles Transpersonal Interest Group, and a regional coordinator for the Spiritual Emergence Network.

Mark can be reached for telephone counseling through his Woodland Hills office, (818) 888-6690. Correspondence can be mailed to 21241 Ventura Boulevard, Suite 269, Woodland Hills, CA 91364, or e-mailed to *markwaldman@hotmail.com.*

A treasury of writings
on the essence of love, intimacy,
and communication,
edited by Mark Robert Waldman

The Art of Staying Together is a perfect complement for exploring the games of love. Bringing together thirty-two renowned authorities to provide a comprehensive view of what people can do to create meaningful and lasting relationships, this book will show you how to establish deeper empathy and trust as you learn how to resolve conflicts with greater ease. Friendship, true listening, gender stereotypes, romantic addictions, spiritual intimacy, and the chemistry of love are just a sampling of the issues that are addressed in this book.

Published by Jeremy P. Tarcher/Putnam
A member of Penguin Putnam, Inc.
www.penguinputnam.com